# Surviving
# Hurricane Katrina:
## One Family's Story

Carolyn E. Dallinger

Cover and layout designs by Erin C. Lain
Photos courtesy of Walter A. Lain

ISBN 978-0-98-325571-0 pbk

Printed in the United States of America
www.blurb.com

blurb.com

# Dedication

This book is dedicated to my mother-in-law, Irene "Madear" Lain, who passed just six months prior to Hurricane Katrina. Her passing made the endurance of Katrina extraordinarily difficult for the family. I believe that Irene's children inherited her strength, and learned through her tenacity and courage in successfully raising her fourteen children, and many grandchildren, in the inner city of New Orleans' 9th Ward.

# Acknowledgements

I really can't find adequate words to describe my debt of gratitude to my family members for opening themselves up to my probing questions regarding a very difficult time in their lives. My admiration and love for them has only grown stronger through this venture. I also want to thank my husband, Walter, and daughters, Erin and Dana, for giving me invaluable advice through this whole process.

# Contents

# Introduction

My first exposure to the unique and intriguing culture of New Orleans was when, as a college sophomore, I met an 18-year-old young man on the green lawns of my small college campus, Simpson College in Indianola, Iowa. I arrived on Simpson's campus from a small Iowa town of 304 people, all white. At Simpson, I soon learned that the group of African American guys, who had come up from New Orleans on the train, was a culturally unique group – they strutted around campus in single file, dancing and chanting Mardi Gras songs like "My Grandma and your Grandma were sittin' round the fire...." I really didn't know what to think of these young men but pretty soon, I was quite taken by one in their group - Walter Lain.

In getting to know Walter, I learned he was one of fourteen children from a family living in the Upper 9th Ward of New Orleans. A fellow college student from New Orleans told me, "They don't let white people in his neighborhood after dark." Walter seemed nice enough and after we dated for many years, I met some of his family who came up to Iowa to attend his college graduation.

Fast forwarding thirty years, Walter and I are married with two girls of our own, celebrating our 25th wedding anniversary this past summer. I am a member of this wonderful family originating from New Orleans. At the time Hurricane Katrina hit, the family almost totally resided in New Orleans; ten of Walter's brothers and sisters and their spouses, thirteen of our nieces or nephews and their families, and my father-in-law.

During each of the four years since Hurricane Katrina's devastating landfall, I have had a strong sense that the story of the survival of this large strong family needed to be recorded. I felt the stories could help others learn the realities of Katrina's impact and generally how New Orleanians are surviving and thriving after Katrina. All the interviews in this book come from my father-in-law Odis or his children, grandchildren, and one great-grandchild.

Qualitative social research is a complex and difficult activity that requires continual reflection on one's methods and the outcomes obtained. Researchers "should continually reflect on their own role in the research process and on the wider context in which it occurs." (Lewis-Beck, et. al., 2004, p. 934) From the moment we heard that Hurricane Katrina had hit New Orleans, through the most recent interviews of my family members, I've been emotionally attached, therefore not an entirely unbiased observer. Each hour that passed after Katrina hit New Orleans, my psyche was totally absorbed in the rescue efforts (or lack of), the whereabouts of family members still known to be in New Orleans, the disbursement of family members around the country, to the eventual rebuilding or resettling of each affected family member.

Therefore I clearly expose my connection to the interview subjects and the subject matter. "It is argued that researchers are always part of the social world they study; they can never step above it in order to gain an Olympian perspective or move outside it to get a 'view from nowhere.'" (Lewis-Beck, et. al., 2004, p. 934) So it is that I share my bias from the beginning, to allow the reader to judge the findings in this context. I believe that my personal connection has provided a level of trust that allowed my family members to be open about their feelings and opinions about many of the research topics.

Even though my own "lenses" have been shaped by being a small-town Iowan, Christian, middle-class female of white European ancestry, I have reached across boundaries into my family's black, Christian, primarily middle-class male and female African ancestry (although it was pointed out to me during interviewing that there is a small amount of white and Indian ancestry in the family's background as well). I do not think these differences have hindered the ability to obtain the stories of my family members but, as I tell my college students, it is necessary for researchers to be open and honest about the perspectives from which they begin their work.

My interviewing was influenced primarily through two theoretical viewpoints. The Conflict theory influenced my perspective in the struggle between various groups in our society. My interview questions undoubtedly were influenced by my perspective of the importance of understanding the impact of struggles between groups of differing economic class, race and power. Conflict theories "help us understand conflict and inequality between persons, ideas, groups, social classes, communities and larger social structures, and enhance our understanding of power structures and the way in which power disparities impact people's lives." (Robbins et. al., 2006, p. 63) I wanted to learn about the impact of race and class from the perspective of those in the midst of the Katrina crisis.

Empowerment theories also influenced my work on this project. I believe strongly in the power of encouraging people to tell their stories and experiences. Empowerment theories provide a theoretical base to address "concerns about social justice, human strengths and resiliency." (Robbins et.al., 2006, p. 125) Those focusing on empowerment theories in their work with others, examine "the causes, consequences, and solutions of oppression and inequality [as] relevant to individuals, families, organizations, institutions, and communities." (Robbins et.al, 2006, p. 121) For these interviews, I hoped that encouraging my family to tell their stories would not only empower them, but allow others to learn about Katrina's impact on this family and the larger community.

Barber, et. al. (2007) explored the use of the narrative approach in allowing survivors to tell about issues of inequality, privilege and disaster in their experiences in Hurricane Katrina. This methodological approach to disaster research provides rich and important data to be obtained about important historical events. (p.101) (See also Montana-Leblanc's *Not Just the Levees Broke: My Story During and After Hurricane Katrina,* 2008.) What I found in obtaining narrative accounts from family members is that the issues of race and class were so intertwined with the actions and reactions to Hurricane Katrina, and the people it impacted, it was difficult to separate them out. One family interviewee exclaimed in exasperation, "Why do people ask the obvious?" when she was asked if race had anything to do with the response, or lack of response, for victims of Hurricane Katrina.

Many studies and historical accounts document the history of environmental racism and classism in New Orleans. Examples include the building of residential housing on top of an environmental waste dump where primarily low-income African Americans lived; the white flight from the Upper 9th Ward after Hurricane Betsy (Colton, 2005); and the lack of levee upkeep and repair over the years, particularly in the Upper and Lower 9th Wards (Cooper, 2006). The resulting 'perfect storm' recipe which was waiting as Hurricane Katrina came in to wreak havoc, exposed a very vulnerable lower economic class and predominantly African American population to suffer the most dire consequences (Erikson, 2009).

Comments, from various people who thought it was horrible to "cry racism" after Hurricane Katrina hit, ignore documentation of numerous policies that have impacted predominantly African Americans or lower economic classes who have occupied New Orleans since its early beginning.

> Racial discrimination takes place not merely through intentional (though perhaps unselfconscious) interactions between individuals, but also as a result of deep social and institutional practices and habits. ... there persist social patterns – where people live, which social organizations they belong to, what schools they attend, and so on – that were built during the hundreds of years where active racial prejudice was the fact of ethnic life in America. These social and institutional structures, in other words, are constructed on prejudicial racialist foundations. (Gilman, 2006, p. 1)

All residents of New Orleans, whether white or black, rich or poor, young or old, were impacted by Hurricane Katrina. However, after walking and driving through devastated block after block, neighborhood after neighborhood, major city section after section, it is very clear who suffered the most losses from Hurricane Katrina. All residents' lives were interrupted, but almost to a perfect 'storm,' those lowest on the economic ladder died at higher rates, lost more property, and were unable to move back to this historical city.

I've tried to keep the unique language and context of the interviews as close to the original as possible. I'm reminded of a conversation that happened this past Thanksgiving in the family's New Orleans home. My nephew Andrew Washington, jokingly exclaimed, "Them grits be wet." My husband Walter and Andrew had a conversation where

Andrew explained that he is literate in three languages: 1) formal English (he has a Ph.D., has been a college professor for years, and now holds an economist job in Washington D.C.),2) black English, and 3) N'awlins (the New Orleans dialect). In developing this book, I've been torn about editing the spoken language of the interviewees. While I recognize that many family members would write their responses differently than their oral conversation to a family member, I have opted in most cases to keep the original language to show the special flavor of the New Orleans' dialect.

An ongoing issue among ethnographers is whether to capture the original spoken dialect or to edit to more formal English. My sincere hope is that no reader will make any assumptions about educational level when reading the New Orleans' dialect, because the assumptions would be wrong. Formal education and "N'awlins" dialect are completely separate things.

Out of the profound loss from Hurricane Katrina, arise these stories of great courage: including saving peoples' lives; compassionate caring for other less fortunate individuals; ultimate despair for the loss of loved ones; to strength and hope to rebuild lives whether in New Orleans or other parts of the country. These stories come from all economic classes and educational backgrounds within our family. The stories show a strong commitment in helping each other out and sharing what little shelter and means that were left. These stories are unique and inspiring on an individual basis but they all have one thing in common – they are one family.

-Carolyn E. Dallinger

# Irene (Madear)† + Odis Lain

3. Louis (Bro)† + **Jennie V.**
Angela
Dwayne
Cynthia
Keisha
**Byron**
**Shavon**

2. **Elsie (Lee)** + Arthur†
Arthur Jr. †
Danella
Tommy †
Vonterris
Drusilla
**Darren**
Keiba

1. **Otis Jr. (June) + Estella**
Wellintgon
**Meryl**
**Shaun + Shannon**
Latoya

10. **Andrew (Daniel)** + Bernadette
Andrew Jr.
Rachella

9. **Raymond**
Raymond Jr.
Ayana

8. **Ruby** + Terrance
Lawrence
Shandrelle
Courtney

7. **Emanuel** + Melva
   **Tanga**
   Emanuel Jr.
   Alisha

6. **Rose** + Henry
   Andrew

5. **Bobby**

14. Pat
    Alex
    Jasmine
    Nijah

4. **Sarah**
   **Sarah Elizabeth (Liz)**

13. **Calvin** + Josie†
    Devrek
    **Alex Nicole**
    Payton

12. **Terry** + Tina
    Justin
    Kelsey

11. **Walter** + Carolyn
    Erin
    Dana

Bold denotes those who were interviewed
† denotes that the person is deceased
* Not all family members are shown on this diagram

# Book 1

Before the Storm

# Chapter 1


## Family Beginnings in New Orleans

New Orleans' culture and its people are influenced by its historical origins from a rich mixture of French, African, Indian and Spanish people. The spoken dialect that results has a unique character of its own.

**Odis Sr.** (90 years old)

If I had to do it over again, I would do it the same way. This place always was called the "Big Easy." Yeah, that's the true name for it, 'cause that is what it was. Big "greasy, easy" I say. But I love New Orleans.

One reason why I love New Orleans? They really done for me and got me in the position and got me movin' forward. I come to New Orleans during the War (WWII). They brought me from Winnsboro (Louisiana), down to Camp Beauregard in Alexandria, Louisiana, then to New Orleans.

New Orleans got me on the Illinois Central railroad. Even two of my brothers had forty-two years each (working) on the railroad. I had just thirty-five years on the railroad before I retired. At the same time, I had sixteen years unloading banana boats on the Mississippi River, here in New Orleans.

I grew up doing farming work in Winnsboro. At the age of nine or ten, I chopped and picked cotton, tended cows, pigs, and chickens. We butchered our own chickens and pigs on the Ellis farm place. I remember killing and butchering chickens and picking chicken feathers.

I brought my wife Irene to New Orleans after we got married on November 15, 1941. I was already in the Army when I got married. We were married 64 years before she passed just six months before Hurricane Katrina.

I always understood that if I was going to make it, I had to make it by myself. That's right. I always did go to prayer meetings and I'm so glad that God blessed me so much. He blessed me with many, many children and grandchildren. I wouldn't make it if it wouldn't be for Him. I think a lot of people, white and black, all people, have been good to me. Very good, very good. That's alright. Yes, indeed. That's alright.

- Odis Lain Sr.

Shavon & her mom Jennie V.

## Shavon
(granddaughter of Odis and Irene, daughter of Louis)

I do understand the mentality of New Orleans people. We are a different breed from anybody else in the country. Some people say New Orleans is like being in your own little island because of our speech and our culture.

Yeah, we don't know how to act when we go other places. There are things that we can get away with in New Orleans that you can't get away with nowhere else. People think it is amazing that we can go to a daiquiri drive-through shop and we can get our drinks to go. They are like, "We can't even bring alcohol outside of a restaurant."

I made that mistake when I went away to school. I asked, "Can I have that in a to-go cup please?" They said, "No!" And I asked, "Why not?" They were like, "Well maybe because we want to keep our liquor license." There are just certain things we are so accustomed to in New Orleans.

After Katrina, the Road Home Program* set up a meeting in a restaurant in Atlanta. They sponsored some New Orleans food and were also showing the New Orleans' Saints football game. New Orleans' people get happy when the Saints win, so I probably saw about three people get arrested that night because they were getting loud.

After the Saints won the game, we were dancing with napkins in our hands, getting happy, and marching out of the building. If we were in New Orleans, that would not have been a problem, nobody would have gone to jail. Atlanta was not playin' that and some of those people went to jail that night just for dancing and getting loud. You do have to know how to act once you leave New Orleans.

New Orleans' food, clothes, and certain items can't be found anywhere else in the country. The food alone would make people come back to New Orleans after Katrina. One of the things you would see after Katrina was so many cars with Louisiana license plates going up and down the Interstate with ice chests just attached to the back side of the car. That way they could get that certain New Orleans' food and take it back with them.

Even before Katrina, if you told someone you were from New Orleans, you were almost like a celebrity. They would say, "Say Baby, just say baaabeee." Especially when I went away to school, they would always ask me, "Why do you always answer your own question?"

The guy I was dating at the time was from Chicago and he just had his own little chant teasing me. He would say, "Huh baaabeee, and you all put 'earl' in your hair. And you can't say 'oil,' you say 'earl.'" I kept going around practicing...

* *The Road Home* program is designed to provide compensation to Louisiana homeowners affected by Hurricanes Katrina or Rita for the damage to their homes. From http://road2la.org

'oye–ell', 'oye-ell', until I could say 'oil' not 'earl.' It took me going away to college to hear other people speak, and then I thought, I have to change the way I talk if I want to be in corporate America. I can't say, "Hey baaabeee, and look at the 'earl.'"

Other places have 'snow cones' and we have 'snow balls.' We have our hot sausage and gumbos. When I'm in Atlanta and people learn that I'm from New Orleans, their first request is, "Let me hear you talk," and the second question is, "Can you cook" because they always want something special to eat from New Orleans.

New Orleans has its own language and a different type of speech. Even when you hear other people from major cities talk slang, it is still proper English. Their English is always very good. New Orleans people have gotten better in their speech, but after you listen to people in other places, you learn that New Orleans people still have a long ways to go.

- Shavon Lain

**Jennie V.** (daughter-in-law of Odis & Irene, wife of Louis)

Here in New Orleans, you are taught to speak to everybody. If somebody is sitting out on the porch, you speak to them. If you pass someone on the street, you speak. You just acknowledge everybody around you.

I grew up in the 9th Ward close to the Lains' house. From the age of twelve until nineteen, we lived in the Desire Projects. Whenever I hear someone say something negative about the projects, I get upset. I say, "You know, back then, it was good people and they took pride in where they lived." You didn't see trash, it was clean and it was just nice.

I remember we stayed upstairs and we had to keep the stairs all clean and swept; we used to mop down the stairs and it was always clean. There was nothing wrong with living in the projects then. It might have had a stigma that you were poor, but yeah, we were poor. We were comfortable and I tell you what, we were better off than a lot of people outside the projects. We had food on our table and we didn't go hungry.

After Hurricane Betsy in 1965, I left New Orleans when my husband Louis was in the Air Force and he came and got us. I didn't want to go, but anyway there we went up to Grand Fork, North Dakota. We had a big blizzard up there. I felt like I was jinxed that year. I said, "Dang, everywhere I go, there is a disaster."

During the blizzard, we were snowed in and couldn't get out. We called the Air Force base and they said they couldn't get out either. We had to wait until they got dug out and then they finally came and dug us out. When we finally got out, we ordered a pizza. We had to walk up an incline of snow to go get that pizza. I said, "We are walkin' on top of cars and stuff, goin' to get a pizza." I made a mis-step and went down in the snow; Louis had to pull me out of that snow. North Dakota had the best pizzas in the world, but after that, we turned around and went back home. We said, "To heck with this pizza, this is foolish."

North Dakota was too cold. I was only there for nine months and I had three kids then - Angela, Dwayne, and Cynthia. So after Louis was discharged from the service, we went to Detroit for about a month.

I didn't know that people were different in Detroit. When I got there, my friend Maxine (who lived in Detroit) and I walked down to the corner grocery. We saw people sitting on their porch and so I spoke to them like we would do in New Orleans. They looked at me like I had cursed them or something.

I said, "Maxine, what is wrong with these people?" She said, "They don't speak to you unless they know you. And if they don't know you, they think you are up to something if you are speaking to them." I said, "Oh, excuse me."

Then I asked her, "Do you speak to your next door neighbors?" She said, "Nope." I said, "Wow, I don't know if I could live like that." Louis wanted to stay in Detroit; I didn't. So we came back home to New Orleans in about August 1966.

When we see each other in New Orleans, we speak. And if something happens, I feel free to run next door to ask for help. I guess we were taught different than other places. It is just a habit, we were brought up to acknowledge someone that you pass. You feel funny passing somebody and not speakin' to them if you are from New Orleans.

- Jennie V. Lain

# Chapter 2

## Flashbacks and Vivid Memories of Another Hurricane: *Betsy*

Hurricane Betsy killed 76 Louisiana residents, most of them in New Orleans, when it hit in 1965. Betsy mostly devastated the 9th Ward which was a mixed race neighborhood until then.

Ten of Odis and Irene's fourteen children were living in the family home at the time of Betsy. When talking about their experiences through Hurricane Katrina, memories of Betsy constantly surfaced. The impact of Betsy is as vivid 44 years later as it was in 1965.

**Odis Sr.**

*"How many hurricanes have you been through?"*
Oooooooooooh, many, many, many, many, at least twelve of them. Several of them I remember distinctly, with Katrina on top of the whole thing. But Hurricane Betsy was big. Some of them were so minor that I didn't pay them too much attention.

After Hurricane Betsy, I got hammers and things and fixed things up myself. One of the reasons why I did it like that -- the professionals know how to do it, and do it like it should be done, but they want sooooooo... much money. I figure if I do it myself, I would come out better.

I wound up realizing that I got my house back and my beds, refrigerator, stove, what have you. I had no money to pay them people. No great big money, no way. I had two jobs, but nary a one of them paid that much. No indeed.

I went down to the SBA (Small Business Administration) and paid that money back that we had to borrow. Paid those notes off. I always try to make it myself if I can. Do you understand?

*"Did you think about leaving New Orleans and going back to Northern Louisiana after Hurricane Katrina?"*
Never did, never did. I went up there (Northern Louisiana) after Katrina, but I didn't stay up there but a couple of nights, days, or weeks. I come right straight back here because this is my house. Just like they up there, that is their house. They have their farms and different things. But I love New Orleans.

- Odis Lain Sr.

**Ruby**  (8th child of Odis & Irene)

As a child, we always liked going to the hurricane shelters (the local school) where we would get a cot to sleep on and they would give us hot chocolate and snacks. We would stay up and play games all night, so hurricanes were kind of fun for us.

I remember when Hurricane Betsy was coming because we were let out of school early that day. School had just started back up for the fall; it was only the second day of school. I was eleven years old and was in the middle school. Our teacher said there was a storm coming and we were supposed to go home.

Nine of my brothers and sisters were already home when I got home from school. My three oldest brothers and sisters were already married and out of the house: Otis, Lee (Elsie) and Bro (Louis). My dad worked two jobs and he was out working on the railroad that night.

The TV was on and they said there wasn't any mandatory evacuations but the Mayor announced that the shelters would be open. The news reporter said that the storm would not hit New Orleans directly; it was going to bypass us.

My mom was calling around to get some more information when all of sudden the lights went out. The winds picked up a little bit but I remember Bobby and Sarah went to bed anyway. Raymond, Rose and I were still up and Mama was up and praying.

The neighbors' shingles started ripping off their roofs as the wind kept picking up. Then we noticed a little trickle of water coming around the front of the house in the ditch.

All of a sudden, we heard mom scream and so we all ran to the back of the house where she was at. We looked out the back window and this big wave was just coming in over the house. The oldest siblings were yelling, "We need to get out of here." Then a truck came by and someone from the truck yelled, "Y'all get out of there. Water is rising. Y'all get out of there."

I wanted to stay in the house and so I said, "We can go up in the attic." Bobby yelled, "No the wind will tear the roof off the attic. We got to get out of here and go to the shelter." To me, as an eleven year old, it didn't make sense to leave our secure house to go out into a flood of water.

We didn't know why the water was rising so rapidly. Since the power was already out, we had lost all communications: no TV and no radio. We didn't have candles or flashlights or anything.

I was in the house screaming. (They always say that I am the emotional one.) I was crying, "No I don't want to go. I don't want to go." Bobby gave me a whack and said "Girl come on, let's go." It was significant to me that Bobby made me go because when we came back to the house several weeks later, we saw that the house got over five feet of water in it and it was actually two inches over my head. As an eleven year old, I said, "Oh thank you God." I thought, "Wow, I would have drowned." I was grateful that Bobby made me go.

We decided that we were going to the local school which was five blocks from our house. We had to walk into this rushing water. By that time, the water was up to my waist. As we were walking, the water was constantly rising. There were four little ones then: Daniel, Walter, Calvin and Terry. Pat wasn't born yet. Calvin, who was only a couple of months old, slipped out of my mom's arms and fell into the water. I remember my mom screaming that she had dropped the baby so everybody dove down and grabbed to save him.

We had this church right behind our house. As we passed the front of the church, a piece of metal that had flown off from a rooftop cut my toe. I still have the little scar on my toe to prove it. But, we couldn't stop to deal with that.

We formed this human chain-link holding hands going through the water. We were also holding on to the fence. However, every property in our neighborhood didn't have a fence. So here we were trying to cross the street and there was nothing to hold on to. We took our chances and went across; this was at Clouet and Tonti streets.

As we were going by the different houses trying to hang on, we came to a lady's house at the corner of Dorgenois and Clouet. The lady came out of her door yelling, "Y'all come on out of that water because you will drown." We yelled back, "We are trying to make it to the school." She said, "Y'all will never make it."

Her house was a good three feet up out of the water at the time. We went in this lady's house and when water started rushing into her house, the adults decided that we should go across the street to Thelma's Restaurant which was two stories high.

By the time we got over to the restaurant, all the bottom floor was covered with water, so they let us go upstairs. The owner of the place was really mean to everybody. He said he would give us a place to sit during the storm, but we had to leave first thing in the morning. He didn't give us any food or nothing. The power was out and his food spoiled anyway.

We were all huddled against the wall in that restaurant; we could hear the howling of the wind and the building was just shaking. We couldn't sleep and the ladies were praying out loud.

Early the next morning, my older brothers, Bobby and Emanuel, said they were going to go find my dad. My mom tried to keep them there, but they went anyway. After a little bit, Bobby came back because he got a really deep cut on his leg.

Eventually, Emanuel came back with my daddy and they were in a boat. We all got out in the boat but it took two trips to get all of us. We went up to Galvez Street bridge where we could get out and walk overtop the bridge. We went up to my sister Elsie's house; she had five of her own kids at that time.

After just two weeks. My dad said he was going to go back and rebuild our house. At first, I was afraid to move back in the house because we heard about alligators being all around. But as little kids, we did what we were told. Daddy said we were going back down to our house and we weren't going to sleep on the floor at my sister's house anymore. All ten kids, and my mom and dad, went back to our house and we slept on a concrete floor. The house was half-way gutted when we moved back in.

I remember President Johnson coming to New Orleans, he was in an amphibian vehicle -- it was like an army tank but it could float on water. Also, the government would drop food from the sky and we would have to go to a pick-up point to get food. I remember having nothing to eat. While we were waiting on the food, another neighbor lady told us, "What y'all think you are - refugees? Get on out of here."

Dad didn't take any money from the government. He only let my mom get some free mattresses and food vouchers. The best thing about Hurricane Betsy was that the water came in and it went right back out. Hurricane Katrina was different because the water stayed.

- Ruby Lain Faiferek

**Walter** (11th child of Odis & Irene)

I was five years old and in kindergarten when Hurricane Betsy came. I remember it vividly. We were trying to get to the local shelter and were just hanging on to the fence. The water was not cold, it wasn't anything like rain water -- it was brackish, brownish water. I was so afraid that we would get too close to the canal and get washed out. That's how terrifying it was.

What I later heard was that all the whites who had lived in the Upper 9th Ward prior to Hurricane Betsy were told about a government program where they could move to Metairie (a Western suburb of New Orleans) after Betsy hit. At one time, if you walked anywhere from Galvez Street to Nichols Street in the 9th Ward, the whole area would have been white. After Betsy, the whites were given an option to move and there was a sudden change. I heard they showed them the flood plane maps and said, "Hey if you stay here, you will be flooded out again." The black people weren't given the same information.

All the people who used to live in the Florida Projects in the 9th Ward, which was previously all white, moved to Metairie. When I was a kid we couldn't go past Miro Street because it was an all white area. So after Betsy, the black people moved in the cheaper houses in the 9th Ward area. The neighborhood changed from mixed white and black, to all black, like overnight.

It was an immediate rumor that they wanted to save Canal Street during Betsy and so they broke the levee below the Mississippi River which caused the 9th Ward to flood. In reality, I don't think they even had a levee system in place in that lower class area at all.

- Walter Lain

## New Orleans' Historial Zoning and Land Ownership Policies

"The nearly complete absence of blacks in the newly drained territory on the lake side of the ridges stems from an explicitly prejudicial real estate system.... Drainage certainly opened new neighborhoods, but restrictive real estate practices closed them to specific groups. The builders and realtors sought more affluent white buyers and developed neighborhoods for them.... Delayed sewer connections reflected a lower-priority status for black and other low-income neighborhoods." (Colton, 2005, p. 99)

Despite plans to systematically drain the city, gaps in the system became apparent in the 1920s. A 1923 assessment of the sewerage system exposed a sizable neighborhood without sewer mains. This area lacking service was a low-lying, largely African American and industrial district." (Colton, 2005, p. 105)

Only in 1958, a decade after the legislature outlawed dumps in the city, did the city finally close the Agriculture Street Landfill. ... Yet after the final use of the site as an emergency dump for debris produced by Hurricane Betsy (1965), neighbors finally ceased their opposition. ... First the neighborhood underwent a major demographic change from the early 1950s to the early 1990s – from white to primarily African American.... The landfill's most vocal opponents in the early 1950s had been largely white – at least those whose opposition was reported by the newspapers." (Colton, 2005, p. 113)

While the dump's development in a largely white neighborhood at the turn of the century was obviously not a case of environmental racism, events following the landfill's 1965 closure must be considered through the lens of environmental justice. The low-income Ninth Ward was chronically denied public services. (Colton, 2005, p. 114)

(For a complete and comprehensive history of the development of land areas, public works, sewers and services in the various neighborhoods of New Orleans read: *An Unnatural Metropolis, Wresting New Orleans From Nature* by Craig E. Colten, 2005.)

# Chapter 3

## Preparing for Katrina: Fight or Flight? *

* A timeline of Hurricane Katrina events can be found on page 362.

**Shaun** (grandson of Odis & Irene, son of Otis Jr.)

I was the offensive coordinator for my son's football team on that very hot summer day of Saturday, August 27, 2005, right before Katrina hit. The boys had a game in Uptown New Orleans. By that time, everybody was a buzz around the city about the hurricane headed our way. People were like, "Are you leaving? Are you leaving?" Our head coach was like, "Nah, I'm not going anywhere, I'm going to wait it out. I was here during Hurricane Betsy and nothing happened and we were alright."

I couldn't say the same thing because I remember hearing about the devastation Betsy did to my family. But I wasn't really concerned about Katrina because we had evacuated for hurricanes before. At the end of the game, my wife Shannon called me and said, "What are we going to do?" I said, "Nothing, we are going to be alright. Man, it's hot today." Then my college roommate, Preston Edwards, called me and said, "Hey Lain, we're going to Houston man, cause Bro, this thing looks rough." I said, "Man what'cha talkin' about?" He said, "Lain, if you ride this thing out, you won't have any electricity for days. It's going to be miserable, you need to roll." I said, "Press, I'm not going to go anywhere man. We'll be alright."

Preston's uncle is a shoe maker in Uptown New Orleans and he was working on repairing my shoes. For some reason I thought, let me get my shoes out of the shop before I leave Uptown. So I got the shoes, went home, and by that time my wife was mad. She said, "What are we going to do?" I said, "Nothing, we will be alright you know."

We monitored the storm by TV. On that Saturday, Mayor Ray Nagin was saying it's a voluntary evacuation. But when I woke up on that Sunday and saw the report and the intensity of the eye of the hurricane, I said, "We got to go." I told my family to pack up.

Now you have to understand what packing up means. We have evacuated for hurricanes before, and we were blessed as a family to own and operate Loews Express Bus Charters and Tours. It was my father Otis, brother Wellington, and myself who operated Loews Express. Loews is an acronym for Latoya, Otis, Estella, Wellington and Shaun (members of Otis Lain's family). My company, called College Campus Tours, was developed within Loews Express, and then it became its own LLC later on.

People in our extended family know that whenever we go out of town for an evacuation, all they have to do is show up at 10901 Chef Menteur Highway (the location of Loews Express and June-el businesses, which are in the same building) and get on the bus and take a free vacation. That can be good and bad because what happens is, it is a free ride, and sometimes it ends up being a free hotel for some.

So Sunday morning, we woke up and I looked around. I was blessed because God kind of spoke to me, but I wasn't totally obedient. I took my shoes and tied them into a plastic garbage bag. I went around and took my laptop and hard drive, boxed them up and took them with me. I put the things on my floor up on my bed. In my office, I put things on top of my desk.

So we were packing up and getting our personal things together. I said, "Let me get the cars together." We had four vehicles: Mercedes, Land Cruiser, van and work truck. So I left the work truck and the van at home and I said to my wife, "Shannon, let's take both of these other vehicles and take them to Loews because that is higher ground in case it floods."

My wife decided to go pick up her father. She told me that God had prompted and led upon her heart to go pick him up because he was in the 9th Ward by himself. So he got his things together and met us at the bus company.

Then my Aunt Elmyr, Aunt Elynda and my Uncle Ed met us at Loews. My Aunt Sarah and Uncle Bobby met us and dropped Liz off. They said they were going to ride out the hurricane and watch it in a high rise hotel. My Uncle Bobby is an ex-sailor and my Aunt Sarah is a doctor. Now if they are thinking like that, have mercy on the rest of the city if they are also thinking like that.

Well my dad and my cousin, Darren Hagen, my Aunt Elsie's youngest son, stayed at the Loews Express building. My grand-father Odis was also at the building but he got on the bus. My brother Wellington and his family got on the bus also. So we had about 22 family members who got on the bus to leave.

The night before that Saturday, we were evacuating elderly homes with our busses; we were also evacuating students from Dillard University and Xavier University. I think a bus broke down so my father and brother had been up all night long with no sleep. So that left me to drive. I drove the bus to Atlanta, Georgia in bumper to bumper traffic; it took us 22 hours to get there. Normally that is a six to seven hour drive.

We went through the Riggolets. We were on Chef Menteur, then the Riggolets is straight out Chef Menteur Highway, then straight out 90. Once we got across, we took

Highway 11. What happened was, we didn't take I10, we took the other Interstate and went straight across the lake without no traffic. But when we got in Slidell, the State Troopers forced us to go 55 North to Hattiesburg to Laurel, Mississippi to Meridian. And so that took a long time because of the traffic, and cars were breaking down left and right. Some people were running out of gas because they didn't prepare.

One thing people didn't realize about New Orleans was that it had a large poverty concentration. My wife called her cousin, Kendra, and said, "You can come with us." Kendra said, "Nah, I'm going to ride it out because my hooptie* is not road worthy." How many people have $200 or $300 just for emergency? Staying in a hotel is expensive. People don't realize, if the hurricane hit on the first of the month when the welfare and SSI checks came in, then they would have had money. But Katrina hit at the end of the month and people didn't have any money left. Kendra rode it out in the Superdome.

We stopped in Meridian, Mississippi at a McDonalds and got dinner and then we continued on until I was exhausted. We stopped in Alabama and my brother drove for about an hour, then he had to stop because he was still tired. Then I drove to a truck stop where we just stopped and rested.

I had developed a lot of contacts through my business, so I called one of my hotel contacts, Barbara in Atlanta, at the Hampton Inn Alpharetta. I said, "Look Barbara, we are evacuating from New Orleans." She said, "Shaun, how can I help?" I told her I needed eight rooms. Barbara said, "No problem." So when we went to the hotel, we got eight rooms for eight days. We were straight.

We picked Atlanta area because I graduated from Morehouse College in Atlanta in 1991, and I had a lot of

---

* See www.urbandictionary.com, hooptie is a junky, worthless car

friends still there. I called Atlanta my second home. It is a funny thing, my wife always wanted to move to Atlanta. So when we got to Meridian, Mississippi, my Aunt Elmyr said, "Let's go to Dallas, where Eileen is (my other aunt)." I said, "Nah, you all sit back, I got this. We aren't going to Dallas." Half of New Orleans was in Houston and Dallas. So I said, "I'm going to Atlanta." There was no question about it, Atlanta was a comfortable place, resources were there, and I know people.

So when we got to the hotel, we just rested. After driving, we checked in and ate breakfast the next day. At 7:46 a.m., August 29th, Monday, I called my father back in New Orleans. I said, "Dad, how is everything?" He said, "Everything is fine. They have a little light flooding in the street, but we're fine in the building." Then the phone went dead.

- Shaun Lain

**Rose**  (6th child of Odis & Irene)


We knew the storm was coming on that Friday, but we weren't paying it a lot of attention because we had maybe two to three storms very close running up to it, one of which was called Cindy.  It had been really hot and I always felt that a hurricane was likely to hit when it was so hot: at least that is my assumption that heat has something to do with the storm actually hitting and hitting hard.

Our regular routine was to gas up our cars in preparation, but at that point, we didn't know whether it was a category five or four or three or anything; we just knew it was coming. So my brother Bobby and I drove around looking for the cheapest gas we could find. By that time, the gas lines were long, gasoline prices were up.  I'll never forget that we found gas at $2.45. Some of the gas stations were going up by 10 cents and gouging the people. Then it hit the news -- don't raise the price on gasoline for people who are trying to get ready to get out of the city. We weren't planning on actually using the cars, but you never know if you might need to.

Another practice that we all do on the day or two before the storm is to run to the store and buy our candles, our batteries, and our matches, bread, sardines, treats, spam, tuna. Most of the things you can keep without refrigeration. The stores wipe out pretty fast. I can't remember at what point we went into the stores, but there was a Family Dollar where I went and got the batteries and stuff like that. We carried flashlights away with us this time.

Another practice is to only pack for three days thinking 1) the day before the storm when we are leaving, 2) the day of the storm and 3) we would come back home the third day. So just in case, I got three sets of clothes. Little did I know that those clothes were the only pieces I would be carrying into the future! It was so weird because I couldn't get back into the house until a month later.

Previous Evacuations

I worked at Loews Express, my brother Otis' business; I helped them with setting up bus trips for people, dispatching busses, and monitoring the building itself. On some days, I spent from nine in the morning until midnight working at Loews. On weekends, we often had parties at the building in the reception hall. That particular weekend of Katrina, we had a wedding scheduled for that Saturday.

The wedding reception actually happened; the people were trying to hurry up and leave after they did their little partying. They didn't try to linger because everybody had to go home and get ready to leave for the storm.

There were at least two incidents prior to Katrina where people had to leave the whole city. One of those two storms was before Madear (mother Irene) passed because she and Bro (Louis) left the city together. Normally Madear would get all her children together or she called everybody and would find out what they would be doing and how they were going to get out.

In that previous storm, they evacuated but that storm didn't hit New Orleans. It actually bypassed New Orleans and the people were very angry because they spent hours and hours in long lines trying to get out of the city. So even when Katrina was coming, everybody was still trying to decide whether they were going to sit twenty-four hours in a line of cars and have the storm hit while they are sitting in their cars. There is always someone with a car that breaks down and the traffic just doesn't move.

At the bus company, during the storm the year before, we helped evacuate people with medical problems and it was a horrendous event because we had no help, no support. A lot of the people were immobile and not ambulatory. They had to be carried and put on seats, and we covered seats with plastic because they were incontinent with all kinds of medical equipment. It took hours to load a bus full of handicapped people, drive them to a shelter and unload them. The bus drivers were upset because all of a sudden they were being asked to be an ambulance person.

## Church Sent Message

For years my church had been showing films and having a meteorologist come and talk to us about how the levee is built like a bowl around New Orleans. They described how if water gets in, it's not going anywhere, anytime soon. They always told us that it would be better to leave and not be there if the water comes in on you.

So earlier that weekend, my church sent out messages for everyone to leave town and that there would be no church. On that Sunday morning, it just felt like a regular day, it didn't really feel like a Sunday at all because nobody was going to church. The Mayor was finally on the news that day telling everybody that this is now a mandatory evacuation, "Get out."

We got a call from some friends in New York and family in West Virginia, and all they had to say was, "Man y'all better get out of there." That was when we learned it was a category five comin' at us. Everyone else was watching the TV and they called Henry, my husband, to get us to leave. So we had our two messages: the church and Henry's friends and family calling and saying get out.

## Family Evacuation

We made plans with all the family to go on a bus at Loews Express. But we were still trying to work to help others get out of the city. People who had not gotten out on their flights by 10:00 that morning were stuck at the airport and were trying to get out some other way. One guy actually rented a bus for about $2000 to get him anywhere away from the city. He couldn't get his flight and he just wanted to get out, Atlanta or somewhere.

We had football teams and baseball teams who we were trying to help get out of town. Everybody had groups that needed to leave the city; no games were going to happen, nothin'. We waited for all those people to help get them out.

I had a girl who worked with me in the reception hall; she was still setting up for an event they were going to have the next day with Richard Simmons. She just knew that they were going to be around these celebrities the next day, wining and dining them. She worked the catering part of events. So she was gearing up for that, and I kept saying to her, "I think you really ought to find a way to get a car and get out of town."

Everyone kept calling other family members and said, "The bus is leaving, the bus is leaving." By noon, we hadn't left because we were helping others to get out of town. So we got in the bus and finally left about 3:00 p.m. So my dad, Shannon's dad, and Stella's mom were the older people on the bus. The middle-aged people were me and

Henry. Then the next level was Shaun, Wellington, Shannon and Andrea. Then there were kids and little children after that. I can't count all the children.

## Nature of New Orleans People

It was pretty sad because New Orleans is the kind of place that people didn't travel a lot. They didn't always have cars. They had a pretty good bus system and they traveled by bus. Well the bus shut down that Sunday and you really couldn't get anywhere. The Mayor said he had busses that would take people to the Superdome, but that the dome was going to be opened up late and it was a place for special needs, not just a place for any old healthy body to wait out the storm. The message was given: "Everybody who can - get out. If you can't get out, then come to the dome, but we can't promise you anything, not even food."

Before the storm, they were fussin' at people about what they would do if the storm might hit. They put out a curfew and you had to be off the street by a certain time, I can't remember if it was 6:00 or 4:00 that Sunday evening. There was a threat given out: "If we pick you up, you are going straight to jail. If you stay and you're caught looting, you're going to jail." They put an extra harsh sentence on it to try to scare people out of the city. They weren't being nice about it at all.

-Rose Lain Watts

### Shannon
(Granddaugther-in-law of Odis & Irene, Wife of Shaun)

We were planning to go to my husband's cousin Keisha's (Lain) baby shower that day. When I left home, it was basically just another hurricane that we had to pack up as usual. But when I returned home from the party, I heard the newscasters and the Mayor getting on the TV. That was when I thought wow, maybe we need to do something about this. At that point I started to have a sense of panic. I panicked and my husband didn't; I think he was out at a football game or something.

The first thing you usually think is -- what do I take? What do I pack up? Do I take our pictures? One of the good things was that I'd just finished enrolling in insurance at my job. I worked as the Assistant Principal at Henderson Middle School when Katrina hit. The new school year had just started, so I had all the kids' birth certificates, social security cards and just all the vital records at my fingertips. So I did take all of that which was very valuable later on.

I took some pictures of the kids and that was basically it, other than a few clothes. It was so funny because it was the beginning of the school year and we had just gone shopping for new school clothes. My daughter, Bria, packed everything, and she was the only one that when people starting giving us clothing, she didn't need anything.

Then once again, we thought it was just an evacuation as usual, as has been a part of our culture forever living in Southern Louisiana. I grew up in Plaquemines Parish. My family was from Bell Chase, a lower lying area that was actually completely wiped out after Katrina. I am accustomed to my mother's side of the family evacuating for every storm, whether it was Hurricane Betsy, Hurricane Camille, whatever. We would evacuate from Plaquemines Parish to the "city" which is what they call New Orleans. But this time it was a little different, especially when we got on the highway and saw the standstill traffic.

I tease my husband to this day because he paid all the bills before we could leave on the evacuation trip. I think back today in retrospect, I was like, "OK you shouldn't have paid the bills." But he is just a creature of habit. Anytime we go, we could be going to Disney World, he is going to pay the bills so we don't spend the bill money.

My dad said he was going to stay and ride out the storm. So I went to bring him some money and some things I bought at the store. But once again when I looked at the news, I thought, oh my gosh, I can't leave him here. So we went back to get him and he actually came on the bus. He was one of the few non-Lain's on that bus.

- Shannon Lain

**Estella** (Stella)
(Daughter-in-law of Odis & Irene, wife of Otis, Jr.)

The week before Katrina on that Monday morning when I got to work, my secretary had the weather channel on. I worked at Delgado Community College as the Dean of Occupational Studies and Executive Director of the High School Program Development. At that point, Katrina was on the other side of Florida, out in the Atlantic Ocean. So I kind of put the storm out of my mind. As the week progressed, we just never focused in on it.

Later in the week on that Friday night, six churches in the area had a revival all together. It was amazing that this guy preached from Ezekiel about how the water was rising -- first at the ankles, then at the knee, and so forth. So the next day, on Saturday, my sister Elynda, her husband and I, decided to go to the dismissal of one of our friends we had grown up with, who had passed. So after the dismissal, they went on to church. I came home.

It wasn't until I sat down on that Saturday and turned the television on that I saw this storm was covering almost the whole screen. That was the first reality check that I had. So I called my mother and told her to get her stuff packed because I began to pay attention and listen to what they were saying.

They were going to start letting people leave from Plaquemines Parish and eventually come on up. I said to my mother, "Well since you live below the Industrial Canal, let me get you tonight and that way, we won't get caught in that traffic."

So, about 1:00 a.m. Sunday morning, I went over and picked my mom up and she had five suitcases packed! I said, "Mama you don't need all this. We are only going to be gone for two days." So I commenced to take everything she had and reduce it down to two bags. She had packed all her insurance papers and everything that she thought she needed. I said, "Look, I'll put that in my garage." But, I didn't, I left it right there on her sofa and I said, "You don't need that."

When we got to my house that morning, we started to talk about what time we were gonna' leave. My mama was there, my sister Elynda came and I couldn't get anything done. I was really just turning around in circles. That was the first time something like that happened to me, but the spirit of God kept telling me, go get your can. I kept a can with birth certificates and all that kind of stuff in my closet. What I did then was to pick everyone up and bring them over to June-El's. I still had not packed a thing.

Then I went back home and tried to get myself together. I was still saying, "Two days, I'm going to pack light." I did put my video camera on the shelf. Why? I don't know because I normally kept it on the floor in the closet. I just kept thinkin' about all those papers, but I didn't do a thing about it.

When we got back to June-El, everybody was assembling. That is when I found out my husband Otis was not planning to go; he was going to stay. I think we had about 20 or 21 people on the bus, I'm not really sure. I think it was about 4:00 p.m. and everybody was finally ready at that point. They had closed off Interstate 10; nobody could leave on the I10 route. We had to go across Lake Pontchartrain on the twin-span.

Shaun had gone across the street to a restaurant and came back with this big loaf of sandwich. I said, "Look, we ought to just go ahead and ride this thing out. Let's go down to the Superdome." Now we had never done that before, we had always gone to Atlanta and turned around and came back home after the storms. So again, I said it for the second time, "Let's go down to the Superdome." Either he didn't hear me or didn't pay attention, but nobody responded. Nobody said a word.

We finally backed out and started down Chef Menteur Highway going north, which I call the back way. At this time, traffic on the main Interstates was backed up way into the city. When we turned on Highway 11, the water was already coming across the road. You could definitely tell that it was flooding at that point; it was the storm surge that was coming in.

So we kept riding on Highway 11 and I just thought Shaun was going to cut off and meet the traffic. But he kept on driving across the seven mile bridge which is normally locked. No one else was on this bridge except our bus. So I'm saying to Shaun because he just kept going, "Shaun, how are you going to turn this bus around or back it up?" I knew we were pretty far out there and I said, "Now it is going to come to a point where that gate is going to be closed and we are going to have to turn around and go all the way back. How are you going to turn this bus around?" He just kept driving and driving.

When I realized that we had passed that lake, I said, "Lord, you wanted us out of here." There was no way in the world that the bridge should have been open. There weren't any other cars. If people had known the bridge was open, they would have been coming on that road. From June-El's to Slidell at Gauss Blvd., we made it in about twenty-five minutes.

*[Otis Jr. speaking: In about four to five more hours, that bridge was totally washed out. On the next day, I tried to cross that bridge and the bridge was locked down. Everything was closed – no crossing.]*

When we got to Gauss Blvd., Shaun hesitated and said, "I ought to go straight down Highway 11 and meet up with Interstate 12." Instead, he went on Gauss Blvd. and then he went Interstate 10 and came back over to Highway 59. Then traffic was bumper to bumper. It took a long time because so many people were traveling in packs. On the side of the road you would see four or five cars pulled over – one car had major car trouble and they were trying to help each other.

We rode all night. By the time we got in Alabama, we were on I65 almost to Huntsville; they were saying that this was where the remnant of the storm was headed. We were in this heavy rain the whole time.

That morning, we were somewhere in Alabama and we pulled in a truck stop. Everyone got out to refresh themselves. I think Shaun or Wellington tried to make contact with Otis. They had spoken to him earlier but now it was after 7 a.m. and we had no more contact with him.

-Estella Lain

New Orleans "is a very poor city. Some estimate 140,000 people do not have cars. About a quarter of the residents have no way to get out. I talked to the mayor a couple of days ago. There is not a plan to use city buses to get these people out."

... -Susan Roesgen, WGNO reporter, responding to a question about why so many have chosen not to evacuate, taken from CNN Reports, 2005, p. 16.

**Tanga** (granddaughter of Odis & Irene,
oldest daughter of Emanuel)

I'm fortunate working for the federal government
and I knew that I would be reimbursed for anything I spent
in evacuating. So I've always evacuated no matter what. Even
during Hurricane Ivan I evacuated and Ivan didn't even come
to New Orleans. I don't fault people that don't leave because
many of them don't have a hurricane fund (money saved to
help pay for evacuation).

But I was fortunate -- my family and my parents
evacuated to Houston. We always went to Houston for
evacuations because of Six Flags. We always see an
evacuation as a vacation. So we packed up things like
swimming trunks. We didn't take anything significant; just
everything that was insignificant. Anything that was fun --
we took.

For some reason, my husband says I'm
unorganized, but I'm 'unorganized organized.' So I had this
mini-briefcase and I often just stuffed important documents

in there, like birth certificates, etc. It was not in any order but it was all in there. Just a week before the storm happened, I got a letter from my mortgage company saying I didn't have flood insurance. I knew we had flood insurance because we just purchased our house the year before and the closing documents showed where they took out for flood insurance. So I knew that we had it, but I didn't follow up with the company, but I did stuff those papers in the mini-briefcase.

When we evacuated to Houston, we only took a couple of things. We actually weren't going to evacuate but as we were seeing the hurricane picture on TV get larger and larger, we said "Let's go." On that Saturday, we were saying, "Let's leave the next day." Then we said, "Let's leave at 6:00 p.m. today." Finally about 11:00 a.m., my clothes were not finished washing, so I said, "Just take these wet clothes and let's get out of here." We did leave Saturday during the day and so it only took us eight hours to get to Houston, which is usually a five-hour drive. But for most people that left on Sunday, it was twelve to twenty-four hours to get to Houston.

When we got to Houston, everything was cool. My brother Emanuel Jr. decided to come up; he lived in Baton Rouge. We had two rooms and everybody was laying on the floor. I had my husband, his daughter and her son, and my two children; six people in one room. Then when Emanuel Jr. came up, they were in the other room.

We all went to the mall. The children went ice skating and we went to the beauty salon; we had a good time. Then we heard the levees broke.

-Tanga Lain Hale

**Elsie** (Lee) (2nd child of Odis & Irene), holding grand-nephew L.J.

It was Saturday and the winds were already blowing. We were at Keisha's (neice) baby shower and we were debating whether or not we were staying or going. We had hotel reservations in New Orleans. Sarah and some others had decided that was what we were going to do.

My husband, Arthur, was already sick; he had been on dialysis for like 28 years at that time. So we had a big discussion whether we could stay or not. But in my heart, it was like "No", I couldn't handle him. I knew that if the lights went out, or an elevator went out, I wouldn't be able to handle him. So the best thing I could do was get out.

It was really a tug of war, but I just really felt like we should not go to the hotel. My husband kept insisting that we go to the hotel. But I just decided, we are going to Houston.

So I made that decision because my daughter lives in Houston. It took us like thirteen hours to get there. We left on Sunday morning. I didn't go the usual way.

We decided to go out on Highway 90; we thought we would beat the traffic. It was just rolling along and shoot, I didn't realize that you are so far off from the Interstate once you do that. We ended up back in the traffic anyway. I guess I should have just stayed on 90 because it would eventually take me to Lafayette. Thank God, we were able to make it OK; the car didn't break down or anything.

-Elsie Lain Hagan

**Raymond Sr.** (9th child of Odis & Irene)

People from New Orleans don't feel too nervous about hurricanes coming. Well a hurricane can strike anywhere along the Gulf Coast, from the tip of Galveston, Texas, all the way around to the Florida Keys. Lots of time, you don't have that direct hurricane force wind. It almost has to be a direct hit and normally it only covers so many miles to get the strongest winds.

That was the unique thing about Katrina. It was one of them hurricanes of a lifetime where it devastated the entire Gulf Coast. I mean it was huge! Katrina stretched so many hundred miles wide and it affected everything – Florida, Alabama, Louisiana and Texas. Devastating winds from Florida all the way to Texas; the whole Gulf Coast got that one. It was just a freak of nature.

I think that Friday it really wasn't a hurricane; I think it was a tropical storm when it cut across Florida. Once Katrina cut across the Gulf, it picked up some steam but nobody really gave it much thought. By that Saturday it got a little stronger, but the TV reporters only predicted it would be like 110 miles per hour. By the time we went to bed that Saturday night and woke up on Sunday morning, Katrina had grown to 160 miles per hour winds and it stretched across the Gulf Coast. I mean, it just got huge overnight.

Ruby had called me early that Sunday morning from California and said, "Y'all get out." So I called my son, little Raymond and told him, "I have a feeling this is going to be a big one." Little Raymond loaded up his car and he took a different route than me, but we were in constant telephone contact. I think Raymond had his SUV and he ended up in Tennessee.

I ended up in Houston; I thought we might stop in Baton Rouge, but we ended up going all the way to Houston. We didn't get there until 12:00 that night. We drove from 3:00 p.m. to midnight; normally Houston is a six-hour trip. But that day, it seemed like it took forever.

Contraflow is good but it still takes a long time. (During contraflow, all traffic is directed out of town on both sides of the Interstate.) You talk about bumper to bumper, stop and go traffic. I think if they would have contraflow for all of Louisiana and Texas, that would be nice. But eventually, all cars were directed back to one side of the Interstate.

It could have been worse than it was – could have been nobody going nowhere. Everybody did get out; it just took a little longer and it took patience. I think people were patient overall. A lot of people were all camped out along the Interstate. At every rest stop, you had people, people, people. It was something else. You had problems like really long lines to use the restroom. People generated a lot of trash. It looked like a traveling carnival, with all the trash, bottles, and picnicking. There were people sleeping in cars.

There was gas available for the cars; we didn't have a gas problem like sometimes. I guess the most stressful part of it was that we didn't know where we were going to stay, and we had a car full of people. We were very tired, it was very late, and we had been driving all day. We were irritable. We didn't know where we could sleep because every hotel we passed was already full. A lot of hotels were charging a premium price -- they wanted $180 and up.

-Raymond Lain, Sr.

**Emanuel Sr.** (7th child of Odis & Irene)

We left that Saturday the 27th. We saw on TV that it was a big storm. My daughter said, "What y'all going to do?" I have two daughters and a son in the middle, and at that time we had six grand kids.

My wife, Melva, and I evacuated and beat the contraflow. We went to Houston and it took us under seven hours to get there. I know in the contraflow it would have taken longer than that just to get to Baton Rouge. My daughter, Tanga, her husband Al Hale, and their two boys; my other daughter, Alisha, her husband and their two boys, all got on the road at the same time.

We pretty much saw on our own that this thing was going to be unlike any other. We was hoping that it would miss New Orleans, but we had started to evacuate every time a storm got in the Gulf; our habit was to get out of town early and beat contraflow.

We left our passports at home; we took just enough clothes for about three days. We figured we would be back home in about three days; that would be the average.

On that Monday night we heard that the levees had broken. I was listening to a radio and someone was reporting that they seen water everywhere and I remember feeling so sad. On TV the next day, they were showing the water and it was surreal. I just know that I was real sad and hurt. I really didn't know what to expect. Our family stayed at that hotel for about six more days and then we decided to pack up. During that time, we had to apply for a FEMA number and so forth.

-Emanuel Lain Sr.

**Calvin** (13th child of Odis & Irene)

I, along with just about everyone in South Louisiana, was watching CNN or the Weather Channel to see what was happening with the hurricane. I started getting calls from family members, nephews and brother-in-laws for a place to stay. Back in 1996, my wife Josie and I decided to move out of New Orleans and we went to Winnsboro in Northern Louisiana. We picked that small, little town because it is the childhood home of my father and mother. I moved my law practice up to Winnsboro that year.

So when we heard from other family members, Josie and I just started preparing for as many people as we could. I don't think we turned down anybody who needed to evacuate. Some people said they were coming but wound up being diverted, going either to Atlanta or Houston. Whoever was able to come, we were able to accommodate them.

My house in Winnsboro is either 100 or 107 years old depending on which document you read. I think it is one of the oldest residences in our town. It is totally wood with the bulk of the rooms having fourteen foot ceilings. The house has what you might consider five bedrooms and three full baths with a large great room – open space with a kitchen, dining and TV area.

We called other family members that lived up in Winnsboro to see if people could stay with them. Like Uncle P.C., my daddy's brother, said he had four rooms available. Then our cousin Shirley and Raeshed had rooms in Shreveport, and so she kept calling to see if anyone needed to come. We had our two overflow places available, just in case.

We wound up with sixteen people in the house, more or less. Most people stayed with us during those first two weeks. After that, people started leaving and going other places. I think a week or so later, Damon and his family went to Atlanta. Then my brother Emanuel followed.

We might have gotten down to about ten people, primarily my wife's family - her brother, Albert and his wife and one of their children, Albert III. Then Albert's wife's mom and dad, also his wife's mom's mom was there. She was elderly, I think in her late 80's or early 90's, and she required home health care. We called the local Home Health agency and we got her signed up. The agency came in and was giving her therapy and nursing aids. She had one of the bedrooms.

Everything just kind of worked out, but we had people sleeping everywhere. My brother-in-law's wife's mother, we called her Miss Bush, would cook every day. That was good because we had all this New Orleans food: red beans and rice, smothered chicken, greens and gumbo. We had a nice sized stove and everybody, under the circumstances, was comfortable. We did a lot more washing clothes; I think the wash machine was going every day. Fifteen people takin' showers - that is a load of towels right there.

I would say the people were calm, once they realized what was going on. My oldest brother Otis was missing, nobody knew where he was at. There was a time we were talking about trying to go down to New Orleans to find him. But everybody was calm and basically taking in what had happened. They were just trying to see what their next step would be. I guess everyone was kind of shell-shocked.

- Calvin A. Lain

# Book 2

During The Storm

# Chapter 4

## Riding out the Storm

A catastrophic hurricane represents ten or fifteen
atomic bombs in terms of the energy it releases.
-Joseph  Suhayada, LSU engineer (CNN Reports, 2005, p. 16)

**Otis Jr.** (June)   (1st child of Odis & Irene)

I should start off by saying that at the time of Katrina, I was the owner of basically three small businesses in New Orleans. One was Loews Express, a bus company with 33 large busses, like the Greyhound buses. We did tours and charters for private folks. Another business was the June-El Reception Hall where we took in people that was interested in weddings and parties. The third business was a campground located in Slidell, called the Pink Panther. It had 78 acres of land; we had campsites for tents, motor homes, and a playground area.

The Loews Express building (also referred to as June-El) is 22,000 square feet. The building was used for office space, for mechanical work on busses, and for receptions. The building, which originally was a General Motors training and testing building, is located on Chef Menteur Highway. That highway was built at an elevated level back during WWII because they needed an exit for hurricanes. That is the one thing they did right.

June-El / Loews Express Building – 2009

My family brought one of the Loews Express busses to Atlanta to evacuate for the storm on that Sunday. That evening Darren Hagan, my nephew, came and we were in the building, just the two of us stayed behind.

We decided that we would ride out the storm because the building was built to withstand a hurricane with up to 200 miles-an-hour wind. We wasn't even concerned about the structure of the building or the height because we did have access to the roof; there was a ladder inside the building if the water should come up.

That night, maybe around 11:00 p.m., the winds started picking up and a window was blown out on the back side, which was the North side of the building. Rain water was coming through this window from the wind. In the early morning hours, we were sweeping water, trying to get everything fairly dry in the building. The floor had just a couple inches of water from those broken windows.

I didn't think that we had a major problem in the city. I was able to climb on the roof and look around and across the street where there was a little trailer court. One of those units was just turned to the side. I thought, oh man the damage wasn't that bad. I mean you had a few things blown around, a couple of tree branches down and pieces of

Busses at Loews Express (2009)

tin came off the roof. When I looked at my surroundings, I thought we are going to sail through this thing. There was no major flooding from the storm itself.

The front part of the building is closest to Chef Menteur Highway. It was like a slope, you can stand on Chef and literally look at the top of the houses to the North as they go down in the neighborhood. So it is a major difference as far as the height. The highest point in New Orleans' East is Chef Highway.

## Taxi disappeared

On the morning after Katrina, maybe around 10 a.m., I decided that I was going to go check on my house which is about a mile and a half away. I went 510 to Interstate 10. When I got to I10, the water started coming in. Around 11 a.m. or noon, I knew that I couldn't go any further, so I turned around. As I was coming back, from I10 to 510, to get on Chef Menteur Highway, I noticed in my rear-view mirror there was a taxi cab; he was about three to four car lengths behind me. The water started coming across that exit ramp and the water was so fierce! I had a 2004 Cadillac that had front wheel drive.

I came from that exit and the water was rushing through. I was plowing through water about a foot deep. If you have ever gone through rushing water with your wheel cocked all the way to the left, you would know I had to go at least 50 miles per hour to keep from getting swept off the road. I'm attributing that I made it only because I had front wheel drive in that car.

All of a sudden that taxi behind me disappeared. When I got to high ground, I tried to look back and I didn't see the cab anywhere. Maybe about a week later, I went back to that site and I saw the cab down in a gutter turned upside down. I don't know what happened to the driver.

I've had nightmares for a long time about whatever happened to that cab driver. I went back and looked and checked. The body was not in the car, but the car was nose down, with the trunk pointed up perpendicular. That was one situation that I thought about for a long time, I think about how I should have helped. I should have been able to help him, but there really, really wasn't anything I could do about it. The water was coming up and was flowing. To me, I was really blessed just to get through before it got worse.

<u>People came to the building</u>

So that Monday, around 1:00 p.m., I was headed back to the building and all of a sudden, we started getting a couple of people coming in: one or two, then three or four at a time. All these people seemed to have animals. I was really shocked to know that many people was left in the neighborhood.

When these people came in, all they knew was that the water was rising. They didn't know where it was coming from or what was causing it. It felt like, man, we went through the hurricane, but then about an hour or two later, the water started coming. Where was it coming from? It looked like the water was coming from the Chalmette area, which is South. Then it looked like the water was coming from the levee area, which is North. It was coming from both directions, it was more than one levee break.

When the people were coming out of their houses, a lot of the water, from what I could see about a block away, was about waist high or up to their chests. It depended on the height of the person. To me, I'm six feet tall, it would have gone up to my waist if I had gone about half a block away. But the farther you went away from Chef, the deeper the water got. The water did not get on Chef Hwy., so the front part of the building was dry. The back of the building seemed like a marina because all of a sudden all these boats started coming in. At the North tip end of our building, we were able to bring people in and that is where they were able to dock boats. Then they were able to walk on dry land from that point.

Most people came just with the clothes on their back. It was like a surprise; some were hysterical, some were in shock. People were just laying out on the grass in front or on the gravel in the driveway. They were standing there for hours, I saw a lot of people that actually slept and spent the night in the rocky area of the drive.

There were young kids, but I would think the majority of the people were elderly. It was a mixed neighborhood, we had a little bit of every background of people come to the building. About half were blacks and half were whites. We had a lot of people that were of higher stature in the neighborhood, but at that point, we were all as one.

The first day people got along real, real nice. I mean it was beautiful. In the beginning, it was a unique experience simply because people really had a chance to tell their stories and just vent and stuff. Everyone was just happy to be alive and get out of the water.

We were up to about 250 people; we had people all over the place, everywhere. It looked like over half of these people had animals of some kind. You know we had people with pot bellied pigs, ducks, sheep, and goats. We had people

Building and parking lot

with a lot of dogs, all kind of dogs. You name it; it looked like it was there. I even seen an iguana. I mean I couldn't believe all these people were willing to risk their lives to stay behind to try to take care of these animals.

I asked the people, "Why didn't you leave?" They said, "Well I didn't have anyone to take care of my dog. I didn't have anyone to take care of my cat. I didn't have anyone to take care of..." this, that and the other. That was the first time in my life I really began to understand how people really love animals because they were willing to give up their lives for them. These people were really strongly attached to their pets.

We had one lady with a pot bellied pig and I told that lady, "Look, push come to shove, we're going to take and barbeque this pig." I was kidding at the time. I didn't know how attached people become to their animals until I told her that. I said it as a joke, but she started crying. I had about ten people trying to console this lady; this went on for hours. I told her I was only kidding because we had enough meat -- we had all kind of ribs and chicken and stuff that was still fresh. Anyway, she said, "He is going to kill my pig." I think she called the pig by name, but never-the-less, it was a problem.

We had a former police chief from a surrounding town. He said, "The law will permit you to take food out of these stores, but don't take nothing else. Don't take any money or break into any machines. Only take what you need to survive." I knew he was concerned about the legal stuff.

I said, "Lord, what am I going to do with all these people?" Then all of a sudden, the food started coming in because we had all these people from the neighborhood, and the stores were around. We cooked a big pot of red beans, I mean a huge pot. It looked like a ten gallon pot full of red beans that came out real good. One of the things we had the first day was food. We cooked and ate and it seemed like it was going to be a great, great time. I had a couple of barbeque grills and I was in charge of assigning tasks to different people. I had a couple of guys barbequing. We had guys come back and say, "What do you need?" We said, "We need barbeque sauce, We need mustard, bread," and they went and got it. Food was not a concern.

We organized people to cook and clean. We organized a counseling section. I had a guy in charge of the bathrooms even though the toilets didn't flush, we tried to maintain it. The problem was, we had too many people to sustain what we really needed to do in that department. So we don't even talk about the toilet and how bad it was and the stench from that deal. Even though we had a lot of Lysol, toilet paper and everything else, there was just no way to flush the sewage. After we kind of closed down the bathroom that evening, I'm not sure how they eliminated. It was quite an experience.

We had all these tables set up in the dining hall. Then we had the formal area where we gave the weddings and we had a lot of room in there where people were able to sit in chairs and some in sleeping bags. We had so many people, a lot of people were outside on the lawn, especially people with animals. We had candles and people were sleeping on the floor, sleeping outside on the grass, and the grounds. People had a way, even though they came with nothing to get pots, pans and sleeping bags. It really wasn't cold, just a little damp. They wound up going back and forth to get stuff that they could salvage. I remember people coming there wet and laying clothes on the ground and the bushes. They had windows down on the busses laying clothes out to dry them out. By night-fall, everybody had dry clothes.

I really, really knew that we had a problem when one guy said, "Look, the hospital is about two miles away." He needed a ride to get to the hospital. At 10:00 that Monday night, I put him in my car. He said he had a severe heart problem and if he didn't get this medication, he was going to die. Chef Menteur Highway was the only route that we could go without having water. We went to several exits on Chef to see if we could get closer. When I realized that I went about two to three miles down Chef and they had water everywhere, I told him and his brother that there was no way that I could help him to get to the hospital. At the time, I didn't know that the hospital was flooded, and what I saw was only the beginning of the flooding.

One lady said, "My mother is dead and I need someone to go back and help get her out of our place." They had several guys wade through the water with her. Her house wasn't that far away from the building, and to find out, the mom was over 300 pounds. They couldn't move her. Other people had to leave loved ones that drowned when they came to the Loews Express building.

Once those people came into the building, I felt like it was my responsibility to try to take care of all of them. I felt like if things weren't right, it was my fault. I had to make sure that they all ate and had water. I opened up everything for them. I had people sleeping on the busses with their animals. I just walked around and was greeting people and was talking to people trying to make them feel at ease; that it was OK. I had all these people calm, they knew my name. I was meeting them for the first time even though they lived in the neighborhood.

I slept inside the Reception Hall, where I put three chairs together. Somebody put my eye glasses in front of me and my eye glasses ended up missing. For the next three or four months, I was without eye glasses. I slept really good that night because I was extremely tired.

## Police Arrival

I guess about 8 a.m. the next morning on Tuesday, a police officer standing over me said, "Are you Otis Lain?" I looked up from my chairs and Lord, he had a gun. It was amazing, everyone was really calm until that next morning when the police came in. There were nine police and they stormed in to the place, screaming and hollering, "Y'all going to drown. You got to get these people out of here." When they started screaming and hollering, chaos set in. The world looked like it was upside down and I said, "Lord, I need help."

The police were saying that the levee had broke and that we had to get the people out of there. They said that everything was going to be about ten feet under water. At that point, we started loading people up on busses.

The police didn't have any vehicles. Where they came from? - I don't know. All nine of them had rifles and were really aggressive. These policemen said, "Look, we don't have any transportation and we need transportation. And we need to get these people out of here."

All these people, I don't know exactly how many but I knew it was about 250 people because when I left, we had three busses full of people. The police were trying to find keys for the other busses.

The police asked if anybody had CDL licenses? It is amazing how things happen because then there were about four to five people step up and say, "I have a CDL." The police said can you drive this bus? I kind of showed one guy a few little things to drive the bus. My nephew Darren was one of the drivers and he has a CDL.

The police decided that they wanted all the vehicles. We had the keys to the vehicles on a rack. They took the rack of keys, went through it and took the vehicles they wanted. They told me, "Look, we need that Cadillac that you are driving." At that point, we had the names of three busloads of people on a card. Once we started loading the people up, and I saw that the police officers seemed like they weren't stable minded; it seemed like they were very excited and you could smell the sense of death in them. Everybody was on their last nerve and it started to be a little chaotic situation.

At first we said, "You can't take your animals on the busses," but shoot, they had chickens, ducks, turkeys and what have you. They got on the bus with their animals and we just got them out of town. Once we got the majority of the people on the bus and it wasn't an ideal thing for me because these police had big guns and they had sweat rolling down on them. Nobody was in charge and it was chaotic. So I jumped in my car and I took off.

But I tell you what, the blessing for me was, once the police came and took over, I felt like it was out of my hands. I was able to take off and I felt like it rolled off my shoulders.

After we left, the police took over the building for a couple of days. They camped out, they had police officers in and out of the building. There was no electricity, no running water, no sewage, but never-the-less, they did what they wanted to do.

When I got back, after a week or so, I had trucks missing, I had cars missing, I had stuff with the steering wheels knocked off. A Rolls Royce was messed up. I had two Rolls Royce cars, one is still in the building now because they couldn't get it started. To me, the policemen actually got everyone excited. They were angry, they didn't have any transportation and all their vehicles were under water, so I was the only one in the area that had vehicles.

When the police came to take over, they took what they wanted. In fact, almost everything on the yard, almost close to 20 different vehicles were scattered all over the place. I never did find a lot of the stuff, and I never was compensated for it. I'm still in a state of shock after these four years to be honest with you.

## Getting out of New Orleans

I went North trying to get to Lake Ponchartrain. On my way to the lake, maybe about a mile from the building, there were moccasins -- black snakes. There must have been about 10,000 of them in the middle of that road! I thought, if I run straight through them, I'm going to kill all these snakes. So I started blowing my horn.

To this day, I felt like what if one of those snakes had gotten under my wheel, inside of my car, or how many would I have run over? I lived with that thought for a long time. But these snakes all looked like they were the same size and all in the middle of the road. I wish I had a picture of all those snakes. Imagine how that street was covered.

I drove down the highway, I saw a fish in a little puddle of water and he was just a wiggling. I think, man whatever happened to that fish? I saw deer. I saw this big boar, a hog as big as the car was running on the side of me. It seemed like he was racing, like he was just going along for the ride. This boar was as big as a horse, he has this tusk coming out of his head. I don't know where he came from. All the animals came to this road. I went through some soft mud when I saw all these animals running crazy with no direction. I said, "Lord, I'm out here by myself, no one knows I'm out here, and if I get stuck, there are only wild animals."

So I proceeded about seven miles going around all these trees. With that front wheel drive car, I was able to plow through stuff that normally I would have gotten stuck. I'm out there in the wilderness with nobody around; no kind of communication. Finally going around trees, scratching the car up, denting it, I got to the end of the seven miles only to find out that the gate was closed and the bridge was out. I said, "Oh Lord, I don't know if I'm going to get back out of here."

On my way out of New Orleans, trying to escape, I had to run through water. The water was at the foot of the bridge at Louisa St. and that was where I saw my limo. The hood was open and the windows were knocked out. And on the other side, I saw my van full of police officers, at least what I thought was police officers going in the opposite direction. At that time I said, "Look, let me just get out of here."

Once I left that building, I was in a lot of water because I just couldn't believe that every street in the inner-city of New Orleans was flooded. Once I got on the Interstate, I got elevated roadway all the way to the Westbank.

## Staying in Baton Rouge

After my little escapade going down and seeing all the animals, I rode around for about three or four hours, just meandering. Gas was at a premium and it was hard to get. I was concerned about running out of gas and getting stuck out in the wilderness. There were real long lines for gas. Ice probably cost you $10 a bag, and gas was $6 or $7 a gallon. I don't know exactly the price. But if you didn't have money it was bad.

To make it worse, everything was bumper to bumper. You had police cars running all over the place. You had stolen cars from the post office, you had stolen cars from the Cadillac dealership. These people thought that they could just take the cars simply because it was an emergency, that they wouldn't be prosecuted; but later on they actually put these people in jail and pressed charges against them.

Some kind of way I ended up in Baton Rouge around LSU. I had two grand-daughters, Meryl and Whitney, in college over there. I walked in to the building lobby and Whitney must have screamed to the top of her lungs.

They must have had about 100 people sitting and milling around, casually reading and talking. When Whitney screamed, "Grandpa, I thought you were dead," everyone stopped and stared. I think it really would have been a Kodak moment.

Meryl came up and made a big deal. Even little girls that I never had seen in my life, came up and hugged me. The girls thought I had drowned in the water and that was the rumor that had gone all over the place. The girls were able to call my wife and said that I was there and was OK.

Meryl was in charge of a dormitory. She said, "Look our students haven't showed up, so you can spend a couple of days here." So I stayed in an LSU dorm for about a week. I had a big dorm room to myself in a dormitory that was full of females. At that point, I just needed some peace of mind. I found that just staying alone, staying with my granddaughters, was rewarding. So I just took off that week before I went back to New Orleans to try to start getting the busses located and figure out where I would go from there.

-Otis Lain Jr.

**Meryl** (great-granddaughter of Odis & Irene, granddaughter of Otis Jr. (June), daughter of Wellington)

<u>Living at LSU</u>

At the time of Hurricane Katrina, I was at Louisiana State University (LSU). I was a resident assistant (R.A.) and I was responsible for about 54 girls on my floor. My sister, Whitney, had just started college at LSU and she was in the residence hall right across from me, literally across the street.

I remember that Sunday before the storm hit. I called my parents in New Orleans and told them, "Y'all better get out of the house, you know." Everyone was kinda' like, "Oh, I'm going." I remember I was going to the Union on campus and I was talking to my step-mom. I said, "Mama, y'all not gone yet?" She told me, "Girl, you know your daddy, he is so slow." Nobody really thought much of it, they were like – "no biggie."

The residence hall staff prepped us and told us, "OK, as R.A.'s this is what you need to do." They made sure we had our guidelines and the whole 'shebang.' That night of Katrina, we checked with our residents to see who was going to stay, who was going to be leaving and where they were going. We did a count and they put us on rotation every four hours.

I told my little sister, "Come to my room and you can just stay with me." Everything was fine; we did our rounds and everything. Then I remember waking up and all the power being out. As time progressed with the storm, I had friends come up and stay in my room. My sister continued to stay with me.

I remember making very, very, very brief contact with my Grandmother Estella. We couldn't talk much, but I found out, that where I thought that they were going to Mississippi was changed to Georgia.

I don't remember how many days later, but I remember watching TV and trying to see a glimpse of what was happening in the East of New Orleans. They never would show it. I was trying to make contact with whoever I could.

I believe I knew that my Grandpa was still in New Orleans at that time and I remember being very upset. But I understood why he stayed, because when you live there, we get hurricanes every year.

I knew that the East was flooded, but I didn't know the condition of the building that my Grandpa was in. I remember, like it was yesterday, I was in my room, and by this time my sister had gone back to her dorm. My sister called me and she was in hysterics, "Meryl... Meryl....wha... wha..."

I yelled, "What, what are you saying? I can't understand what you are saying." She was like, "Merl...Merl... Papa... Papa. He is in the lobby!" I yelled, "What?"

I can't tell you where my cell phone went. I was in my robe, and I remember running downstairs and out of my building to her dorm. He was there. It was just PURE JOY. I fussed at him all in the same breath. My sister was just hysterical. I couldn't believe it; even when I think of it now, I still don't believe it. Who would have thought?

My grandfather had never been to campus with me; didn't bring my sister up to school. Never came into my dorm, nothing like that. I asked my grandpa, "Papa, how in the world? What made you come to this hall?" He said, "I just came on campus and it was the first place I stopped." The good thing was that he paid enough attention that he knew I was an RA and so he knew I worked for the University.

At that time, we had some families come to stay in the dorms. So I spoke to my boss, and I let him know, "I have an empty room and my grandfather is going to have that room to himself." And of course, my boss understood. He said, "That's fine, that's fine." Residential life had sheets and blankets and everything for the people that were coming.

My Grandpa Otis told me about how he escaped and everything. I got him cleaned up and it was funny because it was an all girls dorm. We knew families were going to stay in the extra rooms and so we worked it out. I told him we would get him a cell phone so he could get in contact with people. With him being Otis, he still didn't keep still; he was in and out, going around. I just wanted him to stay there with me, to be safe. I was just nervous but I also knew he is not the type of person just to be locked up in a room.

It really was a moment. I think from that point on, me and my grandfather really started to bond even more. I mean we always have been close when it comes to a working relationship. But this was more personal - a grandfather to granddaughter bond. I fussed at him. Oh, he got it, but it was a blessing because he was OK.

-Meryl Lain

**Darren** (grandson of Odis & Irene, son of Elsie)

I'm a driver for River Parish's Disposal and I've been working there for twelve years. It is a private company and they contract with the City of New Orleans.

I heard about Hurricane Katrina at least four days ahead of time. Everybody was wrapping up their businesses and packing up, hitting the highway, going every which way they possibly could. At that time, I was undecided whether I was leaving or staying. At the last minute, I ended up staying and rode the storm out.

I was up on Chef Menteur Highway at June-El's, my Uncle June's business. I went out to the office there on Sunday and just stayed. June stayed there with me. We were watching TV through Sunday evening and night.

Katrina came close, but it didn't do a direct hit on New Orleans. It was going west, but once it got about 35 miles outside New Orleans, it made a left turn and went up

North. It sort of sideswiped New Orleans and it produced nothing but a whole lot of wind. There wasn't a lot of rain with that hurricane. It was just a lot of wind blowing: blowing trees down, blowing containers over, some telephone poles broke in half like toothpicks.

Uncle June had his radios on because he had busses on the road doing regular trips and he wanted to keep up with everybody, to see where everybody was at. Some drivers called, but he told them not to even worry about coming back in because the weather had been getting really bad. By 2:25 a.m. on Monday morning everything was dead: regular phones, cell phones, electric. There was just no more communication, it was all gone. I was listening to a cordless radio.

A lot of people behind the building in a subdivision got flooded real bad; they got at least six feet of water. Lots of people came around June-El starting on that Monday. People were walking and swimming through it, coming out on boats. About 200 people camped out at the building, June let them stay. The people were mostly middle class, a mixed race background of people. They were trying to cooperate and just trying to find some communication and transportation to get on out of town.

They had stores next door that was closed but the people got as much as they could that was still fresh. So we managed to cook up a lot of stuff for everybody. They needed food. Some slept outside on lounge chairs, some had to sit on the ground and lay their head on their knees. In the beginning they were upset, but in the long run they started smiling; they saw some kind of relief because they got on dry ground.

## Getting out of New Orleans

Me and two others were driving busses out from my Uncle June's business. We had enough people at June-El to fill the busses. June left in his car. I drove the people to

Baton Rouge, Louisiana. I found a lot of water just going down Chef Menteur Highway to get up onto Interstate 10. But by the bus sitting up high, I just had to go real slow through the water.

People didn't panic. I was scared because I was driving, leading the way. I cut all the way to the right where the road was pretty high. I went through the water like that and got up on the Interstate. The other busses followed me. They had shelters set up in Baton Rouge and everybody got off the bus there. The people went inside and registered.

I left Baton Rouge and went to Nichols State University. I didn't have friends there, but there was a person on the road saying that a shelter had just opened up at Nichols State. It sounded like they didn't have that many people yet. I already knew that Baton Rouge was overcrowded.

All the cell phones were out due to the high winds knocking the cell phone towers out. My mom didn't know where I was at. They had telephone service set up over at Nichols State University. They looked up my sister's phone number in Houston on Saturday, after the storm hit almost a week before. That was the first time I was able to contact my mother and she was really happy to hear from me.

-Darren Hagan

# Chapter 5

## The Water is Rising:
## Vertical Evacuation

**Sarah** (4th child of Odis & Irene)


My neice Vonkeisha would soon be delivering her second child, I had delivered her first but I was currently retired from OB/GYN practice. My home was paid for and I had saved enough money to live comfortably. The day before Katrina was to hit, most of the family were having a baby shower. We were having strawberry margaritas, loads of food and all kinds of fun, joy, and laughter. Some people had already left the city -- didn't want to get caught in the crowd.

Katrina had just come into the news two days before. It had started between Florida and the Bahamas. Usually they come off the coast of West Africa so we have two weeks before they get near the Gulf; we have a chance to get use to the idea that a hurricane is coming. So this one was different, this one came up so sudden that I think some people didn't know a hurricane is coming.

Besides they all seemed to curve away from New Orleans (my brother Louis said it had something to do with the barometric pressure from the Mississippi River.) Periodically the family had these three to five day evacuation vacations. Some people would get on the bus -- which usually ended up in Atlanta, some go to Houston or even Las Vegas, or just stay in New Orleans because of first responder jobs or curiosity to see what happens. My brother Bobby and I chose the latter. I secured a hotel room downtown for vertical evacuation.

Everything was rushed on that last Sunday morning. We woke late because we stayed at the shower party the night before. Bobby came over to disconnect and put both computers in the attic. We didn't have much time for preparations. Besides, for the previous big hurricane threat, I had packed my bags and put them in the living room; those bags were still there because the hurricane never came.

Liz was going to go on my oldest brother's bus to evacuate to Atlanta. I packed a few things in my bag and threw a few things on top my bed; I felt that if it might flood, it wouldn't get higher than a few feet or so.

Then I saw my New Orleans Saints football jersey which I had bought for $125. I thought to myself, this jersey is not going down. So I packed it, and my best jewelry. I gave Liz her computer to pack but she started rough-housing and rolling around on the floor with Bobby. As a result, her computer got left on the floor and never put up high enough to avoid the water. My daughter is a "pack-rat" so she did manage to take five duffle bags out.

I wanted to get down to the hotel early because the last time we went down there for hurricane evacuation, we couldn't find a parking space for my car and I knew the parking lot was going to be filling up quickly. When we got there, we got a room on the 30th floor.

The hotel must have expected the refrigeration to go out because that evening they pulled out all the stops and made everything for dinner - oysters on the half shell, key lime pie, all kinds of soups, fancy desserts, etc. It was real, real nice. But there were two separate dining rooms and they separated the people as they got off the elevator. If you were a guest of the hotel, who were 99% white, you were sent one way; and if you were staff or their family members (invited so the staff would keep working), you went the other way. The staff was 99% black. Only the whites were eating the fine things.

When Bobby and I went to the line for guests, the guard stopped us where we saw white people just walking by and not being stopped. Because we were black, we were stopped and had to prove that we were guests. When we were coming out of the dining room, we saw these little black kids, and they saw the chocolate cakes and things we had brought on a plate back to the room. The kids said, "Oooh, where did you get that from?" I asked them what they had to eat and they answered, "Spaghetti with meat sauce, everyone had to have ice tea, and we didn't have any desserts."

They always say to put water in the bathtub, but I fell asleep before I got that done. Next thing, I woke up feeling seasick, because the building was swaying. It was moving enough to bother me.

The lights went out and we walked down to a lower floor in the building and they were giving us a little corn flakes. The hurricane was still in progress. At one point, I had to go to the bathroom. I got lost and ended up somewhere in the hotel where the plate glass windows had blown out. Security came and told us to go back where we had been.

That night when the hurricane was blowing, they wanted everyone to come down to the lower floor, so we did. It was dark with a few flashlights. They still tried to keep the guests separate from the staff. There was one black guy that came in the room where we were waiting out the storm and the white guys kind of ran him out of the area. They didn't want him in there with them.

- Sarah Lain

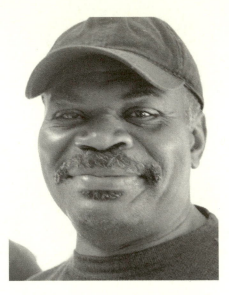

**Bobby** (5th child of Odis & Irene)

I remember telling a couple of people, "I sure hope the hurricane hits New Orleans" because the conditions in the city had become so bleak. The Lower 9th Ward was so bad, and the area around Galvez Street was the same way. There was grass overgrowing the houses. The sewer was actually running in the street; it was literally a third world country in some pockets of the city. Because I had my own computer servicing business, I would drive around the city a lot and see the conditions. I would be like, "People should not let other people live like this. This is inhumanity to man." It was like officials were trying to ignore the poor conditions.

If you go into Metairie (suburb), you might think you were in California or something; everything is so much nicer. For the life of me, I can't understand it, here you have a city like New Orleans with a big Convention Center, the Superdome, the French Quarters, the number one or two tourist city in the country and they can't do any better for these people? The State takes all the money then divides it up to all the communities and gives nothing back to New Orleans, but we have to provide the police force to take care of the problems. Plus all the oil revenues goes to Texas and Houston and everywhere. The State of Louisiana gets no royalties or nothing from that. How does the United States get away with these decisions?

That was why I was going around telling everyone, "I hope the storm hits the city" and then they would replace some of this old infrastructure and repair the streets. But, I wasn't intending for it to be long term, just something quick and dirty.

## Preparing for the Storm

That Sunday morning, Robert Atkins (friend) and Byron (nephew) came by the house. I was sitting on the couch looking at the TV and I said, "Dang, that thing is huge." Katrina covered the whole Gulf. I said, "That thing has the perfect eye." Not only that, it had a muscle in the middle; there was a hump around the eye. I said, "That storm has a muscle - that is a body builder right there."

I went and got the ladder and put it up to the attic. Then I said, "We're just going to ride it out." I went to go get some of my favorite beverages, a couple of bottles of Old Granddad whiskey, and we got us some food. I think I filled the car up with gas. I bought some canned food and water, enough to last a whole week. I know that this area (9th Ward) is prone to flooding and that we could just go up in the attic and wait it out. I don't have an ax in the attic, but I've always felt that I'm strong enough, I could break through the attic roof.

But just in case, I went through and put everything up on top of tables. I took the computers and put them up in the attic. I went down to the shop and put things up high. I did it not knowing that when the water came, it would flip the shelf and everything off it into the water.

I came back home from the shop and my sister Rose called and said, "We are going to go out on the bus towards Florida." I told them that hurricanes go to Florida and hit Atlanta with storms; they should go out West to California instead. No family members was living in Atlanta at the time, but Shaun, who drove the bus, always had a love of Atlanta.

## Evacuation for Storm

I thought about my dad having to ride out the storm, so it was easier to send him on the bus. I packed a few clothes for him and brought him to the bus.

Me and Sarah always had this thing about when a storm comes, we want to get together and see a tornado. We always go to a hotel with a big window so that we can see a tornado. They said they were not going to let people do these vertical evacuations anymore, but we have always done a vertical evacuation by going up high in a hotel. If it floods, you are high above sea level. You never think about a storm knocking over a building or anything like that.

The winds started picking up, so we said it was time to go and we loaded up each of our cars with food and all this other stuff. We really didn't inventory like we should have. We brought a lot of sodas and drink, but we didn't bring a lot of water. If we had brought a lot of water, we probably would have stayed longer in the city. We were thinking the storm would pass by and eventually we would go home the next day. So we went down to the Westin by Harrah's Casino in downtown New Orleans.

## Division In the Hotel

I walked around the hotel and the sign said dinner buffet. There were people in the dining room but there were no blacks and I was feeling out of place. I finally saw Sarah raising her hand and saying this is for the hotel guests. The hotel had this elaborate buffet, with hors d'oevres, all kind of cheese cakes, smoked salmon, crab legs, fillet mignon, some wrapped in bacon. People were walking around serving stuff on their trays. The guests of the hotel was eating fabulous -- it was incredible.

The hotel had this long curtain on one side of the dining room and someone moved the curtain, and you could see all these little kids going like, "Wow, look at all that food." And all of a sudden, the whole curtain slid open. All those employees' families swarmed around staring at us. They were all black. The guests on our side felt like the families were going to break through the glass. It was like a scene out of Titanic.

When the storm came closer, the hotel gave out the routine of where the guests were supposed to go. Most of the higher class people were staying at the top of the hotel. The workers went to lower floors in the hotel. We were very cognizant that they treated some people better than others. It was kind of weird you know.

As the storm got closer, the winds started picking up. We had a really nice room because in New Orleans, Sarah gets treated like royalty. It had a really big window and I drew the curtains back so we could really see all over the city. Me and Sarah could watch the Mississippi River; we could look down into the French Quarter and out to the 9th Ward.

Venture Out

I couldn't hear anything by looking through the window so I said, "Let me go outside." I got on the elevator and went down to the garage level like the 11th or 12th floor and walked out into the garage figuring that I could see around. The wind was picking up and really getting strong. So I went back up to the room.

We had a lot of stuff: two TV's - a battery operated color TV and a battery operated black and white TV; a radio and binoculars. Sarah had her computer and I had mine. We each had cell phones; we were well equipped. Most everyone else only had a cell phone. It is amazing the difference if you have technology. We were just in the room having a couple of drinks.

Later on, I was looking out the big window and I seen these birds flying – they were flying hard but just staying in one spot. So I went back down and out into the garage to see what was happening. The wind was very strong and so I found myself hanging onto car doors. I went to the railing, but all the time, I'm staring at these birds and time is passing. All of a sudden, the wind kicked in just like that. It is a nice little drop over the side. So I'm holding onto the railing and I went to take a step. I realized that the wind was so strong, that if I turned loose of anything I'm dead meat. I was like, "Oh man, I got myself into something. Bad move!"

I had walked around the garage and now the door was on the other side of the floor. I was like, how am I going to get back over there? There was a wind chute right through there. I'm hanging onto the railing and I'm gripping on to the car door. So I finally thought, if I just get down low and drag myself holding onto one car after another. I just kept doing this until I finally got around to the door. I said, "Oh man, thank you Jesus." I thought this is one heck of a storm; these winds are nothing nice.

Back in the Room

After I got back in the room, I looked up and all of a sudden the water was coming through, around the window, and shooting straight across the room. The wind pressure was so high. I also knew that those tall hotels are built so the windows are not tight because the buildings will sway and they have to give a little. But I still thought that the windows could break out.

The curtain in the room was about half an inch thick; it was a real thick, luxurious curtain. So I closed the curtain around the window so it would block the water from shooting. I told Sarah, "If that window does break, then the curtain will catch the glass."

But it really didn't get scary until the power went out. That was when all hell broke loose. Everything went pitch black. You could look out the window and could still see some lights along the river. The hotel made announcements throughout the night, "If you are feeling uncomfortable, go to your designated security areas." After a while they said it was mandatory that you had to go to these places, but they couldn't make you get out of your rooms. But the staff did come around and knock on doors.

After awhile, we got in our beds, then the windows started rumbling, and that was when we said, "You know something, we might be safer in the hallway." So we opened up the door and all these people were in the hallway. There were people laying on the floor; people were afraid and people were praying. Some people were yelling and screaming. We were walking across people, so we said, "Let's go down to the 13th floor."

The elevators were not working, so we had to go up and down the stairwell. Everyone had a cell phone open so it was like a Christmas tree of cell phones. It was amazing how long people's cell phones lasted. My cell phone lasted the entire time and I was using it as a light. We walked down to the 13th floor, they wouldn't let people go lower than that floor.

A large building will build up a certain amount of pressure. If someone opens up a door it is like a plane, you can lose your integrity and all the windows can pop out of the building. So they were trying to tell the people, "Don't open up the doors." But, you will always have a knuckle-head do the opposite.

All of a sudden, the white employees were walking around telling all the black people, "OK the city has flooded, the water is up to the 10th floor of the building." These people were really believing it and I said, "Don't be stupid, how is the water going to be up ten stories." I had looked out the window before I left the room and there was no water out there on the street. There was lots of wind but no water. The employees were trying to terrify the others so they wouldn't go down to the bottom floor and run out of the building.

So me and Sarah just sat down in the hallway with the storm raging. Then someone opened up an outside door and the windows shot out, BAMB. It was only about five windows that broke in the building and it was on that floor. The one giant window in the ballroom had broken out. The wind whipped around that corner and came down the hallway and debris started shooting everywhere. Me and a bunch of the guys grabbed this door and tried to close it. We started piling up things behind the door. It must have taken us about twenty minutes to get that door closed and barricaded so it would block the wind.

After a while, it was so bad in the hallways, I told Sarah, "You know something, I'm going back to the room." I thought I would feel better in the room than with all these panicked people. I decided I would take whatever my punishment would be with the spurting water. A lot of people were getting at one another's throats, you know. You had this one section that wanted to be in charge, another section wanting to be controlling, and another section didn't want to tolerate anything.

At that point, I said, "I don't care, I want to see out the window" when we got back to the room. Water was still spurting, but at least I could look down and see the French Quarter. I saw that there was a lot of wind but no water and no real damage. The Mississippi River hadn't overflowed its banks. The ships rose a little bit in the river, but usually in a big storm they might break away from their moorings. Nothing was floating down the river, so I thought everything was ok. At that point, I just laid in the bed and went to sleep. By the time I woke up later, the storm had really passed.

## Out to Canal Street After the Storm

When I woke up, I went downstairs with my camera. I went on Canal Street and shortly before the storm they had planted all these palm trees. Now they were all blown down. You saw broken windows in the buildings and computers hanging out. No one was running in looting anything. People were almost like after a nuclear explosion -- walking around in a daze, with wild looks on their faces.

I walked down to Claiborne Street and there was no water on the street so I went back and got Sarah. That was Monday and the sun had come out. We walked down all those steps in the hotel. People had started urinating in the hotel because they didn't have any services. No toilets were working.

We walked down to the street and over to Charity Hospital. Ambulances were rolling in and bringing people to Charity Hospital. People said the roof got torn off the Superdome. We walked over there and took pictures of that roof. We went down Loyola Street and all the windows were broken out of the Sheraton Hotel. I said, "That must have been like a plane crash for people in that hotel."

Later, me and Sarah went down to the French Quarter and all the bands were playing in the clubs. A lot of them had generators. It was amazing, Bourbon Street was up and running as if nothing had happened. Some said the clubs had been partying all through the storm. The clubs were serving hamburgers and we stopped and got something to eat. They were still serving hurricanes (alcoholic drinks). It seemed like at least 50% of the clubs were still open -- they didn't miss a beat.

We hung out there for awhile and then walked back to the hotel and up all those flights of stairs to the room. We watched our portable TV and saw the part where the reporters said, "It looks like they have a crack in the 17th St. Canal." We were like, "The storm is already gone. What do they mean, there is a crack?" I was yelling at the TV, "Well put a brick behind it." They said, "Well let's drop some sandbags on it." The Corps of Engineers said, "No we just can't drop sandbags, because we have to do a study."

It was the weirdest thing, it was like there was a group that wanted things to play out. Then there was another group that said let's fix this stuff before something catastrophic happens. I told Sarah let's go home not knowing that the 9th Ward was probably already flooded by that time.

So, I'm lobbying Sarah, "Let's go home, let's go home." But the police were out and they were running most of the minorities off the street, but the whites were getting to walk around everywhere. The police wouldn't tell them anything. I said to some police, "You act like we are going to loot, why do you think that they (whites) are not going to loot anything? That is harassment."

This one Chinese restaurant had opened up on Canal Street and they were selling shrimp fried rice. What they normally sold for $3 a carton was now $25 and they had a line all the way down the street. A lot of the people from the project had not evacuated, like from Iberville Project, and they were in line at this restaurant. When I saw the line I figured they were giving food away for free or something. When I found out the price, I looked at the restaurant thinking all these poor people and you are sucking $25 out of them. You ought to be ashamed of yourselves.

I picked up the pay telephone on the corner and it was working. So I made a call to Walter or someone. I made a few calls on the pay phone and I said to Sarah, "Hey this phone works." When I said that, a lot of people jumped on the phone and started making calls.

Then later, we saw on the TV that they said, the 17th Street Canal is breaking up. This was Monday, so we were walking up and down the stairs in the hotel and the smell was getting worse and worse. People were defecating and stuff. Then they ran out of the food. So they said we could go over to the Hilton to eat.

We were standing in line at the Hilton to get food but right before the workers got to us, they said, "We have to shut down for five minutes to clean up the dining room." As soon as the people came out, the whole ceiling just crashed down with all this water that had accumulated above the ceiling. It was lucky it didn't kill anybody.

## Police Inhospitality

The police officers had set up right in front of Harrah's and had all this food. It looked like they had racks full of all kind of hamburgers, hot dogs, and steaks. The police had all these grills circled around and they were feeding the other police officers and their families. So I walked over to them and I recognized one girl who worked in the police administration. She said, "Oh go ahead and get yourself a hamburger." So I went over to get a hamburger and another police officer said, "You're not with the police department." I said, "I only want a hamburger." He said, "If you touch one of those hamburgers, you're going to jail right now." I said, "Man it is only a hamburger." He said, "Are you gettin' smart with me?" I was like, "No I'm not getting smart with you. It is only a hamburger and you guys have more than you can eat. It is hot out here and that stuff is not going to last that long. There isn't any ice around here or refrigeration." He said, "We have ice, we have all we want."

He called another police officer over and they said, "If you don't move on buddy, you are under arrest." Really I was getting a hamburger for Sarah and so Sarah said, "Bobby, Bobby, that's ok, I don't want a hamburger." I was thinking these police are being foolish but I knew I didn't want to go to jail.

The weird part about it, we went down to the Hilton and there was this guy on the street. He was telling everyone, "We are still in the eye of the storm. This is the largest storm in history." Because people did not have any communication, some people were believing him and were running around in a panic and saying another wave of Katrina was coming. Sarah and I were laughing because we had been watching TV. But I told Sarah, "You could see what the world would look like with no communication. Eventually, it seems like it would be lawlessness."

Mostly people were level-headed. I was more worried about the police because they were the ones that were agitating the situation. The people weren't thinking about nothing, but the police were so busy asserting their authority, "You know there is a curfew. We don't want nobody on the street." They had such selective enforcement. Most people just wanted to get back to their houses.

Then to find out later, the police were the ones busy doing the looting. They must have been busy trying to cover up their own little trails. The police were a diversified group, about 60/40 black to white. The fire department was about 50/50 white and black. The police chief might have been black, but the hierarchy in the upper management jobs were white. You would think that since the police force was integrated, the way people were treated would be different. But then it deteriorated into what I call a 'third-world mentality'.

White police were always like that when I was growing up. You had to say, "Yes sir, no sir," no matter what age you were. But black police took on that same persona; they wanted to be called, "Yes sir, no sir." During the storm, it seemed like it went to another level. It just magnified itself.

That is the main reason me and Sarah decided we better get out of New Orleans. We were not scared of the people; we were scared of law enforcement. The police were gettin' out of hand. They had guns, all these weapons, and it semed to me the police were ready to shoot people. They were really freakin' out.

Guests in the hotel had free run to go wherever they wanted to go. So at that particular time, me and Sarah was saying like, "They might want to take us and drag us into the Superdome, you know." They might say, "You guys don't look like tourists." It was kind of weird, like you had a ton of whites as tourists; what happened to those people? They definitely didn't bring them to any shelters or anything. But they did get them out of there somehow.

One thing about New Orleans, police have always stood guard at all the banks; they know where all the money is and they had access to all that. So as soon as all those lights went out, I heard police were the ones breaking in the banks. A bit of this was shown on the TV, but not much. The police would shout, "Get out of here, this is police business." They were perpetrating this lie, creating this false idea that people were out there looting. Some places, the police officers were saying, "Go ahead and go in there and get what you need to eat."

Right after the hamburger incident with the police officers, I walked down to Poydras Street and I said, "Sarah, look down there. That is water coming up the street!" And she said, "Sure is." You could see down to Charity Hospital from the Hilton. We had walked down that street on Monday evening taking pictures and there was no water. But now, on Tuesday, you could literally see the water coming up slowly. It wasn't a big wave, but you could almost see it rising.

Getting out of Town

We decided to go ahead and take Sarah's car and leave mine at the hotel. It was pitch black in the hotel; you couldn't see nothing. There were two tracks of people in the stairway – one going up and one coming down, and this was going on all the time. It was so startling in that stairway, because you would get so close to someone -- within inches -- and all of a sudden your eyes would light up seeing someone up close.

Then you heard people calling out, "Who are you?" and "Coming through." I had to carry all the stuff and heavy suitcases down those stairs and to walk up that many flights over and over. There were a lot of people just sitting down on the stairs and a lot of people were getting delirious from going up and down those stairs. They were saying, "I can't do it anymore"; they were crying.

A lot of time you had to go all the way down to the bottom to get something and come back up, like to go find drinking water out on the street. There were people urinating in the hallways and that was awful. The employees finally said that they were going to shut down the hotel on the next day, Wednesday.

As we were driving down the ramp of the hotel, we could see people breaking into other people's cars, busting windows and trying to get a car to escape the city. Everyone was trying to get transportation to get out of there.

At that point, we didn't know people were at the Convention Center. To get up on the freeway, you drive down Tchopatoulis Street and go around. So we was going down to the freeway and we saw all these people at the Convention Center. I said, "Wow what is that? All these people." But they weren't beating on the car or nothing. Most of them would wave a little bit. They didn't know what they were getting ready to descend into. Even so, a lot of trash had built up already. There was a mass of humanity even on that Tuesday.

People were gravitating to the Convention Center all the way from the east, and the 9th Ward. The Superdome was already locked down; they weren't letting people out, but they weren't taking anymore in either because they had met their capacity. The only place left to go was the Convention Center.

It was hot right after the storm on Monday, and Tuesday was even hotter. All those people at the Convention Center and the sun was beating down on them. Most of them couldn't even get in the Convention Center to get out of the sun.

## Forced Back From The Bridge

I wanted to yell out the window at the people, "Why don't you guys go across the River? It is clear over there." I had been looking at TV and there was no flooding happening over there. Little did we know, we were driving around going slowly through the crowds because it was almost like Mardi Gras, but instead, you had all these zombies, like they had been traumatized. You could already see that they were out of energy because it's hot; it was 90 degrees and it looked like the people had already hiked 30 – 40 miles; it looked like they couldn't take another step.

We did see a small stream of people trying to walk across the Mississippi River Bridge; that is a long walk in itself. But we got there and saw all these police officers on the other side of the bridge. Then we seen some of the people coming back across the bridge towards downtown. Me and Sarah were saying, "Why are they coming back this way?"

So we drove down there and the police stopped us but then they told us to go ahead. If you were in a car, they would let you through, but anyone walking, they would turn them around and say you have to go back. It was hot, I know the heat from the concrete was not nice. You couldn't even sit down on it; it was too hot. But the police were turning them around.

We had an air conditioned car. That's why I really felt sorry when I saw the police turning everyone around. I wanted to tell the police something, but Sarah said, "Now you know you always get in trouble Bobby, I can't get you out of jail." I was saying, "Man that is cold blooded turning those people around." On the other side is Algiers, and that is still New Orleans. They should have let people overflow there and at least they could have let them sit on the grass or something. The police were so busy "protecting" their malls and businesses. The bad part, later on those businesses ended up being torn down anyway.

The police acted like material stuff was more important than human life. These police were armed to the teeth. The military hadn't come in yet. They were all local law enforcement.

A lot of those Gretna police have always been like that. When I was growing up, if you were black, you stayed out of Gretna because they didn't tolerate your presence. You could see that mentality again: *"This is our Gretna. We are going to protect it beyond our borders. We don't want you people coming in here. It's not about security, it's not about safety, it's just about this is our neighborhood and we don't want you in it."* But New Orleans is a big city across the Mississippi River, it is huge. Still, they had all those people at the Convention Center and they wouldn't let them over. That is when you really say, that is inhumanity to man. It was really tragic.

-Bobby Lain

"Monday, August 29, 2005: It's still a two-hour wait before the eye wall of the hurricane gets to New Orleans. Water gushes down the streets like waves on the ocean, coming up through the manhole covers....

Reporters begin to hear that bodies are floating in the water. Police cannot reach their rescue boats, which are in flooded areas, in order to use them for search and rescue, leaving the populace largely on its own."

CNN Reports, Katrina State of Emergency, p. 20 & 21

# Chapter 6

## Rescuing the People

❧ ❧ ❧ ❧

The greatest threat from hurricanes is not wind, but storm-surge, which accounts for most of the damage and deaths caused by hurricanes.      (A Failure of Initiative, 2006, p. 51)

Katrina makes landfall in Louisiana at 6:10 a.m., but the flooding of residential areas in greater New Orleans actually begins an hour and a half earlier. Between 4:30 and 5 a.m., levees ... breach.
... A head of water almost 20 feet high destroys houses in the immediate vicinity of the breach and pushes others off their foundations. The Lower Ninth Ward begins flooding extremely rapidly, and a barge drifts through the major part of the breach, breaking the top nine inches off the already-failed concrete wall. All areas east of the breach flood to about 12 feet above sea level; since these areas lie below sea level, their houses are totally submerged. (NOVA homepage, 2005)

❧ ❧ ❧ ❧

**Byron** (grandson of Odis & Irene, son of Louis)

<u>The Storm</u>

On that Sunday night, when I got off of work at Pacriani where I unloaded ships, I went to my girlfriend Julia's house. Her brothers had already put her and her four kids on the bus to send them to the Superdome. I was like, "Alright, Cool" 'cause I knew they would be safe. It was just us: me, my girlfriend's two brothers and one of our friends at her house in the Lower 9th Ward. That was when everyone was telling me, "I don't know how to swim." I was like, "Cool, I got ya."

We were on the St. Benard side of the Industrial Canal. I was on Roman Street just a few blocks away from the Industrial Canal in the Lower Ninth Ward where the levee broke.

A lot of people felt that the hurricane wasn't going to hit us. On Sunday we were saying, "This thing is going to turn around and not hit us." We were watching the TV news and the reporters said this thing is turning. But the power went out and after that, we didn't hear any updates about the storm.

The power went out about 2 a.m. and we sat out on the porch looking up at the sky. It looked like nothing was coming. We were like, "OK man we are going to go inside and go to sleep." We went in and slept for a good hour and when we woke up, all of us went outside and we didn't see any rain coming down. But we looked at the ground and we saw water coming up the street so we ran back inside and got our tennis shoes on. We got a bed sheet for the ones who didn't know how to swim so they could hold on to it and get across the street.

Mike, the guy across the street, had a boat and we called him the night before. He was like, "Man if things go wrong, come over here and get in my boat." It was frightening 'cause as we was leaving the house running to get across the street, I slipped on some rocks and I was going underneath the water, which was about up to our knees at that time. The ones that couldn't swim picked me up. They said, "Man you can't go anywhere – you are the one that knows how to swim." I said, "Alright, alright, cool."

First we went inside Mike's house and lifted up all the TVs and put them up high on top of stuff. So we took the ones who couldn't swim out of the house and put them on the boat. The ones who could swim went back in the house and waited until the water started rising too high.

Water was rising kind of fast; within half an hour the water was over the top of the door in the house. We put life jackets on the ones who couldn't swim. We had to swim out to the boat and pulled the boat over close to the house and got the rest of them in the boat.

We got along-side Mike's house and was between the house and a big tree. We was holding onto the edge of the house along the roof because that was how high the water was. We hung on to the roof until the rain stopped; we

Mike's rebuilt house and tree behind it

stayed like that probably about three to four hours while the storm hit. Right before the rain stopped was the first time I seen the waves in the water. I said, "Boy if I had a surf board, I could be surfing right now." That was how big the waves were.

When day broke, it stopped raining. We saw a Mercedes Benz floating up the block. We joked, "OK, let's let this car pass first." It was unreal. Then we went out in the water. We seen a house that had a second story that was above the water, but the group didn't want to break in nobody's house. So I was like "cool."

We saw a church around the corner that had high steps up to the first floor of the church. So we went into the church. We stuck people in that church so they would be out of the water which was about nine feet deep then. We were saying to them, "You are all secure and nothing should happen to you in the church."

I went back to the church months later and it was no longer there. I think other people said that the church fell down. I said later, "We must have been blessed, the church stood for a reason that particular day."

## Finding Our Dog

I had to kick into survival mode. When the water came up so fast, I left our two dogs in the house. After I got everyone safe, I got Mike and told him I have to go back to my girlfriend's house to get the dogs. I went in and had to make it all the way to the back of the house. The little dog, just a puppy, was alive floating on top of luggage. I had to push a floating refrigerator, a deep freeze, and a sofa out of the way so I could grab the puppy.

When the water came up, we had to leave one of our bigger dogs chained up. If we let him run around, we wouldn't have been able to find him because that was the type of dog he was. But the water came up so quickly, I couldn't get back for him in time. I reached down for the chain and felt to the end of the chain. I took the chain off his neck and I picked his body up and put him on top of something, but I knew that he was already dead. It was like I couldn't take him and so I put him up high.

I brought the puppy across the street to the church. There was a store on the corner that people were going in to get food. We went in there and grabbed what we needed; I got dog food for my puppy.

## Saving Others

After dropping off our group at the church on Monday morning, I walked out to the front and looked out the front door. They had people in their houses screaming, "Help, help." So I yelled out to them that we would come around with the boat. They were on their roofs and the water was way up to the roofline. By the time Mike came around the side of the church with the boat, I was already swimming towards the people. I saved a few; I started picking them up and putting them in the boat and we brought them back to the church.

I seen houses pushed to the side, like a house would be in the middle of the street blocking the street. I wasn't in too much of a panic. I had to keep my composure to keep the rest of them cool, because if I was going to panic, then they would also panic.

There was this old couple, a woman in a nightgown, looked like she was cold standing on top of her roof. She was crying for help. She was able to get through a hole in their roof because she was a slimmer woman, but her husband was chubby and he got stuck in the roof and couldn't get out. So I told him, "Hey man, I'm about to jump in the water and I'm going to come underneath of you and feel where you are at. Hey man, once I pull you down and out, hold your breath. I'm about to go underneath this water and if you start fighting me, kicking me, or whatever, I'm going to have to let you go. I can't save you if you fight me." I had to swim down in the water to find a window that was open so I could get in the house and swim to find him. This man was in his 60s, if not older than that. After I pulled him out, the others pulled him up on top the roof.

When they came 'round with the boat, they pulled him in the boat. I really wasn't thinking during all this; I knew how to swim and I did what I had to do to help people. I could of looked at it like I should just save myself, but I didn't at the time.

When we heard someone scream for help, we would go to them and rescue them. Then we would go to the next area to help someone else. We could only go so far with the gas we had in the boat. After that, we saved the ones that we could save. We brought them back to the church.

We went driving around in the boat looking for missing family members. One guy was handicapped. He only had his kneecaps on up; he didn't have any lower legs. We found him like two days after we first got out of the house and helped save him.

There were only two boats in the area – one guy didn't have a motor with his boat but only had one paddle. I think his paddle may have just been a board that he found. We told him to hold on to a rope and we towed him in back of our boat with our motor. We started doing it that way to help load more people in the boats and save more people. I would guess that we brought over 200 people from their houses to the church or later, a school, but we weren't keepin' count.

### Martin Luther King Jr. School

On about the third day, we brought the people we put up in the church to the Martin Luther King School right there on Claiborne Street. It is right across the street from a police substation, sitting on the corner. It is two stories high and the water was overtop the first floor of the building. There was a man on top of the school and he yelled out, "Hey man, bring those people over here." They had a lot of people climb up this ladder on the side of the school building, but

Martin Luther King Jr. School

Ladder survivors climbed

we had a lot of old folks too. We had to help them climb up there to get in the school.

After they got everybody over to the school, we were still going around the Lower 9th Ward in the boat to find people. We had to lift heavy downed power lines above our head – passing it from one person to the next to get the boat under so the lines wouldn't get caught in the engine. All the power was out in the city.

We would go find people and bring them to the school until we got low on gas and then we would go search for another boat. If the other boat had the same type of gas we needed, we would siphon and use the gas. That way we could still keep searching for people because no officials were coming in the Lower 9th to help rescue people. We kept saving people for about three days.

We didn't see Wildlife and Fisheries boats come out to help search until about the fifth day. When the Wildlife and Fisheries people got out there by the school, they kept asking us to leave, but we were like "Nah." Since they were not saving these people, we would bring them to the St. Claude bridge and drop them off. We would bring the Wildlife & Fisheries boat to the school and tell them to take the people from there. They had all those boats and wouldn't give us no gas. So we were like, "We're going to do what we're going to do."

There was a police substation across the street from the school. I took the boat that we had been towing, got in it and paddled across the street. I pulled that boat up on the steps to the substation and went up the stairs. They had a vending machine with chips in it, so I broke into it and grabbed everything I could – chips, snacks or whatever. I took them back and gave them to everybody at the school.

There were close to 200 or more people at the school. The cafeteria was on the first floor and had been destroyed because it was underneath the water. I woke up one morning and said, "We need some food." We knew the corner store was under water. The roof was open on that store so I went in there and I grabbed what food I could grab. Everything was floating but it wasn't that much. I told my friends, we have to get these people out of here because we don't have that much food and they can't hold out that long.

One night a good twelve to fifteen Wildlife and Fisheries boats came to the school. They said, "We need you to come out of there because we are going to transport you all." We were like, "Hey, does anybody want to leave tonight?" Some people were like, "Yes, we will leave." We told them to come back in the morning to get us. So we started sending people out that night. A lot of people wanted to stay in the school but we didn't have enough food. We told the people that we were about to leave and they had to leave too.

That's about when we seen helicopters coming over our head. People were waving and doing what they could to get the helicopter's attention, but they just kept going. I thought it was messed up. Seeing all those people that needed to be saved, and we were trying to save people, but the helicopters were just flying over. At some point, we decided that we had to try to save ourselves too. A person can only do so much. We did what we could for the people. No help was coming at all.

## Apartment Building

We decided to leave the school and that is when we got over to the St. Claude Bridge and walked down Poland Street by the military base. It just so happened that one of the guy's girlfriend had an apartment across the street from the military base and the power was still on in that apartment. It still had running water, so we showered and cleaned up. They really didn't have much flood water in that area because it was high ground.

The apartment was just down around the corner from the St. Claude Bridge. I ran across my Uncle Daniel (Andrew) who is a fireman; he was up there on that bridge. We did talk, but he asked if I was staying and I said, "Yeah." He said that he had to stay because of his job but I should try to get out. I told him that I was about to go do 'what I do' – I just left him and went back to where we were staying in the apartment. We got some food and ate until the food ran out.

Apartment building Bryon and others stayed in

We had about six people then at the apartment – including the dude with no legs. At first, when we got the guy out of the boat, we carried him over the St. Claude Bridge and I believe it was someone from the Fire Department that gave us a wheelchair. It had been left on the bridge. We put the dude in the wheelchair. After that, we went down to the apartment and we stayed there a couple of days. We were debating whether we were going to the Superdome.

When we got across the canal at the St. Claude Bridge, they had a clothing store on the corner. We saw people looting and going in there. We said, "We need clothes too," and so we went in and got the clothes we needed. We got shirts and changed clothes. We didn't have anything with us when we left in the middle of that first night and had been wearing the same clothes all that time. We brought the clothes back to the house and washed the old clothes up because they had Katrina water on them. We hung them out on the gate to dry out.

There was a restaurant right next door to the apartment on Poland St. and we broke in there to get something to eat. We started barbequing meat. When we went to cooking, we fed a few other people and kept some food for ourselves. There was a restaurant right next to the military base. The whole time we were there, we had a neighbor with a boat and we were like, we will bring this boat over by us in case some more water will come.

After that, they told us that the 17th Street Canal broke and water was coming. I don't lie, that was the time when a lot of the people went to panicking. I kept telling them, "The water isn't coming, they are just telling us that so we will leave." That was about five days after the hurricane but we had no communication and no way to really know what was happening. It seemed like they weren't trying to find ways to communicate with the people.

Naval Port of Embarkation Building
Across the Street from where Byron stayed

We saw the military at that facility across the road from the apartment letting people in for those couple of days, so we went over there to see if we could get in there to stay. They were like, "Oh no, we ain't letting anybody in." We said, "We just seen you letting people in." I guess it was their family members or other military; I don't know who they were letting in, but they sure wouldn't let us in.

We stayed about two days in the apartment. On the second day, all of us didn't take a bath that particular day because we said we could wait until the morning since we had water and power. But when we woke up the next morning, we had no water or power.

Once we got out of the Lower 9th Ward, we seen that Canal Street in the downtown area was dry. We got upset because we figured they were trying to save the businesses on Canal Street so that is why the water came at us in the Lower 9th. So we felt that was how they planned it. On Canal Street we barely stepped in a puddle of water around there.

Back on the morning of the storm, one of the guys felt that he had heard an explosion. He heard something go "boom." We said, "Hey man, stop clowning around." We thought that maybe a barge had probably broke the canal or something, but we weren't sure.  There always was talk that they would blow the canal in the 9th Ward to save the French Quarter.

-Bryon Lain

❖ ❖ ❖ ❖

The flood of 1927 was the first natural disaster in recorded history to have such dire consequences for African Americans, it displaced approximately 330,000 African Americans.

To save New Orleans, the leaders proposed a radical plan. South of the city, the population [was] mostly rural and mostly poor. The leaders appealed to the federal government to essentially sacrifice those parishes by blowing up an earthen levee and diverting the water into marshland. They promised restitution to people who lost their homes. ... The city fathers took years to make good on their promise[s], and few residents ever saw any compensation at all. (Rivera, 2007, p.26)

At the time of the levee's destruction (1927), there were few concerns about the welfare of the African American population residing in the marshland used as drainage. (Rivera, 2007, p. 506-507)

❖ ❖ ❖ ❖

# Chapter 7

## Down and Out at the Convention Center

"'I have not heard a report of thousands of people in the Convention Center who don't have food and water.'" – Secretary of Homeland Security Michael Chertoff; Statement made on September 1, 2005, four days after Hurricane Katrina hit New Orleans.

(CNN Reports, Katrina State of Emergency, p. 56)

People initially went to the Convention Center after the breaches of the levees late Monday night or early Tuesday morning. As the floodwaters rose, people left their homes and headed for higher ground. The Convention Center is near the Mississippi River levee, one of the higher elevations in New Orleans. The National Guard estimated that there were 19,000 people there. Conditions in the Convention Center were notably worse than the Superdome in several ways. Like the Superdome, the Convention Center had no electrical power, no lighting, no air conditioning, and no functioning toilets. But unlike the Superdome, the Convention Center had no authorities or security on hand, no weapon screening, no food and no water.

(A Failure of Initiative, Final Report of the Select Bipartisan Committee, 2006, p. 118)

**Byron**
(grandson of Odis & Irene, son of Louis)

<u>Convention Center</u>

We were still at the apartment building and this one friend with a U-haul truck came by the apartment. I told him to take the puppy somewhere and drop him off to keep him safe. I had kept that little dog with us all the time up to then.

It just so happened that the friend passed back by the apartment with his U-haul and so we told him, "Take us out of here." But instead of takin' us out of the city, he dropped us off at the Convention Center. We got there about five days after Katrina had hit.

When we got to the Convention Center, the people were sleeping inside, outside, in the neutral ground, and across the street; the whole Convention Center area from Harrah's Casino on down to the end of the Convention Center had people sleeping. The majority of the people at the Convention Center were black, although we ran across a few white folks. They were mostly lower income. We were like, "Man, all these people stayed behind?" We were shocked.

We staked out a spot outside the Convention Center where our group stayed together. From a corner store we got food, cigarettes, wine, beer, anything to keep our composure. We could also trade the liquor for other things. We shared some of the food and water with an older lady and some kids who were staying around us.

There were thousands of people there with no help: no facilities, no food, no water. There was nowhere to go to the bathroom; we just had to go find a spot to go to the bathroom. I never thought that this would happen here in America; they have resources in this country to help these people but I'm like it was the President's fault, the Mayor's fault and the Governor's fault! All of them were at fault for not helping us in such humiliating circumstances.

While we were at the Convention Center, other people would bring someone out there that had died and throw them up there on a pile; there was a lot of older people dying. I saw dead bodies moved out of the Convention Center.

Before the busses came, we were walking around the city trying to find us a car so we could get out of there; that is how bad it was and we were well into our second week after Katrina. We were looking all over to find a car.

It just so happened that there was cars in the Convention Center parking lot that had been damaged. We was trying to see if we could get one of those started, but then we saw the military helicopters coming in and I felt that the military were going to get us for trying to steal a car. We were afraid we could lose our lives.

We heard through word of mouth that a lot of people were killing other people too. People said they caught one guy that had raped someone and they beat him up and killed him. I heard stories about the Superdome and that people were getting raped and killed there. These stories passed mostly by word of mouth from people at the Convention Center. I didn't think they had any reason to lie about that.

Some nights you would be asleep and you would wake up and hear some water coming up the street. I heard that the military were just messing with everybody. They were putting this rushing water sound on a loud speaker or something, making it sound like water was actually coming. They did this about every other night. I wondered why they were doing this to these people who had already been traumatized. We were like, "These people are playing these games."

The worst thing I saw was when the military shot a man at the Convention Center. The military would walk through the area with their rifles drawn. They made everybody get up off the ground and stand up. We were saying, "For what reason are they doing this?" They weren't trying to save us, the military were pointing guns at people. It seemed like they were just messing with the people. The military were not bringing anything to us like water or food. It seemed like they could have put some people on their vehicles and driven them out.

When the military started shooting, everyone got really nervous. They were about half a block away from us. We just seen the man had his hands up in the air and then the military shot him. We said to each other, "They shot that man for no apparent reason." Basically we just lost all hope then.

People were saying to each other, "Oh man, they are going to kill all us now." I was just trying to get our group to keep their composure. Some people went to cracking up. One guy I was with started saying things and crying – he was just cracking up before my eyes. I had to step up and do something. I would pull someone to the side and try to calm them down by talking to them. They would start crying and saying things like, "I don't know where my kids are at. I don't know if they made it out safely."

<u>Contacting Others</u>

The busses finally started making runs out of the Superdome. The Superdome people got out first before they moved the Convention Center people out. We kept seeing busses passing by and we were like, "What's up? We should be over at the Superdome." Two more long days passed before they had came and got us from the Convention Center.

We went across the street and that is when the pay phone starting working and we went to calling people collect. My girlfriend and her kids had been at the Superdome during the time I was in New Orleans but we had no contact during that whole time. When we did finally get in contact with them, I think they were in Texas.

My girlfriend's brother went to call his baby's mama who ended up in Oklahoma. We got her to start calling everybody else. That is when we started finding out where everybody was at. I told him to tell her to call my people and tell them I'm alright. She did it.

Later when I talked with my family they said, "Boy, we were worried about you. Nobody heard from you and we didn't know if you were killed." People said that they saw me in the Time Life Magazine. Later on my partner showed me the picture and I said that it didn't look like me. He said that it was me because that was exactly what I had been wearing.

## Leaving on busses

Then the busses finally came, picked us up and brought us to the airport. All six of us were still together. When they finally took us out to the airport, they took the back roads and you could see people everywhere; people were still all along the highways. The best thing I saw during the whole Katrina experience was when they were transporting everyone out on those busses. I was so happy that they were getting us out of there.

They flew us out on an Army plane to Arkansas. We were supposed to go to Texas, but I had to use the bathroom right before loading and so we missed that flight. The others were mad at me. The group had formed a strong bond together because of what we had gone through. This was our family and that was how we were looking at it then.

Although I was happy to get out, I still to this day have never found out what happened to my puppy. I miss my little dog too.

- Bryon Lain

❖ ❖ ❖ ❖

"BLITZER: What is it like inside the Convention Center? There are thousands of people inside. ... Are there any National Guard personnel, any troops on the scene?

RAY COOPER: Yes. There's troops passing by with their weapons like a show of force and stuff, as if I'm in Iraq and stuff. I'm ex-military. I know what they look like. And that's basically what it is."

(CNN Reports, 2005, p. 71)

❖ ❖ ❖ ❖

CNN reported there were still 2000 people at the Superdome on Saturday, September 3rd. That more than 75,000 meals were served outside the New Orleans Convention Center from Friday, September 2nd to Saturday, September 3rd.

(CNN Reports, 2005, p.176)

❖ ❖ ❖ ❖

# Chapter 8

## A New Social Order

The unanswered question everyone is asking, however, is why military transport planes can't come and airlift people out – out of the drowning city, out of the stifling Superdome, out and away to shelters in neighboring states.

(CNN Reports, 2005, p. 40)

❖ ❖ ❖ ❖

The U.S. government has received offers of aid from dozens of nations across the globe in the aftermath of Hurricane Katrina, the State Department said. Neither the White House nor the State Department has said whether these offers have been accepted.

Reports of aid or supplies offered from:

Afghanistan, Albania, Argentina, Armenia, Australia, Austria, Azerbaijan, The Bahamas, Bahrain, Bangladesh, Belarus, Belgium, Bosnia and Herzegovina, Brunei, Cambodia, Canada, People's Republic of China, Republic of China, Colombia, Cuba, Cyprus, Czech Republic, Denmark, Djibouti, Dominica, Dominican Republic, Ecuador, Egypt, El Salvador, Equatorial Guinea, Finland, France, Gabon, Georgia, Germany, Greece, Guatemala, Guyana, Honduras, Hungary, Iceland, India, Indonesia, Iran, Iraq, Republic of Ireland, Israel, Italy, Jamaica, Japan, Jordan, Kenya, South Korea, Kuwait, Latvia, Lithuania, Luxembourg, Malaysia, Maldives, Mauritania, Malta, Mexico, Mongolia, Nepal, The Netherlands, New Zealand, Nicaragua, Nigeria, Norway, Oman, Pakistan, Palau, Papua New Guinea, Paraguay, Peru, Philippines, Poland, Portugal, Qatar, Romania, Russia, Saudi Arabia, Singapore, Slovakia, Slovenia, Spain, Sri Lanka, Sweden, Switzerland, Thailand, Tunisia, Turkey, Uganda, United Arab Emirates, United Kingdom, Venezuela, Vietnam, Yemen

Sources: CNN; NY Times; BBC, Wikipedia, See sites: http://edition.cnn. com/2005/US/09/04/katrina.world.aid/ (http://edition.cnn. com/2005/US/09/04/katrina.world.aid/) ; http://www.nytimes. com/2005/09/04/international/americas/04offers.html?_r=1 (http://www. nytimes.com/2005/09/04/international/americas/04offers.html?_r=1) ; http: //news.bbc.co.uk/2/hi/americas/4210264.stm (http://news.bbc.co. uk/2/hi/americas/4210264.stm) ; \ (http://en.wikipedia. org/wiki/International_response_to_Hurricane_Katrina) l "cite_note-Solomon_2007-48"

## Robert
(childhood friend of Bobby the 5th child of Odis & Irene)

I was out there cutting grass, doing my normal routine the day before Hurricane Katrina, but I said to myself, no hurricane is coming; once in a lifetime is enough. I was thinking about Hurricane Betsy and I thought God is not going to punish New Orleans twice. So I stayed with my regular routine. My sister came by and she said, "Man y'all are cuttin' the grass for nothing." I said, "What are you talking about?" She said, "Katrina is coming directly here. We are getting ready to leave. Do you want to come?" I said, "Nah, I'm going to hang in." This was on Sunday.

So I went around the corner to the Lain's house and they were packing. Bobby and I have been friends from the sixth grade when we were in the same class at school. I just lived around the corner from the Lain's and have gone over to their house all my life.

Bobby didn't want to leave the city and he was going to put his father Odis on the bus to get out of the city. I said, "Man, I'm hanging, I'm staying Bro." We were just laughing around. So I guess Sarah enticed Bobby to leave and he went up to Canal Street in the hotel.

I went around the corner and went to Winn Dixie grocery store. A friend and I got us a couple of stuff; we fried us some chicken just in case. Everyone in Winn Dixie was saying the Superdome was the place to go. I said, "Hell if I'm going to the Superdome." From past experience during another hurricane 'false alarm,' I experienced the chaos and the way they treated the people in the Superdome. I refused to go through that again.

So my partner and I knocked around and I said, "I'm going to take a nap." This was maybe about 8:00 p.m. About 12:00 that night, he woke me up. He said, "Bro get up,

Rebuilt house Robert and others stayed in after Katrina hit

touch the floor." This time when I touched the floor I said, "Nigga did you piss on my floor?" He just looked at me like I was crazy and said, "No man, it is the water comin' inside." I got up and started grabbin' stuff. I had a flashback from Hurricane Betsy and knew how fast things happened then.

I went to the bathroom and flushed the toilet and more water was comin' up faster and so we just grabbed some stuff and got outside. The water was about two foot high then. There was a two-story house next door to me. I looked over on the other side of the street because there was a two-story house over there also. I said, "That is too long to walk. That water is comin' down the street like a tidal wave." I told him, "No, right here Bro, right next door."

By the time I got to my gate, the water was up to my chest. I had to drop everything that I was carrying and swim next door because I was half way there when the water rushed in. As I was going upstairs to the porch of the house, the water was constantly rising. The water stopped just at the top step on the stairs of that porch. It was about ten feet high then. I would say it took only about 15 to 20 minutes to get all the way up to that top step. I looked down Clouet Street and I seen those waves just comin'.

In that house there were two separate apartments connected by the porch. When we got there, I started praying, "Please Lord don't let the water get any higher because I don't have anywhere else to go." The water stayed right there at that top step! It was a four-plex with two bedrooms on each side, upper and lower. The lower apartments were flooded by that point. My partner had the next door apartment and I had the other side.

There was a freezer full of food. The gas was still on and the water was still runnin'. We didn't have any electricity though. So we were straight for about three to four days. We fried food and we ate pretty good. We was alright.

So the next day, about 11 a.m., you could hear people hollering for help, it was chaotic. It was hot for the people that were on the roofs and the attics. I had another

"Air Force One flies over New Orleans and the Gulf Coast hovering for 35 minutes at 1,700 feet. President Bush is able to see the Superdome and the flooded neighborhoods" on Wednesday, August 31, 2005.   (CNN Reports, 2005, p. 45)

partner and he was staying about three blocks down. He had a boat and he came by the apartment and asked, "Hey man, can we bring a couple of people to stay with you all?" I said, "Yeah, I guess so."

Before you know it, we had Miss Williams who was maybe 75 years old, and Miss Eunice who was maybe 65 years old. The craziest thing was, prior to the storm, I had asked God to send me and my partner two females. Well he sent me two females - two senior citizen females. Lord have mercy. Being a bachelor, I asked for it. But I found out you need to be more specific what you ask for. Two female senior citizens came and they kept us balanced though.

There was a dude from the roof on the corner hollering for help and they brought him to stay with us. We had ten people total staying in those two apartments. We had five on one side and five on the other side with the porch connecting the two sides.

That water was nasty and I saw dead dogs and cats floating around. I got out there one time - I went to the corner on that little boat and I seen the family in that house had tied a lady family member to their porch. She was swollen so I didn't get that close. The rest of them was in the attic in that house but she couldn't fit in the attic and so she drowned. Her family didn't want to lose the body, so they tied her to the porch. That was a terrible sight.

We didn't have any electricity or communication, no access to anything that was going on in the city. We did see Helicopter One with Bush flying across the city. Miss Williams said, "Look, our President." You could hear people hollering, "HELP, HELP!" The helicopter just flew right on and we didn't get any kind of signal that we would be gettin' any help or nothing. It was ridiculous. I wasn't surprised at the time. I said, "They're just going to forget us anyway. We're black people, so we're not on their top priority anyway."

I only knew the 9th Ward was flooded; I didn't have any information that the rest of the city was flooded. The only information we would get was from the dudes in the boats. They told us that on Claiborne Street the water was pretty low; on Poland Street the water was high.

## New Social Order

It was like a little picnic on an island in our apartments.   Everything was organized and everybody had duties to do like clean up, cook, etc. That was until Knuckle-head came; he was the dude that was on the roof hollering for help. He was a youngster.

The outside temperature had to be in the upper 90's and humid. In the attics, God knows what temperature it was. It was hot in the apartments, and we were staying on the second floor. We didn't have no fan or nothing. If it was this hot in the apartments, just think how hot it was for Miss Eunice. Before she got to our apartments, she was across the street in her hot attic with another young man.

When they turned the gas off, that was about Tuesday or Wednesday, then they cut the water off. We had to go to Plan B; we couldn't just stay there. My ex-brother-in-law came by there on top of about ten boards of plywood that were tied together. The boards had floated from the railroad track. He said, "Man you can't stay here. You have to find some transportation and this is the best I can do." I said, "How are you going to get this to go in the direction we want to go?" So someone found a couple of poles and we used them for paddles. We were just floating in the street – that wasn't a problem because the water was so deep.

## Leaving The Safe Haven

We said we would put four people on our plywood boat at a time. You could go down to Claiborne Street and there was dry land there.  So we put the ladies first and took them down there. Then he brought the plywood back and we got on.

During our ride, Knuckle-head didn't like how I did things and he didn't want to listen to anything. He was young and wild but he didn't have any survival skills as a whole. He really only wanted to listen to himself talk.

The ten of us had made a bond and commitment to each other. Whatever we would do, we would be stickin' together regardless. Wherever they would send us, we were not going to let them divide us up. So we all got out at Claiborne and Clouet at the bridge overpass.

At the bridge overpass, there was a National Guard helicopter bringing people up into the helicopter by climbing a ladder. The helicopter couldn't land because of all the telephone wires. So they let the ladder down and everyone had to climb up.

There was a lady climbing up the ladder and she fell off the ladder. She fell on the concrete bridge and I just seen all the blood and everything just splatter. This was the first day I really seen someone die in front of me. There was a lot of people on the bridge. I'm afraid of heights and I had seen the lady fall so I said, "We have to come to Plan C now, because I'm not getting up on that ladder."

The old Palmer School where Robert and others stayed

### Living at the School

There was a school just two blocks down from the overpass. We could see a lot of people down there, so I said, "Man we might have to go over there by the old Palmer School until somebody comes to rescue us." A lot of people from the neighborhood that I knew, had broken into the school and had made a shelter. They had it pretty well organized.

I seen one of my partners; he was running things at the school. He said, "I'm so glad you are here." I asked, "Why?" He said, "Man, I need some help; we need to organize these people and they will listen to you. You ran the homeowners association." I said, "Alright." They had about 300 people over there in the school.

We used the same program we used in the house. The men would go out and get the food and bring it back. The women would prepare the food. The rest of them watched the kids. They had senior citizens there also. It worked out pretty good.

We didn't have no gas or no water at the school. But everyone put their heads together; they got charcoal and they were barbequing everything. If they weren't barbequing, they had the big pots from the school and they made a fire and cooked our food. And still, there was no communication, no radios, no nothing.

## Communication at Last

About four days later, somebody brought a portable radio. That's when we heard Mayor Nagin tell the President to "Get off his ass." The people were cheering you know when they heard that. The last day we was at the school, there was this elderly white man who died at the school because he ran out of medication.

They woke me up that morning and said, "Hey man, come out here." I had been sleeping like a baby; finally got a peaceful night of sleep. I came out there and seen the body and said, "Man you called me out here for this? What do ya' want me to do?"

We didn't know how long we would be at that school so I said, "There is one thing we can't do and that is keep this dead body in this building because we will have an odor. We have young children and old senior citizens, so we just can't let this happen. Why don't y'all wrap the body up and put it on the push cart."

They said, "What ya' going to do then?" I said, "I'll think of something. I'm going upstairs to freshen up and I'll be back." I went upstairs and I thought and thought about it. Finally I thought about the first police precinct that was just about three miles down the road.

I thought if I could get someone to row the body down there, then we could talk to the police officers about what to do with the body. So we got the body and went to the first precinct. That's right there on Rampart Street, about two blocks from Canal Street. So we pushed the body over there in the boat.

The police officer said, "What's this?" I answered, "It's a dead body." He said, "We ain't worried about no dead bodies; we're worried about the living." I said, "Well, what do you want me to do with it? Why don't y'all take it and do what you do with the other bodies."

He said, "We ain't takin' that dead body." I said, "Y'all not? I can't take that body back to the school because other people are living there and it is unsanitary." He said, "Man, I'm tellin' you, we don't want that body."

I thought to myself, I have enough headaches and so I said "OK." We took that body and left it on the neutral ground (grassy median in the middle of larger streets in New Orleans). My ex-brother-in-law said, "Man, that's cold Bro. You gonna' leave that body there?"

I said, "David, this is survival time. Just think about it. That body is nothin' but a shell now. His soul has gone to heaven, hell or purgatory now. This ain't nothing but a shell Bro. He was made of dirt, he will return to dirt." I said, "Don't worry about it. That body will start stinkin' and they will figure something out to do with it. Just block this out of your mind and let's continue on with our mission."

That was a hard decision. To show you how God works in mysterious ways, He put that thought in my head at that time. So when David asked that question, I was able to answer right off. Later, a reporter asked me if I was angry about that situation and you know what my answer was? I didn't have time to be angry. I didn't have time to think about whose fault it was. The only thing that crossed my mind was survivin' and makin' sure that everyone surrounding me worked together as a team. But being scared or pissed off? I didn't have time to think about stuff like that. I was in survival mode trying to protect myself and others.

Get What You Need

By this time the National Guard knew we were staying in the old school and they told us, "Y'all can go take anything: food, water, what you all need to survive. We understand that you can't stay there without it." We had detergent and bottled water to clean with and to drink because the school didn't have any running water.

I seen people walkin' down the street with televisions. I said to one young man, "Where is the electricity at? Man, what'cha gonna' do with a television? I can understand you need to take food, but what are ya' gonna do with a television and a sofa? I don't get it."

The young man said, "Man, I'm going to stash this." I said, "You're going to stash it where? Man do you realize there is nowhere to take it? That makes no sense." He stuck his middle finger up at me. He was a young guy. But all kinds of people were taking stuff, all races.

Taking things was not in my survival program though. I felt guilty about takin' even food. There was a grocery store on Dauphine Street. Now it didn't flood or anything but it had a freezer. Ernest and I were walkin' and it was our duty to go out and find food for our ten people that day. We seen these white people goin' in this grocery store on Dauphine Street. I told him, "Man there is something good in this store. Ernest, why don't you go check it out."

Ernest said, "I'll go check it out only if you go with me." In the back of my mind, I said that was stealing. But I got into my survival mode and said to myself, "Do you want to survive or do you want to die? Do you want to starve to death? Remember, when you get hungry, you are not pleasant to deal with." All these thoughts kept going through my mind so I finally said, "Let's go see Bro."

They had baby back ribs still frozen in the freezer. We had to find a curtain to put all the stuff we got to take it back to the school. We were about one and a half miles away from the school. The National Guard came and said, "It looks like y'all need some help. Put this stuff on the truck man. I'm going to bring you back to the school." The National Guard already knew who we were and so we stuck it on their truck and they took us back to the school. If we had pushed that all the way back, it would have taken hours.

By the time we got back to the school with the food, the people was cleared out. So, we ate good. We had soap and everything we could think of to survive. I had liquor on my boat. We had a little nice time that night. We took our little drinks and went to sleep. That was about Thursday or Friday.

On Friday, a helicopter came and dropped food off on top of the school because they couldn't land. So they were just droppin' food and water, sodas, different stuff on the roof. Of course the people had already been cleared out by then.

## Rumors of Gangs and Shooting

The whole time we were by the school, I never heard those rumors about gangs and shootings that I later found out was on the TV news. I didn't see any guns, shooting or anything. There was only one fight that I witnessed. Well, I didn't see it personally, but Knuckle-head was fighting with someone over some food, and I found out about it later.

We had a rule that after the food was prepared, the senior citizens ate first, the kids ate second, then the women ate, and finally the men ate. That was the way we had it set up. But Knuckle-head decided that he brought the food and supplied it that particular day, so he wanted to eat first and it was the females turn to eat. So one word led to another and they came callin' me. By the time I got there, Knuckle-head had been hit on the side of the head by a female. I said to Knuckle-head, "You should be ashamed of yourself, you know the program and the rules. From day one, you know that senior citizens eat first, then the kids, then the women, then we eat." He complained, "But I got the food."

We had about seventy kids at the school. To be truthful I don't know who organized it, but during the day time, they put the kids in different rooms and played games like they were in school. I thought it was a great idea. It kept the kids occupied because the school we were staying in was an elementary school and so there were supplies. This kept the kids occupied and kept their education going at the same time. I always used to say, "Idle minds are the devil's workshop." Everyone was trying to do something positive and to stay busy.

We naturally had some disagreements but everyone handled them intelligently. They seemed to know that it was important for survival. Most of the people I was dealing with had gone through Hurricane Betsy, so they had prior experience and it was nothin' new to them. I thought that helped a hell of a lot.

We kept the school clean. In fact, before we left the school, we cleaned it again. Everybody worked together to get it cleaned up. We used the 'Katrina water' from outside in a five gallon bucket to flush the toilets manually. That way everything kept clean. There was a warehouse right there on St. Ferdinand where we got all the personal hygiene stuff we needed like toilet paper, paper towels, and stuff like that.

Escape the City

That Sunday evening, the National Guard finally came and got those of us that remained, not with a helicopter this time but with the MP trucks. The ten of us all got on the truck and went down to the Convention Center. Then we went from the Convention Center to the airport. When we were outside at the Convention Center, it seemed like thousands and thousands of people were waitin' to get on the bus to get out of there. We didn't stay at the Convention Center but it was only about forty minutes before they put us on a bus to go to the airport.

Now being at the airport was another experience. Whew. They said the Superdome was a mess. The airport was dirty as well; it was unbelievable. I didn't want to use the airport bathrooms. I walked in there and I couldn't stand it. Now we kept the school running and clean with no professional people around. Why couldn't they do that at the airport?

I used to work at the airport and I knew where all the employee bathrooms was and they was all nasty also. I could understand the public bathrooms would be dirty, but they should have been able to get some kind of way to keep the employee bathrooms clean. They still had running water and the toilets flushed. I know they had a lot of people to deal with, but they did not put a plan in place to deal with cleaning the bathrooms.

The people in charge didn't even tell us where we were going, they just made us get on a plane without telling us. We found out it was a U.S. Marshall's plane and they were transporting prisoners. All ten of us were still together. Miss Williams told them, "Y'all can't divide us. You can't separate us. I don't care what y'all do, but we are stickin' together." That was Miss Williams' job to make sure we kept together. She would have none of letting anyone separate us after all we had been through. So we stuck together and got on the plane.

My curiosity was killin' me now. I said, "Where the hell are we goin'?" So I went up and asked the pilot. He wouldn't say until the plane took off the ground, but then he said, "We are going to Phoenix, Arizona." I guess they thought that everyone would try to get off the plane if they told us before the plane had taken off.

I found out that Knuckle-head's greatest fear was flying. I'm kind of evil sometimes, so I thought it was 'pay back' time for all the headaches that Knuckle-head gave me in those ten days. So I started telling him all kinds of horror stories about air pockets and that the plane was going to go crooked. I told him that it was a possibility that we were overloaded with people and that the lightning might come out of the clouds and hit him because he was sitting by the window. He kept saying, "Don't do that." He got so paranoid, that he said," I don't want to sit here by the window no more."

The MP heard me tellin' Kuckle-head all these stories, so he said to Knuckle-head, "Let me see if I can find you another seat." Half an hour later, the MP took him and moved him to another seat. It took about six to seven hours to fly to Phoenix. We got to Phoenix at 1 a.m. on Monday morning and they had the red carpet all laid out for us. The Assistant Mayor of Phoenix was black and she was right there when we got off the plane at 1 a.m. They treated us really nice.

-Robert Atkins

# Chapter 9

## A Broken System

**Andrew** (Daniel)
(10th child of Odis & Irene)

On August 26, Friday, we were watching the Saints game. The game went off and they said Katrina is headed this way. It was supposed to be going to Florida, but it came to New Orleans instead.

On the next day, I was at work, at Tupelo & St. Claude, where the fire station was located in the Lower 9th Ward. I work for the fire department as an fire engine driver and also drive my own cab part time. On that Saturday, I knew it got serious when they started shuttin' down everything about 4:00 p.m. On Sunday, the fire department gave us a break and let us go home to get prepared.

My family evacuated and said they were going to Memphis. On that Sunday, I was trying to get them out of the city by driving ahead in the cab showing them my little secret shortcuts; and all of the shortcuts was crowded. We

Andrew with the fire engine he drives

left the house at about 10 a.m. and the next thing, it was about 2:00 p.m. and my family was just getting to Kenner which is only about ten miles away. The last time I saw them was at Williams Street and I10.

I came back down to our house. Didn't put nothing up. Left the cab right there. I just acted like it was another storm because I didn't really think it was going to hit. It had been like 40 years since Hurricane Betsy hit and so there had been a lot of storm threats in all those years, but no damage.

I was about to do some things around the house like put the garbage out and put anything that might fly away in the shed. I didn't get to it because my employer called and said, "Come back to work." The sun was still shining ya' know. I got back to work and it started to get cloudy. Driving back to work, I could see people out there barbequing and going to the store getting drinks, chips, snacks, and so forth.

## Naval Port of Embarkation

At the fire station, they told us to move our cars to the Naval Port of Embarkation. I said the car would be all right where it was at. I didn't believe that it would flood because the area by the Engine House is zoned like "X"; they don't need flood insurance. Never-the-less, I moved my car.

That was Sunday night about 6 p.m. We put things up high on top of the refrigerator at the fire station. Then the weather just started getting bad; it was deteriorating. About 8:00 p.m., they sent us to the Port of Embarkation on the other side of the canal. The fire department brought in everyone from all the 3rd Fire District and they had sleeping bags, cots, and blankets there for us. Fifty of us firefighters were over there -- all three different platoons and three different shifts. The department had little snacks, food and generators for us. It was like we would stay there and go home the next day.

We went to sleep and about 5:00 in the morning, the wind was like full throttle, blowin' hard. It was just one hard blow without lettin' up. The facility was made of concrete and about five stories high. It is right near the (Mississippi) river and so the land was high. We could see the water blowing sideways. We didn't really notice that it flooded because the street was dry, but we looked across the canal and the river was high. I said, "Wow." You could see the top of the levee, but the water was like just a foot under the top. It never did come over the top of the levee though.

My cell phone wasn't working by then and I hadn't heard whether my family made it to a safe place yet. The only phones working was Verizon and Alltel.

Later on Monday about 5 p.m., we took a ride with the fire truck and went down to Canal Street. There were wires and tree limbs in the way, but no water. A few people were walking around. Some palm trees had blown over.

We went down to Broad Street and nothin' -- just a little water in the street. You had a lot of tree limbs down, so you couldn't drive down some streets. I think we went to Broad and Orleans and water got kind of high for the engine to go through. We didn't want to get stuck because the water was above the wheels about two or three feet high. It wasn't fifteen feet or nothin' like that, but it was enough that you could get stuck. So we came back to the Port of Embarkation.

## St. Claude Bridge

I think it was the next day, Tuesday during the day, we went to the St. Claude Bridge and there were thousands of people. It looked like nobody left the city. Whatever the people had gone to sleep in, that was what they were still wearing. A lot of people at the bridge were sick and needed medicine. They had no food and no water. They were tellin' stories, "Oh my mama is dead."

It looked like nobody left the city. It seemed like hundreds of Wildlife and Fisheries boats were backed up in the water. The people didn't know where to go -- they were scared and just wanted water. The officials were telling the people to go to the Superdome. There were supposed to be National Guard high terrain vehicles, but the Guard only had about two or three of them. They were taking the old people first. It took an all terrian vehicle about half an hour to go to the Superdome and come back. But there were about 5000 people out there on the bridge.

Some people had diabetes. I knew they weren't going to make it because they looked like they were about to pass out. They didn't have their medicine. The heat was about 90 degrees that day.

Out of all those thousands of people up on St. Claude Bridge on that Tuesday, I saw my nephew Byron coming. We stayed there and talked awhile. I told him, "Byron, go to the Superdome." Then Byron said, "I'm going to go back over there to help rescue others." So I said, "Bro, you are going to get hurt you know." The water was like thirteen to fifteen feet high then. That was the last time I seen Byron. I didn't have any way to know what happened to him after

St. Claude Bridge where Andrew saw Byron

that. I just kept thinking Byron didn't have a boat or anything --- just him. I worried about him and told him to not go, but he still went. Byron just went back into all that water.

Then, it got dark that evening. That was when it really got crazy because the National Guard stopped bringing people to the Superdome. People were stuck. It was dark, all the electricity and lights were out. People had no water, they were scared and didn't know where to go.

We (firefighters) was at the Naval Port of Embarkation and we had generators. Some National Guard were there also. The people knew we had water and they just wanted water. The people wanted to come in because they saw lights in there and they didn't know where to go.

There was a trouble-maker in the crowd trying to stir the people up. It really was just one of them that was making trouble. But the rest of the people just wanted water and somewhere to sleep. The National Guard took a position on the people with their M16s. I was inside the building and could see they had about 20 National Guard, but they made it look like it was 300 of them. It looked like the military were going to take out the trouble makers first.

The National Guard made us (firefighters) leave, they didn't want us to see because they were about ready to shoot those people. The Guard were like, "Ready, Set," and the next step was "Fire." But they didn't want us to see, so they took and brought us firemen across the River. They brought us to the West Bank, which took about two hours. The National Guard, which was about half and half white and black, young people, police or school teachers, grocery store clerks, you name it from all over the country.

The thing is, while the firemen was there, the National Guard stood over us with armed guards, guardin' us, but we really didn't notice it at first. They were acting like we were going to do something, but we were just firefighters. The Guard was watchin' us and keepin' us in one place, I guess in case we would steal something. We had about 50 firefighters, no more than 100, in the kitchen on the floor.

The National Guard changed the password every day. The firefighters said, "Wow, this is not working." The Guard wanted to be in control and was trying to push us around. The firefighters had to do what they said. The Guard would tell us, "Be here in five minutes" and then we would get there and have to wait there for an hour. The National Guard was bossin' us around and we really wasn't getting along with them.

I wanted to get my car out of the parking at the Naval Port of Embarkation and have it available on the street, but the fire department wouldn't let us get our cars out. Later on, some people were lootin' cars and taking cars just to get out of town. If that would have happened to my car, then I would really have been stuck -- so the department did help me save my car.

## Rumors

There were all kind of rumors that people were driving around with assault weapons just killin' everybody on the sidewalk. There was one rumor that on the expressway, by the Oakwood Shopping Center, people were just shooting firefighters. We could see some smoke. CNN reported it on TV and us firefighters could see the shops that were burning. We found out later that the part about people shooting wasn't true.

Another rumor going around was that the people at the Convention Center were shootin' everybody. That was on CNN and the radio at one point. There was also a rumor that babies were being raped at the Superdome. We found out later that wasn't true but those were rumors at the time and you didn't know what to believe.

The firefighters didn't even know that most all the city was flooded at that time. It was like 80% of the city was underwater but we didn't see that where we were at; the firefighters just saw that the streets were dry. In Algiers

(West Bank), we didn't have a drop of water -- we didn't know.

The fire department was rescuing people and fightin' fires. A lot of people panicked because they didn't have insurance and saw the house was under fifteen feet of water, so the people just lit it up. You couldn't do nothing about that. The firefighters couldn't fight all the fires because we couldn't get to them.

## Grids on Houses

Several agencies were doing searches from house to house. They painted grids on the house when they went door-to-door to search for people. The grid explained who did the search, the date they did it on, and if they found anybody. That is a standard method for any type of crisis and rescue workers have to learn that in training. That was nothing special for Katrina. You just don't see that too often.

Like "DFW" probably stands for Department of Fisheries and Wildlife or something. The State Police, Fire Department and other agencies did the inspections. It also could have been anybody from the federal, state, local or private levels. At the bottom of the grid was the bodies found. There are a few houses with marks on them down the street; most of the houses with grids are demolished or painted over by now.

## Police

The police got crazy. I heard they was lootin' and stealin'. The police cleaned out Wal-Mart, they stole cars and ATM money, looted and quit their jobs. It was so easy for them. The police would take everything though, like brand new cars from dealers, Cadillacs, Corvettes, Chevrolets. The police would go in the dealership, take the keys, and drive off.

"The first slash of the X was made when they entered the building.
Once the team exited the building, they completed the other slash.
At the 12:00 position is the date they did the search.
At the 3:00 position is the number of hazards found.
At the 6:00 position is the number of victims found.
At the 9:00 position is the team that did the search."

> (Ruel Douvillier, Urban Search & Rescue Team, New
> Orleans Fire Department, in When the Levees Broke, Spike
> Lee, 2006)

Tree & wall with marking "1 Dead"

A former New Orleans police officer has been sentenced to eight years in federal prison for helping to cover up the deadly shootings of unarmed civilians after Hurricane Katrina. The sentence against Michael Hunter was nine months above the maximum recommended guideline. Hunter is one of five former officers who have pleaded guilty in the shootings that happened a week after Katrina hit.

-Des Moines Register, December 2, 2010

I heard police were stealin' stuff like catalytic converters. They would take a torch and grind it off. Why would they jack the car up, cut the catalytic converter off? What is the most they could get – like maybe $40? Here there was a brand new car, and they would do $2000 of damage just to get a couple of dollars for the metal. It made no sense.

I heard that some police still had their police cars stashed. They would come back into the city, come get the car, get the uniform on, and get whatever they wanted. To get control of it, I heard they (police department) just flat out fired 300 police officers. I think it could have been almost half of all of the officers during October and November.

The department also changed the police uniforms from blue to black. They said it was because the police had lost their uniforms but I think the real reason they changed them was because a lot of police had quit but still had the uniform. The department changed the radio and changed the cars to Impalas.

I believe the police thought it was the end of the city and they were just getting what they could. They thought the city was gone and they didn't have no more jobs. Several police thought they would have to go somewhere else and get a job and they just didn't know. It was so chaotic and no communication. But officers are now back in the blue uniforms, they just changed it a couple of months ago (summer 2009). At the time, the department had to distinguish the good ones from those that would come back in and loot and steal in the city.

I had needed some shoes, that was the only thing I wanted. My shoes got wet and the soles came off. Every time I brought a brand new pair of shoes back, someone would take them. So that was the only thing I needed. But I heard some police were taking plasma TVs. Now what are you going to do with five plasma TVs when you don't even have anywhere to stay?

The difference between the police and the firefighters is that firefighters don't panic. Plus, the department was keepin' us together. Another thing is that we don't carry weapons.

The fire department would give us things to hold on to, like they started paying us double, that was nice. The overtime was quadruple. That can take your mind off a lot of stuff. Also, the Red Cross and Walmart would come in and give us gift cards; that would make things easier. It wasn't a lot, but it did help out. One time Red Cross gave me a $1500 gift card and Walmart gave me a $300 card. Those were given to all firefighters.

## Devastation

The devastation of the city was like a bomb hit it. Around here (Lower 9th Ward), there were houses on top of houses; houses on top of cars; cars on top of houses; houses on top of trees; houses in trees; and houses six blocks away from where they had blown.

I saw a floating body, and bodies are still being found. There were people I knew who had died. There were people that I had seen the day before barbequing and then we would see the circle on the map where they found bodies and I realized, wow that was where those people were barbequing.

## Seeing My House

At first I didn't believe my house would have flooded. I had to park and walk about eight blocks to my house in about three feet of water. That was the lowest part right there seeing the water in the house. The water was like black and you could see dead pelicans, dead birds, dead dogs, nothin' livin'. No birds flying, no insects, nothing.

When I went back to my house the first time, I saw a limousine of June's stuck with not a scratch on it. But like two days later, I saw that same limo on South Claiborne; it was smashed on all four sides. It was like someone had dropped it off a ten-story building. It looked like somebody took a bulldozer and just kept repeatedly smashing it as fast as they could go. I never saw anything like it but I knew it was the same one. They left it right there.

That's what happened to most of June's busses, they just kind of disappeared. He had like 40 busses and all of a sudden, they weren't there anymore. When I would see one, there would be wheels and parts missing. The police confiscated some of the busses. The ones still in the lot today are the only ones June got back.

On the way to my house, I heard they had about ten people got killed on Danzinger Bridge on Chef Menteur. I went there and I could see shot gun shells and bullets still there, but there wasn't nobody still there.

Then I went down the street going to my house and I could see the water gettin' up kind of high. Two guys came out there and said, "Let's take his car." I was just by myself. All of a sudden, I made a U-turn with my car. I wasn't going to do it on my own, you know. I was just going to go right through them, but maybe they were going to car-jack me.

After that, I went around to Jordan Street, that is right near the Canal. There was debris on the street, so I worked my way through the mud and water. I could see all the levee breaks and the railroad tracks washed out.

## First time leaving New Orleans

My cell phone wasn't working and I didn't know where my family was for quite awhile. I thought they were in Memphis. Then I thought, oh they went to Jackson. But when I was finally able to talk to my family, come to find out, they went to Houston. I got off after about ten days of working straight and went to Houston to see my family. They were staying at a little hotel.

Houston was more organized than Mississippi or Tennessee. My family was able to get Red Cross help and get a voucher for a hotel. All of a sudden FEMA was going to pay for the rooms. After that, our family went to get an apartment. The management charged us $200 for an application. So we paid that and then we went the next day and the managers wanted three months' rent just so they could reject us and keep the $200. It was a scam you know. The management didn't tell us that when we filled out the application. They had our credit application and our driver's license numbers. That is what I wanted back and the managers wouldn't give it back. They had a copy of a photo ID on each one of us. So we got ripped off that time. All of a sudden there were over 200,000 New Orleans people in Houston and the businesses were trying to get all this money from the New Orleans people.

When I got to Houston, that was the first time I found out most all of New Orleans was flooded. On the TV, I saw the people evacuating by helicopters. I saw on CNN that there were cars way down I10. People getting out of helicopters, and helicopters getting people off the roofs and dropping them right there on I10. People were being born right there on I10; people were dying also. People were getting off school busses at the airports and didn't know where they were going: Iowa, California, Atlanta, New York, anywhere. Some evacuees are still in other cities and never could come back to New Orleans.

Evacuees were leaving Baton Rouge because they weren't getting the benefits. I heard the government would not consider you an evacuee if you stayed in the state, so you had to go out of state. If you left the state, then you could get food stamps, unemployment, an I.D. In Baton Rouge, I heard evacuees weren't gettin' nothing.

## Coming Back to New Orleans

Firefighters had to come back to New Orleans to work and we stayed at the Holy Cross College for about a month on Woodland and DeGaul. Then the city government had us living on the ship. For two months, it was like I was the only person in the world. I would ride around down Claiborne and I was the only person. I was able to do that because I had the firefighter I.D. There was nobody until about October, then I could see State Police and National Guard. The city was under a curfew and people couldn't get back in until November. So for September, October, and part of November, it felt like I was the only person in the world. I just couldn't believe the devastation.

I had to fix my house, I worked so hard for it. I hate to let things go so easy. Everyone else was fixing theirs. I had my job and that was what kept me here. I mean it wasn't bad because they brought in gasoline. Gas tanks were brought in and then you could fill up. That would kind of ease things. Then the phone started working. I got kind of worried because the phone bill got up to $800 and then the phone company said they would give a break. Food wasn't a problem. Just looking at the devastation, that was the shocker.

I used to get off work, drive to Houston, then come back. At first the department was givin' us four days on and then four days off. I liked that. But then we went back to our regular schedule which is twenty-four hours on, and then forty-eight hours off. I would do the twenty-four hours, then go to Houston, come back, then do another twenty-four hours. I've driven back and forth to Houston over 200 times. I don't ever want to go through that again.

You say you will never do it again, but then Hurricane Gustav came last year in 2008. Gustav was worse than Katrina because a lot of people took all the water and bread at the grocery stores; it just wasn't available. Then the electricity was out for about two hours a day, and TV was off for a whole month. I was just in the house in the dark and I couldn't sleep all nights.

You could see the power company starting to turn on people's lights little by little, they would get a half block closer. It seemed like my house was the last one to get the lights turned on. Gustav was worse for me. Katrina did the damage, made the poles weak and everything, but Gustav just pushed them over. The utilities were made weak by the termites and then Katrina. But Gustav came and just finished them -- it just knocked over the wires and stuff.

I wish my family would move back to New Orleans. The family saw something better in Houston: better schools, more opportunities. I have thought about leaving, Houston and New Orleans are about the same. But I have this job here that keeps me here. The age is the factor, otherwise I would have been gone four years ago. If I was under thirty, I wouldn't be sittin' here in New Orleans, but I'm 52. In Houston you have to be 35 or under to get on the Fire Department. In New Orleans you can be 60 and still get on the job. I guess you kind of get used to the family being gone. I figure they are gone, it is 2009 now, it's been four years.

Yeah, it does take a lot of strength to go through it. I used to be driving on the highway a lot -- it would take five hours to drive to Houston and that would take up a lot of time. Now, I don't even think about it, just click in a radio station.

- Andrew (Daniel) Lain

# Book 3

After The Storm

# Chapter 10

## Returning to Chaos

Dallinger (on right) & college students gutting an apartment
building during Spring Break 2006

Mold along the wall

Devastation in the Lower 9th Ward (March 2006)

Debris on the street after college students gutted an apartment
building during Spring Break, March 2006

Walter (Dallinger's husband) gutting an apartment
building with college students in March 2006

## Sarah
(4th child of Odis & Irene)

After spending a few days at Calvin's in North Louisiana, Bobby and I went through Baton Rouge for twenty-four hours. I slept on a sofa and had a hissy fit with State Farm trying to get some money for my living expenses since I had paid premiums for that coverage for twenty-five years.

We then went toward New Orleans to pick up Bobby's car which we had left in the hotel's parking lot. Metarie was allowing people back in, but not New Orleans. So coming east on the Interstate, there was a checkpoint. Bobby and I knew we could not get past that checkpoint so we took a back road. This took us in a roundabout course so that we had to cross the Mississippi River twice. Then we had to cross the major bridge from the Westbank to downtown New Orleans.

We got on the bridge and it was eerie being the only car on this eight-lane wide bridge going across the river. There was this burly, redneck Jefferson Parish sheriff's deputy. Remember the bridge originates and ends in Orleans' Parish. I had heard stories of how these white deputies had pointed guns at black people to keep them from crossing this bridge. I had to think of how to get past this one person. I knew New Orleans was off limits to general people. My brother was driving my Mercedes. The deputy waved us to stop. I pulled out my medical license and my driver's license. We let the window down and I handed both licenses to him. He handed them back and waved us on. There was no verbal exchange whatsoever.

We came across the bridge a couple of blocks from the Convention Center which had only recently been evacuated. Three blocks before we got there, we could smell it! It was the worse stench I have ever smelled and being a doctor, I have handled lots of bad smells. It was the stench of rotting bodies, trash and excrement. This was compounded by the fact that the weather was still stifling hot. I thought it was like something out of the Peanuts comic strip, like Pigpen when you saw the dust rising off of him. It was the rise of stench. As long as I live, I will never forget that smell; it was a terrible thing.

We were headed toward the hotel, but a block before we got there, the Army guard stopped us. He told us we couldn't go to the hotel because it was a government facility. I said, "No it's not, it is a hotel." But at the other end of the block from the hotel, you could see them bringing boxes out. So I guess they were storing some kind of papers there. The Army was occupying that whole section of the city.

Bobby and I told the guard that we wanted to get my brother's car. He said that it was impossible. Finally I said that I was a medical doctor and we needed to get the car because I had to get a computer out of the car that had some information that I needed.

He said we had to talk to Lieutenant Rogers. We said, "OK, where is he?" He said that Lieutenant Rogers was down the block. When we found him, he was a tall, good looking guy, but he had this 'little honey' and she was leaning over him. He was blushing because she was leaning over him and he had been paying attention to her. She also was trying to get to the same place as us to get her car. She was using all of her "assets" to get there.

Lieutenant Rogers wasn't going to tell her no, so he couldn't tell us no because we were right there beside them. So he said, "OK, I will take one of you up there." So I stayed in the car and my brother tells the rest of the story about getting his car.

-Sarah Lain

## Bobby
(5th child of Odis & Irene)

I said to Sarah, "Hey Sarah, you're a doctor, they're gonna let you in the city." So we got in her car and we drove back down to New Orleans. There were still a lot of people lined up on the freeway. This was about three or four days after Katrina and the water still wasn't down. They weren't letting people back in the city but we knew the Uptown wasn't flooded.

We went around the back way and we got waved through. A lot of vehicles and cars were blocking the freeway. Sarah showed the guard her doctor's card and he let us in. It was pretty easy.

We saw all this military stuff parked on the side of the Interstate. We saw tons of helicopters flying all over the place, a lot of them had guns; it was like a war zone. It was like 'Welcome to Viet Nam.'

It was one of the funniest things in my life when we went back to the hotel to get my car. Anybody in the city could get free gas so we filled up the car. As we drove around there were a lot of military which made us nervous, but they didn't harass us at the time.

We drove around the hotel building but they said to wait right there. We told them that we had to pick up my car. He said, "Well you really can't do anything around here because it is dangerous and you need a military escort." Another lieutenant came down and he said they were cleaning out the building. All my life I had seen this one building in downtown New Orleans, but I never knew what it was because it never had a name on it. Come to find out, it was an FBI/CIA building that was totally dedicated to covert activities. So they had all these moving vans and people dressed in black; they looked like aliens from outer space because they were in special uniforms. They were moving all these boxes and putting them in vans.

When we came, they had to move all these vans and secure them because they thought we were special envoys because I was with Dr. Lain. They figured if we got in past the clearances, we must have special papers. At first the people said we couldn't go in the hotel because it was high security and important things were going on. One little guy said, "Man, it is the FBI and the CIA, you really don't want to be messing around here."

That is when Sarah came and told them, "Hi I'm Dr. Lain and this is my brother." She went off a little bit like my mom would do when protecting her children. She had a little of my mama in her; she did the 'Irene Lain' on them. So, the battalion showed up, it was about twelve soldiers and a lieutenant.

My car was up on about the 10th floor, so they sent in two soldiers and they ducked down and carefully advanced up the parking ramp. Then they sent two more soldiers who passed the first two and they did their little squat with the automatic weapons.

We were walking behind these soldiers doing this all the way. We got up to about the third floor and we were watching all this ahead of us. I was thinking to myself, this would take us all day getting up to my car like that. They were doing one row of cars at a time.

I hadn't really been thinking about what they were doing until all of a sudden, it just hit me. I burst out laughing and I said, "This is funny." The lieutenant looked at me and said roughly, "What're you laughing at?" I said, "You guys think we are in Viet Nam! Do you think there are going to be terrorists up these steps?"

He said, "Well, you don't know who might be behind these cars. They might come out shooting." It was the weirdest thing. That is how bad things can be when there is no communication going on. I thought if people had been hiding behind the cars, wouldn't they have starved to death by now? At least, they would be begging for water by now, all these days later.

All I said to them was, "They might have starved to death by now." Even the soldiers said, "Yeah, man he's right." After that they sort of relaxed and everyone just walked on up. Then the lieutenant said to the soldiers, "Just go on about your business" and he let them go. I said, "I know where the car is." He said, "Well let one guy go up with you." I said, "Whatever."

I thought to myself, I'm not scared of anything around here, I was born in this city. These guys were from other states and all they could believe was what they had heard on the news, that everybody has a gun and they were shootin' down there in New Orleans.

First Sight of House

The city government kept the people out of New Orleans for about two months before they started letting residents back in to go to our houses. It was amazing how fast all the mold had taken over. The temperatures were running in the high 90s. I think it went into a dry spell right after the storm and it might have lasted all the way into December without a rain.

When I first saw the house, it looked hopeless. The refrigerator was suspended in the air -- I was trying to figure out what was holding up that refrigerator. The thing was lifted horizontal, four feet in the air with nothing under it and nothing around it. It was incredible. There was water still running from broken pipes in the house and about a foot of sludge on the floor from the residue left from the water leaving.

The water itself had been all the way up to the ceiling. Matter of fact, it was maybe two inches into the attic. Sheet rock had fallen from the ceiling and no pictures were on the wall. My mom had all these pictures of the family all around the whole living room. A few places where the sheet rock was still on the walls had some picture frames left still hanging but the actual pictures washed out blank, you couldn't make nothing out of it.

When I came back into the city, I said, this is what it probably looks like after a nuclear explosion. Everything had like this 'moon dust' on it out in the street. It was like a real thick dust. They had like big swans and birds that you normally would never see. I asked myself, "Did these birds escape from the zoo? Did they fly up from the Gulf? Did the hurricane bring them in?"

Then I saw spiders in all kind of colors: red, yellow and blue. I ain't never seen these animals before. I saw a whole lot of new stuff -- it was incredible. I saw weeds and grass growing that I had never seen before. It was like all this alien stuff invaded the area. The storm almost literally brought in new species, new plants, and new insects. When I was gutting houses and taking stuff out, I'd think, "I wonder what I will see next."

## Decide to Rebuild

I thought to myself that my family's house has always been here. It was built right here and I just had the inclination to rebuild it. My dad had bought the lot and had contractors come in and build it as a three-bedroom house in the beginning. Everyone in the family was saying, "You have to tear this house down; there is no way you can salvage it. Don't waste your time." I kept replying, "I can fix it."

It was a lot of work but I knew I could do it. When it was first built, it was smaller. They had doubled the footprint of the house over the years, but I just knew I would always rebuild it.

At first I was commuting from Algiers on the West Bank from Tanga's house. Really you didn't want to get caught in the area of the house (9th Ward) after dark. Literally, it was like the wild-wild west right after Katrina. Everyone's sense of alertness was heightened. It was very, very weird when you don't have no lights in the city.

Everything was pitch black. At the time, I could just walk outside and put my hand in front of my face and not be able to see my hand. That was how dark it was by the house. As far as you looked down the streets all you would see was blackness, except for the railway down there, you could see some light there.

I found myself working on the house and then I would go to the front door and walk outside just to look to see if anything was moving out there. Then I would go back in to do more work. I felt like one of those little animals in Africa that popped up to look around, make sure there were no predators around to pounce on me. I know some people got robbed and things of that nature. You never realized how scary life could be after a catastrophe without any light.

-Bobby Lain

Sarah and Bobby Inspecting Sarah's House

## Otis Jr. (June)
(1st child of Odis and Irene)

### Coming Back to Find People with Guns

I stayed away from New Orleans for about a week or so, then I came back to check on everything. What really, really got me was at every turn there was somebody in uniform with a big gun. In the evening, it seemed these people would shoot and ask questions later. I was a business owner trying to check on my businesses but the city wasn't allowing general people to come back and forth. It was a Gestapo-type of environment. They was saying that you have to have special approval for everything.

After the storms (Katrina & Rita), a group called Blackwater had these cars with tinted windows and I heard they were just shooting at the people. You talk about being deathly afraid -- I went down to New Orleans a couple of times and I said over and over to myself, "Lord, I shouldn't even think about what I have lost. Let it go."

### Lawlessness

For a long time, over three months, the police kept a van of mine and used that van until they got new equipment. Every other week we would ask, "When are you going to return the van?" The police would say, "We are not ready to return it yet." Now how do you get justice out of that? What do you do and who do you talk to? We had a mayor who everybody hated now because he said that the city will be 'chocolate' again. We had police officers out of control and in fact, during this time, a police supervisor told me that one of the officer's shot himself at my building. We had death and destruction all around us and it was survival of the fittest.

I felt like a lone ranger, my job was to stay out of harm's way. I kind of got an idea of what was going on with my stuff in the businesses, but then I realized, I had no control over none of it. And the money I had left in my pocket, I was paying to people just to keep them happy.

At the same time, when the phones came back up, I had people calling me looking for refunds. At that time, I was thinking that I was still in business and could afford to give these people money back from cancelled trips. So I was paying out money and not receiving any in return. Other people that owed me money, refused to pay me though. To this day, we have not collected from a lot of these people.

I heard all these stories about people shooting at other people. It was like the military shot and killed people, but you will never know about it. The people who came to help (military) were the worst ones. I heard there were some people on the Danzinger bridge with a guy who was trying to escape, and the military just shot at these people. Those are stories that will never be told. The bad part about it, it looked like everyone had guns except me. The military were taking guns from everyone else.

Thinking back about it, it really feels like I had gone through a war. It was so similar – I saw the guns, the dead bodies, people on the rooftops with guns, and helicopters flying all over.

One of the things that really sticks in my mind, was when I was able to get on the freeway high rise, the portion that goes towards the dome, and there were all these people on the roadway. The people were yelling, "Mr. help me." I had tears, sweat, chills, and I was like, "What can I do?" The really sad thing about it was, when I got to the top of the bridge, just before getting to the Mississippi River bridge, these helicopters was dropping water down on the bridge and guess what? The water was breaking when it hit ground. To me it was stupid, they could have gotten down closer. They were dropping water down to people and the bottles were just splattering everywhere. People had to defecate on the bridge and they had to sleep on the bridge. And then they couldn't get off the bridge on one side because the military were shooting at people.

Then as I drove out of New Orleans, there were all these busses lined up with water and supplies, coming from all over the country and world, and the check points weren't letting them in.

When you start reflecting on this stuff, you think, how can I explain this to others to make them understand? I saw the Blackwater people, and to me, it was nothing nice. I saw all the people coming in from the military and National Guard service, and most all these people were young, I mean about 20, 21, or 22 years old. To me it wasn't like any of them were concerned about saving lives, mostly they seemed concerned about what kind of hell they could raise.

## Louis searching

I learned afterwards that my little brother Louis was trying to find me. For two weeks, a lot of people didn't know where I was or even if I was alive because the communications system was bad. It must have been about a month after Katrina when Louis wrecked his Mercedes trying to find me. At that time he was going through medical problems (cancer). We had grown up doing things together and he thought if he found me, his life would have been OK. I didn't find out until later that when he was trying to find me, he actually slept in his car and it was cold. He also slept in the building on Chef (June-El) for a while when he was looking for me. That was sometime in October.

I didn't find Louis until sometime after that when his condition had deteriorated to a point that he was confined to a bed. I later learned from a preacher I heard on the radio, that sometimes it is best to keep your mouth closed. I'm embarrassed to say that I didn't know that then, so when I found Louis I said, "Man, come on and get out of the bed, let's go shoot some pool." He looked at me like he thought, "Man, don't you know I'm dying and you're acting stupid."

## Stealing Property

For days after Katrina, and even up to this day, people went inside the Loews Express building and were taking stuff. People also went inside the Pink Panther Park and were just taking stuff.

I had a lot of sleepless nights, a lot of times I did whatever I could to avoid confrontation and blood-shed. I was at the park, and I found that all these people came in and were just squatting in the park – not paying anything. These were supposed to be people cleaning debris and stuff up after the storm -- they weren't ideal citizens. Some of these people came from jail and they would attack people right to their face. My mother always told me to be careful of who you make friends with because not everyone is friendly. Nevertheless, we had good people and we had bad people in the park.

I met people from all over the country and everybody was running to New Orleans thinking they could make the fast buck. Some people bought millions and millions of dollars of equipment and they never got the contracts. A lot of people got contracts and didn't get paid. A lot of other people got paid and didn't do the work.

The sad thing about it was that for a long time there was no law and order, nobody was there to say this is right and this is wrong. I can't imagine that the lawlessness of the wild, wild West was any worse than New Orleans after Katrina. I learned how to survive by just avoiding those people. I would go into several places and see the stuff that I actually owned. Believe it or not, I went into the store across the street from my building and I could see my chairs lined up around the wall in that restaurant. But what was I going to say?

## Getting Busses Back

When my busses were used to evacuate people out of New Orleans right after Katrina, I was trying to give the people a phone number and procedure to follow to get the busses back to me. But at the time, we were more concerned to get them out and I said, "Call me." But everybody didn't get the instructions because the police came in hollering and getting everyone excited. They were saying things like, "Hurry up and get on the bus because we are going to get washed out. We expect twenty more feet of water and it will be over top the building." Everybody was getting in a panic. I was taking names of people that got on busses at first. But after I saw the situation was getting to a point where you couldn't talk to people because of the panic caused by the police, I got out of there.

Each driver we found for a bus made the decision of where they wanted to go. If his family said, "We want to go to Dallas" that was where they ended up. The busses ended up everywhere -- one was in Houston, Texas, another one in Lake Charles, Louisiana, another in Shreveport, Louisiana, and yet another bus ended up around Dallas. I had to spend money sending people all over the place to get these busses back. I went with drivers to try to get equipment back.

I had the most problems getting the bus back that ended up in Memphis. One guy I knew had a son who was a great basketball player for LSU and went on to play for the pros. His family decided Memphis was where they wanted to go and that bus ended up at a USA Bus place in Memphis.

The first time I tried to retrieve that bus, I contacted the company and they said it was in Jackson, Mississippi at the bus station. I went to Jackson and contacted the police department and we went all over trying to find the bus. Come to find out, the bus was nowhere in Jackson, Mississippi, the bus was in Memphis. So, I went to

Memphis to the USA Bus company and asked for the bus to be returned to us. I believe that the people at USA Bus decided that they thought I was not the type to be able to afford to own a vehicle like this. They said that I would have to prove that this was my vehicle.

I wound up having to call in the dealership where I purchased the bus from to get them to fax over information concerning my ownership. USA Bus didn't think I could afford the bus just based on my looks. I guess to them a man of color didn't look like I should be able to purchase a $400,000 vehicle. I said, "Not only do I have one bus like this, but I have 30 like this. I have limousines and like twelve to fourteen minibuses." It was not like this one bus defined me.

Then after all of that, USA Bus wanted to make a deal with me that since New Orleans was flooded out, I should leave the bus there and they would maintain and keep it for me. I said, "No." Under the circumstances, I needed to take my bus and get out of there. This ordeal was so disappointing because that is when I knew I was in trouble -- everything that I owned and did from that point on, I had to prove to people.

My nephew Darren brought one of the first busses back to Loews Express. Darren told me, "On the way back to New Orleans, I saw one of your busses in Beaumont, Texas and it was just sitting there on the corner."

So we went and looked for this bus in Beaumont. We spent days trying to find this particular bus and the only reason we kept missing the bus was because right next to the hotel, there was an overpass on the incline. Unless you were in a high vehicle, you couldn't see the bus. So Darren saw it from the bus he was driving back to New Orleans but when we passed in a car, we passed it up several times even though we were going back and forth. It was really disgusting because Darren was giving me instructions on the phone and I was in the area, but I would get off the exit looking everywhere and then get back on not seeing it. Some kind of way, one time I was in a van and higher up off the ground, I was able to look over and I saw the top of the bus. That was maybe the third trip. So I finally found that bus.

There seemed to be some kind of episode with every bus that we were trying to get back; it wasn't easy. It cost me a lot of money. I had to fly people to Dallas to pick up a bus. First of all, they had to get instructions and had to find it. They had to get transportation from the airport. I spent a lot of time and money to just round those busses up and bring them back.

In New Orleans itself, a lot of people called me and said, "I see your bus over here." One time, someone said, "Your bus is up on Napoleon Ave." I went and found the bus in the middle of the neutral ground.

There were about six or seven mini-busses and a van that I found around the city. I had a GM truck that I never did find. There was a couple of major things that came up missing.

The police had taken a lot of vehicles and I never got paid for those. One time I looked over on the other side of the road and saw a brand new limousine I had with a bullet hole in it. Anyway, I discovered later, the one that was brought back was shot up and the one they kept was destroyed and wound up in the salvage yard. I found a limousine two years later that they sent to my house with a statement saying it was salvage. I ended up giving it to those people simply because they were looking for a lot of technicalities and charges. I thought, if I take this piece of junk, what am I going to do with it? I also had a vintage Rolls Royce which ended up in Baton Rouge.

The police force called me (how they got my cell phone number I don't know.) At the time I was coming from trying to pick up a bus from Dallas and I was on Interstate 45. On the phone they said, "Otis Lain, we know that your busses were taken from you. We are calling to find out if you want to file a complaint." I said, "Look, let me get back to you. Who am I talking to? I've been driving all night and I'm barely staying on the road. Let me call you back.

I think it was the next day that I had an officer call me and say, "Look, man, they are trying to press charges against us, Coach Lain. We don't need to go through this because it was a disaster and we needed the transportation." (I used to be a high school coach in New Orleans and he used my old title Coach Lain.) The next day I called the police officer back and I said, "Look, I don't want to press charges, I mean, you can do what you all have to do."

This is New Orleans and I knew what might go down. I didn't want to press charges because I knew that people knew me and I didn't know them and it is a back and forth situation. I'm thinking that it was going to be a big court case and it was a situation where I had police names and numbers on a piece of paper. At the time during Katrina, I had asked what is your name, and wrote it down in case I had to go back to this.

What I found out was that there is no such thing as justice, you just try to survive. It wasn't necessarily safe to go on with a big court case and I never could understand why people feel like getting even is just locking a person up. I also knew at this point, no judge wanted to touch this stuff, because who do you sue? How do you sue, what do you do about it? Even though they acknowledge they took some stuff. I decided all I could do about this was pray.

The insurance company, believe it or not, didn't pay for anything. They were saying that for each vehicle, I only had $14,000 of damage and my deductible was $15,000. I think going to court at that particular point was not an option for me because I wasn't able to get anybody to litigate anything and I felt like I was wasting money.

### Use of Busses After the Storm

A little while after Katarina, Wellington, my oldest son, received a phone call requesting some of our busses to work up in Alexandria. He was in charge of dispatching busses. He told me, "This guy wants five busses to work in Alexandria." I found out every bus in New Orleans had a job and they had a thousand busses that met up in Alexandria.

I told the guy, "Look, I got nine busses available that I'll send to you." We sent those busses up there and we stayed on that particular job for about three months. We stayed onsite transporting Army people. We picked up people and brought them wherever they assigned us. There was one bus that caught on fire and we went and brought them to safety. In the end, I've yet to get paid for all that work.

Then another hurricane came along and we worked in the Lake Charles area. We were at McNeese State University and spent time working there. Everybody spent time on the busses; we took showers at the college or at the truck stops. We ate a lot of MRE meals (Military Meals Ready to Eat.) We did whatever they assigned us to do. We were dealing with military personnel and they made various assignments for us. They moved a lot of people to Shreveport.

However, it was like a pyramid scheme. The people that were on the top got paid, if you were on the bottom it trickled down. So if you were last in line, it was possible that you didn't get paid at all. We got paid for just a fraction of the work that we did. When I asked if they needed those additional busses and they agree, I was expecting to get paid for that. The money got tied up with people who didn't own busses. Somehow they were getting commissions off of my busses. That was a nightmare.

I had a lot of people working; they were doing other jobs like electrical jobs and what have you. I managed to pay these people to keep them employed. This must have gone on for a month. This was the bus side of it, mass confusion, nothing really went smoothly. In fact, I had people in hotels from Lake Charles to Mandeville, spread out all over the place in Covington and elsewhere

I usually was in my car rushing from place to place and we had to do business in cash simply because communication wasn't quite right and the banks weren't quite right. Business was 'cave-man style', I was operating out of my pocket on the front seat of a bus trying to make sure that people were fed, had places to stay and something to eat. That was my responsibility.

-Otis Lain Jr.

**Darren**
(grandson of Odis & Irene, son of Elsie)

After driving the bus of people out from June-El, I stayed at my sister's in Houston. I came back to the New Orleans area on September 14. I was 30 miles west from New Orleans in the area by the job site, River Parish Disposal. My workplace didn't really get too much damage and no water there. They used the front office for us to sleep in. The workers had blankets and pillows laying on the floor.

About a week later, my company took a warehouse next door and converted it into a house for us workers. They fixed it up with beds, air conditioning and carpet. It already had a bathroom set up in there for showers. So that was home then. It was like twenty-two of us staying at that house. I felt very upset at the time because we just couldn't be at home, but everybody got along and it wasn't no problem. Even with twenty-two of us there -- we were all cooperating.

They could only take the individual workers in the house; a lot of workers left families behind. The families had been displaced to all kinds of places from Katrina. Every little chance the workers got to get off work, like having a weekend off, they went to visit their families. It was mostly men that were staying at the warehouse because they were the drivers of the trucks.

We was working a lot of long days -- seven days to catch up (picking up the garbage) and sometimes sixteen or seventeen hours a day. It took a long time to catch up and try to regroup to get more people to come back into the city to work. More people did come in as time went on but we still had a lot of long days.

At the time, I managed to get into the city with the work truck. The National Guard let me in. When I first saw the city, it was like, "What happened? How could this happen?" It looked like a war came through the city and just took it apart. It smelled real horrible from a lot of chemical plants; a real raw smell, like rotten egg smell. The water stayed up so long it turned the sidewalks and the streets different colors. It was a strange color that you had never seen before. The plants and vegetation were all turned upside down and turned brown. Everything was dead.

I came straight out to see what my family house looked like and what kind of damage there was. We had furniture thrown up every way and turned upside down. There had been four feet of water; the water pushed the doors open. It was very upsetting and devastating to see the house like that. I was the first one to see it and I had to tell my mom about it.

You couldn't stay in the city, you just had to go in and assess your property and go right back out. My dad was very sick at the time when Katrina happened; it really made his condition worse because he was very stressed about it. Not until the end of September or early October could owners really start cleaning up and throwing things out.

As part of my job, I drive around the whole city. I saw the amount of garbage from the very beginning, in-between, during the clean-up, and towards the end. I was working through this whole time.

I saw FEMA and other clean-up crews working. People from all over the country, and all over the world, were driving in the city taking pictures with their camcorders. They wanted to be up here, say they saw the devastation, and go home and say, "Yeah it actually did do a whole lot of damage." Those people irritated me.

Sometimes I did get tired of a lot of people coming down doing documentaries and reports from a bunch of universities. They wanted to see the Lower 9th Ward, Lakeview area, and 17th Street Canal. The Lower 9th Ward was really bad; Katrina just took it out all together. It was unbelievable, something you had never seen in your life. They had stuff turned upside down, houses literally coming up off of their blocks and into another house. They had a straight hit of water that just pushed everything upside down and over.

People got irritated, tempers were short, and attitudes got bad in the city right after Katrina. People just couldn't come to grips with it. It was just something they had never seen in their life. They were just getting angrier and angrier every time they looked at the devastation.

I heard a lot of reports about the levees; they did a study on it about three years before Katrina saying that all the levees were in bad shape. Nobody really did respond or do anything about the report and there was just years of laziness and neglect. Now everyone was paying for it.

-Darren Hagan

**Tanga**
(granddaughter of Odis and Irene, daughter of Emanuel Sr.)

<u>Lack of Contact was Torture</u>

After staying at the hotel for seven days during our evacuation, we said, we can't do this forever. Our family split ways; I went to Atlanta area because my husband had a brother there. My mom headed to my Uncle Calvin's place in Winnsboro, Louisiana. My brother was able to go back home right away because he was in Baton Rouge, he had insignificant wind and hail damage to his home.

After we separated, we were unable to talk to each other because of the lack of phone service. The cell phone lines didn't work. It had been like a week and I didn't know where my mom was, and I didn't know what she was doing. She had been bouncing around to so many different homes, I didn't even know what they were going through.

Our family is real, real, real close -- like we talk to each other two to three times a day, not every other day. During this time, we were not able to talk to each other; that was like torture. I didn't know where my sister was either.

Eventually I found out that everybody migrated to my brother's home. At that time, he had like over seventeen people there, so it was rough for them. The way I learned they were there was when my aunt, my mom's baby sister, called me and some kind of way, she was able to put us on a three-way phone call. Tears just rolled down my face when I spoke to my mom. It was very emotional and every time you ran across someone, it was emotional.

<u>Helpful Church</u>

I have to thank this one church, McDonough Baptist Church in McDonough, Georgia. The church opened up their doors to the Red Cross and when we were evacuated, we walked in and they had a system ready. They said they had been preparing for this for years. This was before I knew what type of damage I had at the house.

I came in and a person came up and showed me how to rotate to the different stations, so not too many people would be at one station at a time. So every other person would go to different areas. Sometimes you went in and got a meal first, you could stop off and get canned goods or any type of dry foods or any type of clothing. They had toys for the children, milk for babies and pampers. I mean this church was so wonderful.

I saw one of my ex-coworkers there and we just hugged and cried together. It was just two weeks after the storm, on Labor Day weekend. We cried and then we would see somebody else and we cried again.

They would give us numbers and we would sit down with the Red Cross and fill out our information. The Red Cross gave us a check there on the spot. After we got the check we would have to get in a bus to go cash it right away and the bus had a SWAT caravan. They had SWAT members on top of the bank, across the street, and everything. Now some people I heard got credit cards or debit cards, but we had to get a check. I felt very thankful for the help but if they would have given us an option and say you can go anywhere to cash the check, I would have opted for that. But, there were a lot of the elderly and maybe someone might have taken advantage of them. This was their way of added security and I appreciated their help.

## Helping Other Family Members

Just the year before Katrina, we had moved into our home on the Westbank of New Orleans in Gretna. We were there less than eight months at the time of Katrina. Our home had minimal damage - roof and wind damage, missing windows and things like that. We were fortunate.

Sometime in September, about two weeks later, we went home and all our lights were out. We saw all the electric trucks around and went in the house and all of a sudden the lights came on. When we first went in the house, we made the fatal mistake of opening the refrigerator and the stench of that went through the whole house. I believe you can still smell the stench to this day. No matter how much we painted the walls, used that chemical stain and smell blocker, it still smells.

So the insurance company came out maybe the last week of September to assess the damage. Because my husband works in construction, before we got our insurance payment check, we just went on ahead and repaired the roof, so at least we could stay in the home. The windows weren't fixed or anything but everyone who stayed there didn't mind. They just needed a place to stay. It felt great to help provide for the other family members, especially for my parents, because my parents do everything for me.

Our home became the 'safe haven home', so many of my family members stayed there. As of October 3rd, my parents moved in and then other family members would come and go. My Uncle Bobby moved there and others would stay when they came to check on their homes in New Orleans.

-Tanga Lain Hale

**Rose**
(6th child of Odis & Irene)

I believe it was like October 5th when I got back to New Orleans. For a time, the city kept us out on purpose but when we got back in the city, there were all these guards. We tried not to take certain exits because there was a guard at the end and you didn't want to have any run-ins with any armed guards. It was very frightening to drive around the city at that point; there were no people. All the trees were gone, there were no birds, no cats, no life; it was dead and gray.

I didn't think it smelled as bad as after Hurricane Betsy. After Betsy it smelled like the bottom of a dried-out river bed where you had oyster shells and other stuff. After Katrina, the smells were worse when you got close to a house. Later there were lots of mold and mildew smells; you had to wear a mask. It was frightening because you didn't know what was leaking. It also looked like the bottom of a river bed because Katrina left a gray soot on everything.

When everything dried, there were just cakes of mud a little less than half an inch thick on everything. I did pick up some of the dried mud from my porch and it was obvious there was oil in the mud. I picked it up in case they wanted to analyze it later on. There were lots of rumors about how toxic the place was and I couldn't identify the smells; we just knew the smells weren't healthy at all. We were afraid to breathe.

The other part that scared me a lot was when I tried to drive down the streets to see how the other areas were making out, like around Franklin Ave. I had some friends around there and I went to check on their property. The streets were all tore up. There was still water bubbling up through the ground.

You didn't know which streets were gonna' just sink because New Orleans has a lot of canals under the streets. We've had other times when the streets have just broken up and you had to be careful not to fall in. So there was all these streets cracked up -- you couldn't drive anywhere because it was a hazard.

When you came into New Orleans, there was no food in the city other than you had to go downtown. There they would give you plates of food and they would give you gasoline.

My car was parked at Loews Express and it survived. It looked like it might have floated a little bit or it might have had only a foot of water that didn't ruin the car. I went to get my car to drive it back twenty-two hours where we were staying in Maryland. There were other people that I tried to give a ride. So we went to check their houses out. Everything had mildew and mold and nothing could be saved.

One lady's house had been built four feet off the ground on pilings, like mine was, but her house was uptown. She got just two feet of water. My house was four feet off the ground but I still had six feet of water and my water (measured by the waterline where the water sat for days) was like up over my head in my house. Just the thought of that, how would I be in a house that I felt secure because it was built four feet off the ground already, and now it had five feet of water in the house.

Everything had rusted - the air conditioners and the fence were all rusty. But the contents of my house had floated, and then when the water finally went out, the contents blocked the door. The contents were just piled up blocking the door; some kind of way it looked like the water may have been sucked out when it finally left because of the way we couldn't open the door.

So we went in through the window and we got a ladder. I brought two friends and my son, Andrew, to help me too. I guess I kind of knew I couldn't do it by myself. We picked up an aluminum ladder out of the yard. I can't remember why that ladder was clean enough for us to crawl across. We searched for whatever we could find to get up to the window. We put that ladder in there and Andrew crawled across that ladder to get my lock box. I had a lock box with some bonds, birth certificates, and marriage license in it and now I only regretted that I didn't take other important papers off the wall. The lock box was on a shelf in the closet where the water didn't get up to that shelf.

We had some other important papers like loan documents and all kinds of bank papers which we had put up on a high shelf in the back room. All those cabinets had hit the ground, so none of the papers were saved by putting them on that high shelf.

By that time, you couldn't save any of the clothes that were on the shelf. There were some bags attached to the clothes on hangers that still had water in them from the storm. So the smell then was terrible ... you couldn't breathe. And, there were too many big horsey flies everywhere, it looked like a plague. I had to get that box out of there because it was all I had left.

So we got the box and my son said, "You can't save anything." He knew I would have been trying to save books, but they would have been just mush... and it was very unhealthy. The mold was so horrible; the sheetrock fell off the ceiling. Some of the sheetrock bent some of the prongs on the ceiling fan, so part of the ceiling fan was still there, but the blades were broken. The boards beyond the sheetrock had all kinds of cracks. You could actually see the sky because a lot of the roof was gone.

The houses stood, but most of the churches had been hit as if every church had its own tornado. Somebody explained that because of how churches are built, they don't have enough support and they collapse. They are long churches with a middle that is not completely supported, so they fell down in the middle. The brick fronts were just shattered on a lot of churches.

We stayed by Tanga's on the West Bank for a few days. It usually floods when it rains anytime over there, but they don't get that Betsy, Katrina flooding, the kind where you might drown in a flood. Over on the West Bank, everybody had a blue roof. We called it the "blue roof" because when everybody had roof damage, they had to cover it with blue tarp that is tied down. So at that time, everybody had the blue roofs, their refrigerators were on the side of the street, and they were trying to do their repairs.

There were people on the West Bank, but still there weren't enough restaurants over there for everyone trying to get food. Grocery stores weren't available either at that time. We would try to go to Walgreens, to Rite-Aid, or to Walmart, none of those stores were there anymore. So when you came into New Orleans to try to take care of your property, you had to make sure you gassed up somewhere, like in Baton Rouge.

Baton Rouge was another nightmare because of all those New Orleans' people evacuating to Baton Rouge; the traffic was thick with people everywhere trying to take care of business. The government was actually pretty nice to us because they let us get our medicines for free and they helped us to get access to things we needed.

-Rose Lain Watts

**Jennie V.**
(daughter-in-law of Odis & Irene, wife of Louis)

I first came back into the city to get the bedroom set from upstairs. We were sleepin' on an air mattress in Atlanta. I told Anne (Angela) that we can rent a U-haul and get both of the bedroom sets and the stuff from upstairs in our house. One of my bedroom sets was brand new and I didn't want anyone to steal that. They had already knocked the door open and everything.

It was horrible coming back into the city. It was so depressing, it made me want to cry. The oak tree on the corner had fallen into our house and made a hole in the living room. It looked horrible. You look at it now and you would never believe the mess that it was in at that time.

Students came from all over the country to help gut houses during Spring Break 2006 – many slept in tents

I started rebuilding the house after Louis my husband passed. He died in March of 2006 (just six months after Katrina). You know we had people from all over come to New Orleans to help. The people that gutted my house was volunteering with Catholic Charities and these people came from Michigan.

To rebuild the house, I did the general contracting work myself calling each individual person for each job. I felt that when you contract someone to do the general contracting, you are paying them extra money, for what? I figured if I could get my own people, I could do my own contracting. So I was lucky enough to do that. Some family members, like Damon, told me about the guys that do the sheetrock and the people who hang the doors. I got a lot of recommendations and advice, so I was able to do it myself even though it gave me big headaches.

My daughter Keisha and her husband Charles recommended a lot of people to me also. They started

Students standing in line to get an outdoor shower
Spring Break 2006

rebuilding their house first, so as they found people, they told me about them. Everybody was just waiting on their Road Home money.

I got a FEMA trailer but I didn't get my Road Home money until March or April. It seemed like it took forever to me. From about April until about September is when I got into the house. That's because I was out in that FEMA trailer on the lot and I was constantly walking through to see what they was doing. I tell you, the Mexican workers were great; they worked hard. I had no complaints about the Mexicans. They listened to me and they did what I asked them to do.

Other workers seemed to tell me what they wanted to do – not the other way around. I said, "Hey look, this is my house. This is the way I want it, and I want you to do it this way." The Mexicans made sure that they got it right. I liked that.

I got my cabinets from some Vietnamese people. They did OK, but they didn't get me the particular granite that I wanted. They got something else and tried to tell me it was the one I had asked for. I said, "No, I know which one I picked out, it didn't have any black in it." In the end I said, "Well, I'm not going to worry about it." By then, I was tired.

I could have killed my plumber. I was so angry with that man it brought me to tears, I swear. I don't know what was wrong with him, but he didn't do anything right. I had to get someone else out here to "undo" some of the things he did. I was really upset with him. In the beginning, I thought he would do good work, but I don't know if he had a personal vendetta against me, because around here he sure didn't do good work. The other guy I finally called did everything. He hooked up the sinks and he didn't charge but a small portion of what the first guy charged who messed everything up.

-Jennie V. Lain

## Estella
(daughter-in-law of Odis & Irene, wife of Otis, Jr.)

The first time I went back into our home, I was with my daughter Latoya. It was in October and Latoya and I drove down to New Orleans from the Atlanta area. In the mean-time, Otis was always back in New Orleans.

We drove down and when we got to Mississippi, you could really see the devastation from Katrina. Very few people were even traveling at that time. Then we came through Slidell because this was the only way you could get across because the Twin-span was out of commission. We were just in awe and really saddened to see the state that the whole Highway 11 was in at that time; I could not believe it.

My sons, Wellington and Shaun, had already gone back into the house earlier and retrieved some papers I was able to salvage, dry out and make copies. One of them was my marriage license, everything was washed away except the number on my marriage license. It was a blank sheet of paper with a number on it. I was able to get another copy of the marriage license from that number.

When Latoya and I finally got to our home, there were some things that I wanted to put my hands on, things that I had gone off and left. We were there trying to pick up what we could. We spent maybe two days and my good friend, Sheila, accommodated us.

We didn't realize until it was dusk that nobody was on the street but us. I said, "Latoya, let's get out of here." By the time we got to Chef Menteur Highway it was black. No street lights -- no nothing. This was in middle October. I took pictures of the house and the community.

At that point I retrieved some things that were dry. One of the main things was a Bible sitting on top of my counter which was kind of high; we would sit at it with bar stools. The water was maybe about four feet high but the countertop was dry.

When I got back to Fairburn, Georgia and I was thumbing through that Bible, I found some notes that I had written on Jeremiah 29:10 and the following verses. Verse 11 is my favorite. I began to read and the Lord said, "Wherever I plant you, your sons and your daughters, let them marry, plant, build until I change it. Again 'I know the plans I have for you, plans for good and not for evil.'" So when I read that, I knew that I was to stay put in Georgia; that settled it.

Of course we went back to New Orleans a couple of times to our house. I said, "Lord, I can't buy all new clothes and I need some church clothes." Everything in the closet was ruined; it had been wet and now had lots of mold. I went through those things and I said, "Just allow me to get some things that will be serviceable." I had some nice suits and I knew I wouldn't be able to find them in my size. They really fit me and since I'm an elder, I needed those pulpit type skirts that are long enough for church.

I got everything I thought I needed. Latoya took the shoes she wanted because at that time I couldn't wear high heels anymore. I took all the shoes that I could wear. I went to the FEMA office across the river in New Orleans -- that was a God-send. I talked to this lady and explained that I had some clothing that had mold. She sat down and gave me some information on how to clean these things. The answer was simply to clean them with Pine Sol.

I spent about two weeks working on those clothes in the garage and then I put those things in the dry cleaners a little at a time. The Pine Sol killed the mold. The dry cleaners worked with me because he ran them through several times to get the smell out of them. This man ended up doing a beautiful job. He took a special interest; he didn't charge me an arm and a leg -- maybe $7 for three or four pieces and that was unheard of. Finally I got all those things cleaned and I had clothes to wear. I always find it helpful to pass along the Pine Sol tip given to me.

-Estella Lain

**Elsie**
(2nd child of Odis & Irene)


I couldn't stop crying when I first came back into New Orleans after the hurricane. I just walked around in a daze; I could not believe the devastation I saw. Roads were all buckled and houses were just torn up. I must have made six or seven trips before I finally decided to start guttin' my house.

I initially had no intentions on coming back to rebuild. But then I decided, am I going to live my life like this? The longer we left the house sit, the worse it was getting. So that is how we really made up our mind that we would go on back.

My house ended up damaged more than I initially thought. It is two stories and we thought the upstairs was fine since the flood waters didn't get that high. I thought I could come back and live upstairs while I got the downstairs repaired. But in the process, the roof was more damaged than I thought, so I ended up losing three rooms' ceilings upstairs.

When I found out I couldn't move back in upstairs, they had already gutted downstairs. That wasn't until 2007, because we were only in the house six months before my husband Arthur passed; he passed in 2008.

There was only one way into the city. We couldn't go the Slidell way because that bridge was out. I came back to the city pretty often but I always had to come by myself. It was just hard dealing with this whole situation because I knew that I didn't have any help. I just had to buckle down and make up my mind to do it myself.

I saw people, who were mostly men, and it was clear they didn't have nowhere to stay. I could tell that the color of their skin had changed and they were real poor and skinny; it was easy to tell that no nourishment was going on. If the person didn't go and find one of these wagons that was feeding people, there was nowhere to eat. Everyone had to eat and gas up before they came into the city.

Metairie was about the best place, on the way out of town, where you could stop at a gas station and get something. Or you could go into a section of town where Red Cross would feed people everyday. The stench and the mold was just everywhere and that made it hard to eat. There were also flies everywhere and that made it hard to eat too.

When I came back into the city, I really went down to Mississippi with my brother June and we would go and hang out. He would have a hotel room and I would go down there. I was really in-between trying to transact business because I had to show proof that I owned the house. I had to try to get to city hall during the daytime to get permits to start working.

Once I got the permits, then I was coming back and forth because I got somebody to start working on some of our property. I would try to check on them and check on the neighborhood. At first I was trying to see who was coming back because that was important in determining whether I should come back or not.

My husband and I missed New Orleans. I couldn't really make up my mind because I had four daughters that all stayed in different cities; one in Houston, one in Las Vegas, one in Washington D.C., and one in Georgia. So I couldn't make up my mind which town I would like to stay in.

I really liked Las Vegas but I figured that is not the place to be. I liked Houston and I was trying to get my daughter Drusilla to decide. But I didn't tell her what I wanted to do about getting a larger house there with her, so she never knew. I didn't want her to make up her mind that way. I would say things like, "Girl don't you want to put this house up for sale?" She would answer, "Oh, I like my house." So I wasn't about to talk her into moving out of her house. I only recently told her my idea that we buy a bigger house and move in together.

Drusilla was sad when we left. She had been a very good hostess while we stayed with her and she really helped me with her daddy and his medical issues. I could come and go, she really gave me the help I needed. I could run down to New Orleans, or run out of town, or whatever.

-Elsie Lain Hagan

## Emanuel Sr.
(7th child of Odis & Irene)

During the evacuation, we were staying in a Holiday Inn hotel in Houston. That is where my daughter booked the hotel. We wound up staying there about six days.

After those six days, we left the hotel and went to Winnsboro, Louisiana and stayed at my Uncle P.C.'s house for about two nights. Then we went to Baton Rouge and we stayed at my son's house, Emanuel Jr. for about two nights. He had a lot of people including his in-laws -- his wife's mother, her husband and sister. His wife doesn't have any other siblings besides her brother, but she had two cousins who had children and spouses. So their house was getting pretty crowded.

Emanuel Jr. made room for us but then my youngest daughter Alicia and I decided to go to Atlanta. Some how I had my daddy's medicine with me in Baton Rouge, so we had to make a trip back through Winnsboro to give him the medicine on our way to Atlanta. It was at least two hours extra going that way. We just dropped the medicine off and kept going.

Then we made our way to Atlanta and arrived around September 9th, which had been my mother's birthday. We went to Atlanta and stayed with my wife's brother, I think it is called Snellville, Georgia, a suburb of Atlanta.

We came back to New Orleans on October 1st and stayed with my daughter, Tanga, who had a house on the West Bank. Her house had wind and roof damage but no flood damage. It was overwhelming and sad to see the city after Katrina. It was dark and there were no lights at all. Only a few places were open for business. Uptown didn't get any flood water and my work place at the Sewage and Water Board was flooded out. They reopened the building but the basement needed a lot of work.

I felt like I had lost everything. My house was flooded out but my brother Bobby told me, "You will be better off in a year. You will get everything back." He was sort of right; we got a lot of stuff back. There are some things that can't ever be replaced, like your books, pictures and personal stuff. Some of the people that we were associated with never did come back. Unfortunately, some of them drowned and we just miss some of them that moved elsewhere.

-Emanuel Lain Sr.

# Pictures taken within months after Hurricane Katrina

Devastation along street of family home in March 2006

Small grocery store (The Sweet Shop) down the street
from the family home, March 2006

# Chapter 11

## FEMA Trailers &
## Cruise Ships

## Report: FEMA mishandled toxins in trailers

NEW ORLEANS 7/24/2009 — The Federal Emergency Management Agency didn't react  enough to reports of toxins in trailers housing victims of Hurricane Katrina, endangering the health of thousands of victims across the Gulf Coast, according to a new report by the Department of Homeland Security Office of Inspector General (http://content.usatoday.com/topics/topic/United+States+Department+of+Homeland+Security)

... Other findings include:
• FEMA officials announced they had found hazardously high levels of formaldehyde in occupied trailers in February 2008, more than two years after the first storm victims were housed in them.
• FEMA caused a two-month delay in trailer testing in 2007 because it didn't have a public communications strategy in place for Congress, the media and trailer occupants.
-Rick Jervis, *USA TODAY*"

## Jennie V.
(daughter-in-law of Odis & Irene, wife of Louis)

Well I'll tell you, I first stayed in my daughter Angela's FEMA trailer. She was trying to get it changed over to my name but FEMA wouldn't do it. Angela's trailer was real bad; you couldn't even stay in that trailer the smell was so strong. My eyes and nose were burning so much. I would feel it; my eyes and nose would start burning until all I wanted to do was get out of the trailer.

I called FEMA to tell them about the smell. This was before the information about formaldehyde in the FEMA trailers came out. I told them, "I can't stay in this trailer." They said they were getting a lot of complaints about that. So they told me to open up all the windows and air it out. I did what they said and eventually I was able to stay in there.

I did get real sick when I was in that trailer, but it was my back -- my sciatic nerve. So I don't know if it had anything to do with the trailer or not. I also had a rash all over my arm and shoulders. The doctor gave me some ointment to clear that up. The doctors said it was 'Katrina rash' but of course they didn't put that in my records. I got sinus headaches and I never had sinus headaches before either. But finally the headaches cut out, but every once in awhile I might still get a headache. I never had that problem before living in the FEMA trailer.

Finally FEMA sent me a trailer under my name. That trailer was second hand. So I moved into it from Angela's trailer. Since the trailer was second hand, I guess the smell had already left it -- I didn't have no problem with it. Then I moved into my house when it got finished.

-Jennie V. Lain

## Elsie
(2nd child of Odis & Irene)

I stayed with one daughter for a year and the second daughter for two months. Then my husband Arthur and I came back and stayed in the FEMA trailer for nine months.

I applied for a trailer when I originally found out that they were offering trailers. It took a while for them to get the trailer to us. I ordered a handicapped accessible trailer because of my husband's condition. We probably would have come back to New Orleans sooner, but the trailer didn't come until like July 2006.

My son Darren got his FEMA trailer before mine. We both had our trailers on the same property line. That way, when we were working on the house, we were right there together.

-Elsie Lain Hagan

## Darren
(grandson of Odis & Irene, son of Elsie)

It felt different to live in a FEMA trailer. It felt only a little like home. I didn't get in the trailer until about August 2006, and didn't get out until around January 2008, when my family's house was ready to move back in.

It felt strange because we had never lived in a trailer before. My family used to go camping during the summer months a long time ago, but living in a FEMA trailer wasn't like setting up a tent and sleeping on a campground.

My trailer worked out OK -- I didn't have any problems with it. I got my trailer on the property before my mom & dad's trailer got there. It took at least another month after they delivered the trailer to get the lights turned on and the propane tanks delivered. It was hard for my mom and dad to live in their trailer because my dad had health issues, but they managed to make the best of it.

-Darren Hagan

## Otis Jr. (June)
(1st child of Odis & Irene)

The only thing I got from the Federal government was a FEMA trailer. The FEMA trailer was parked on Chef Menteur Highway on the side of the Loews Express building.

I spent a lot of time in that trailer. It seemed like every other day, FEMA had a different person knock on the trailer door to check on stuff. They would see if the windows were screened, check to see if I had gas, check to see if all the mechanical parts were operating right. I had to sign forms, but I think the FEMA worker just wanted to make sure that I was still there.

I've always said, "One of the things you never want to do is get involved in a government project." The government spends more money in one month checking up on everything than you can imagine. It was the worst thing that I ever experienced in my life.

-Otis Lain Jr.

## Bobby
(5th child of Odis & Irene)

I liked my FEMA trailer. There were problems; it wasn't the best of quality. But it was the first opportunity to stay right next to the house and that way I could accelerate my repair work.

On the property next door (to the family home), a FEMA trailer came for Raymond. Then a trailer came for Pat (lived in the house on the other side of that lot) and my dad moved in that trailer. Finally, my FEMA trailer came; we had three trailers on the same lot.

Matter-of-fact, me and Robert Atkins tore down the house on the back of that lot by hand. That house was leaning and when they pulled in the first trailer, we didn't want that house to fall over on the trailer. We just kept taking down a little of the house at a time so they would haul

FEMA trailers beside family home 2006

that off (with the garbage pick ups.) That way we had a place to put all three trailers when they brought them.

One neighbor got his trailer a couple weeks before me. I think we got the first trailer in January 2006, and the utility company wouldn't turn on the trailer electricity. FEMA would lock the trailers up and not let anyone in until the utility company hooked up the power to the trailer.

The utility company tried to channel the power to a trailer when one came in, but we still didn't have any street lights. It took another five months before we had street lights. We broke in the trailer lock and started staying in the trailer before we had electricity to the neighborhood.

I kept calling the utility company on the phone and lobbying them for electricity. They started turning on little neighborhoods down by the river, then out by the lake. There would be a trailer with lights but the neighborhood had no lights. You could see trailers with lights on – like being out in the wilderness with a light in the distance.

When we were living in the trailer, there were people going around kicking in the doors and burglarizing trailers. You just hoped that you were not home when they would do something like that. But I never did have that happen to me. I heard that it was happening in New Orleans East. The burglars were looking for money. It was just so easy to knock the door open of a FEMA trailer when you were gone. There wasn't a lot of security in the trailers.

People were also tearing out the electrical wires (in a partially repaired home) to sell the copper that was worth no more than $50. Here you might have just spent about $3000 to $4000 to put the wiring in and they would do about $100 worth of work to pull it out. It defies all logic.

The FEMA trailer allowed me to really accelerate the work on the house, so I was very thankful for that.

-Bobby Lain

Water line above student's head where water sat in
family home for several weeks

## Raymond
(9th child of Odis & Irene)

I drove back into New Orleans for the first time at night. I really didn't have nowhere to stay or spend the night. The trailers weren't delivered yet. I was basically homeless.

Emanuel was on a cruise ship when I came in. I called and asked him, "Where can I stay?" He said I could spend the night by Tanga's across the river. I think Bobby was staying at Tanga's house also. So I ended up going over there and Al, Tanga's husband, let me sleep on the sofa.

I woke up that next morning saying, "I got to find me some other place to stay." I went over to the FEMA office and told them I had no where to stay. I think they put me up in a hotel. It was hotel, hotel, hotel. I got sick of hotels. I was in the hotel for about three or four months, then finally I got a FEMA trailer. But then it took another month or month and a half to get electricity in the trailer.

Once I got in the FEMA trailer, I stayed a month and it didn't agree with me. The FEMA trailer had chemicals and as soon as I got in the trailer, my eyes started burning. Before they came out with the info that the trailers had formaldehyde in them, I had already had a reaction to the trailer.

I also had to get out of the trailer because it had a ply board bed which was too hard and there just wasn't enough room for me. I want to have and use stuff and there was no room. Some people liked the FEMA trailers and some people didn't. Not everybody had a reaction, like Bobby didn't have a reaction. Daddy and Bobby, they loved their trailers. Sarah came and she lasted about a day in my trailer I think. I let her stay in it and she didn't like it.

I really didn't have any problems fixing my small one bedroom home. It's a shotgun double house. I basically put in most of the sheetrock. I just fixed one side (of the two units). It is four years later and that other side still is not fixed yet. I'm still working on that house trying to get it to where it was pre-Katrina.

There was a lot of devastation all over the city -- a lot of poles and trees were laying in the streets. The whole city had a stench about it. It was all in the air because you had a lot of people putting out refrigerators and they had mold and mildew and spoiled food. They had a lot of maggots. They asked that people tape up the refrigerators but a lot of the tape fell off and the doors came open.

We were driving out in East New Orleans and we saw a pack of dogs chasing behind these two chickens. This one chicken flew up and was on top of this burglar-barred door and the dogs were at the bottom just waiting. It was like in a jungle -- survival of the fittest. Another dog ran up with a chicken in his mouth, it was a game cock. These dogs looked ferocious.

You didn't see a lot of pet dogs but I did see a lot of rats. For some reason the rats survived; they can swim and climb. The rats survived, but probably more dogs drowned. It seemed like rats just took over the city.

-Raymond Lain

**Sarah**
(4th child of Odis & Irene)

They offered me a FEMA trailer. They went to my address and did all of the markings, putting down flags and markings for its placement. All of this eventually weathered and blew away. But still FEMA would call periodically and say "your trailer is on the way." The trailer never came. In reality, subconsciously I really didn't want to live in a FEMA trailer. First, my house is located on a lonely corner and I would have been isoolated by myself out in the dark. The trailers weren't safe or very secure and there was lawlessness and insanity running rampant.

I decided to pay for an apartment. Until I could find one in a neighboring parish, I tried staying in Raymond's trailer. I felt physically ill, my head hurt, my eyes burned and my throat was raw. I left town for two weeks, somehow the freezer door fell open. There were some steaks in there. When they thawed, the flies came in, it was during summer.

When I returned, there were about two million flies in that FEMA trailer. It was like a horror movie because the flies had defecated all over everything. Everything was covered with this foul, red slime. I tried cleaning everything with Lysol but I had had enough and passed the trailer on to Raymond's 22 year-old son. A year later when they took that trailer away, they still had dead flies in the window sills.

-Sarah Lain

## Andrew (Daniel)
(10th child of Odis & Irene)

Cruise Ships

The city put everyone (city employees) up on Carnival Cruise ships for four months, from October to February. There were two ships; the police had one ship and the rest of the city workers and employees lived on the other ship. I was on the same cruise ship with my brother Emanuel. He worked for the city's Sewage and Water Board. Emanuel and his wife, Melva had a larger cabin on the outside of the ship. I had an inside cabin and couldn't use my cell phone because I couldn't get signals.

Living on the cruise ship was like going on a cruise. It was the same thing every day -- they provided all the food that you normally get on a cruise ship. Well it wasn't the lobster, but the rest of the food was the same: the steaks, the gumbo, all the salad and everything. The gumbo on the cruise ship had muscles and Dungeness crab in it; it was different from New Orleans' gumbo. At 3:00 to 4:00 in the morning, you could go get pizza, sandwiches, breakfasts, omelets, and all the salad you could eat.

The only good thing was that I was in a room by myself. Another person was supposed to be in my room, but they never showed up. It could have been three or four people to a room; even two people would have been uncomfortable. I was by myself and it still was uncomfortable; I was sleeping on a bunk.

The TV only got about three channels and not any local channels. Sometimes the Saints would play a game but I couldn't get it on my TV, instead they would show the Giants or some team from another part of the country. If you wanted to go watch the Saints, you had to go find another TV somewhere. They didn't have the entertainment like on a cruise either.

I really didn't sleep there too much because I was on shift at the fire station and then went to see my family in Houston on days off. February 24, 2006 was my last day on the ship. They put us out of the ship and the cruise company took the 300 million dollars and split. They haven't been back to New Orleans since.

## FEMA Trailer

After the cruise ship, I was lucky to get a FEMA trailer thanks to the Fire Department. FEMA said I had multiple claim numbers so that would cancel me out and I couldn't get nothin'. Then FEMA would give me another claim number and it would show up as multiple numbers again. It was a crazy cycle.

So finally the Fire Department got me a trailer in Harahan and I stayed there for about eighteen months while I worked on repairing our house in the East. I would come from Harahan, by Huey P. Long bridge out in Jefferson Parish (west of New Orleans), to work on the house by myself and that was like a 40-minute trip each way.

The FEMA trailer was comfortable - it was built for four people. It would not have been comfortable for four people though, mostly I was by myself. That trailer was identical to the one my daddy had.

The water was the worst thing, I only had four gallons of hot water in the trailer. During the first month, my head was spinning and it smelled like glue. But no one knew it was formaldehyde. All of a sudden though, the smell dried up and went away.

To keep the trailer, it seemed like every week you had to write letters about what your plans were for rebuilding ... what you were working on in your house, stuff like that. It was a lot of pressure. It looked like some people were stealing trailers and still getting rent vouchers. But FEMA was putting pressure on me.

I got my house fixed, it took 790 days. I counted the days before I slept again in my own home. I moved in that FEMA trailer on February 22, 2006 and stayed there for eighteen months; I moved out of the trailer on October 24, 2007 and back into my own home.

-Andrew (Daniel) Lain

**Emanuel Sr.**
(7th child of Odis & Irene)

My wife Melva and I stayed in our daughter Tanga's house for about two weeks. We had visits from some of my brothers and sisters. Tanga was one of the only relatives that had a house up and running.

After about two weeks, me and Melva were both able to get on the Carnival Cruise Ship. We stayed on that ship for about two months. The ship was docked here in New Orleans and it was for first responders, police and fire, and city workers.

The city had also set up tents as temporary facilities for people to stay in, but they didn't have any room in the tents for the families to stay. The city had temporary facilities for food and porta- potties also by the tents. There were cots to sleep on in these tents. Some families got separated but I wanted my wife to stay with me.

-Emanuel Lain Sr.

*The Times-Picayune, Sept. 15, 2009*
For the first time since Hurricane Katrina left tens of thousands of families living in FEMA trailers, a federal jury heard allegations Monday that the government-issued shelters exposed Gulf Coast storm victims to hazardous formaldehyde fumes.

# Chapter 12

## School Upheaval

**Sarah Elizabeth (Liz)**
(granddaughter of Odis and Irene; daughter of Sarah)

At the time of Katrina, I was like fourteen years old and was going to St. Mary's Academy in New Orleans. I was in cheerleading, dance, piano and gymnastics when Katrina hit on August 25, 2005.

People really didn't think the hurricane was going to hit New Orleans. At school, everybody was praying on it to hit because they didn't want to go to school for a few days. Then it finally hit and everybody was mad because they didn't want to leave the city.

I did learn that I was able to survive Katrina. I thought we were going to drown at first because we had to evacuate immediately. I went on the bus with Auntie Rose. It was one of my Uncle's busses from Loews Express. All the family got on the bus and we left. I was sad because I couldn't bring everything. I lost a lot of stuff. I had movies, CDs, clothes and a lot of stuff that I lost.

Katrina had strong Category 5 winds and the levees broke. The first time I saw my house was when I came back from Atlanta; it was a disaster. My dresser was knocked down, my bed was broken apart and stuff was just all over the floor. There were leaves all over the inside of our house. I thought it would never be able to get fixed again.

I went to three schools after Hurricane Katrina hit: Holy Names Catholic School in Oakland, California; Skyline High School in Oakland, California; and Peach County High School in Atlanta, Georgia. When I went to the new schools, I only was able to continue dance out of all my activities. Mostly, I didn't want to be in activities anymore. I did play the violin at Holy Names in California. It was hard to change schools and having to meet new people because you had to start all over again.

I get worried about other hurricanes coming, but really not worried enough. When Hurricane Gustav came last year, it just did wind damage. It was a Category 2 and it didn't really flood. But for the next time, I'm praying that they fixed the levees and made sure that floods don't happen again.

I do feel stronger because I went through Katrina. I learned that I could get through it even though I lost a lot. Actually, I'm glad that Katrina took some of my stuff because I did have a lot. Really, I had too much stuff; you could hardly walk through my room.

I'm praying another Hurricane like Katrina don't come because there is no place like home, like New Orleans. I'm very glad to be back in New Orleans. California wasn't doin' it. Atlanta didn't do it. Although I did have some fun when the hurricane hit because we were traveling all over the place, I'm glad to be back home in New Orleans now.

- Sarah Elizabeth (Liz) Lain

## Shannon
(granddaughter-in-law of Odis & Irene, wife of Shaun)

To survive through an experience like Katrina, I think the 'survival of the fittest' mentally and spiritually were important. At that point, age didn't really matter because the younger people had to keep the older people sane as it related to their mental state. Maturity played a big part, at that particular time, because throughout the course of the first couple of weeks after Katrina hit, everybody had their breakdowns at different times.

Then a lot of the emotional stress was basically going stir-crazy because we were in the hotel with all our family members. The kids were running out of things to do; we were brainstorming about what to do because we had never been in that type of situation before.

Then it really hit some of us when everybody started going their separate ways from the hotel. We did take into consideration that we were part of a large family, but at the end of the day, we had to think about our immediate family and what we were going to do. So, it was like we were together, but then we had to divide up.

At the time we were in the hotel, we had Liz with us, so Liz went with Rose. I think Rose and her husband and Grandpa Lain went by Calvin's house. Everybody decided that this was best and then the group got smaller. So the '3-day vacation,' that we always look forward to during hurricane season, changed into 'OK this is about to change my life.' Another fearful thing was that our money started to dwindle. There's only so long you can stay in a hotel; there's only so much you can eat out. It was funny, we started out in the vacation mind-set that we were eating out, then I think by day five, we were buying sandwich meat and bread because we realized we would have to hold on.

We learned some valuable lessons as it relates to something as simple as not having a local bank. We banked with Liberty Bank which is only in Louisiana. So we couldn't tap into our funds because there is no Liberty Banks anywhere else. I think I was at a credit union and after awhile, we had to plan on how we were going to survive. Of course it didn't matter to the hotel that we didn't have any more money. We moved from being able to get in to our checking account, then we started using credit cards until they were maxed out, and so that was scary.

We frequented Walmart a lot. Walmart really benefited from the storm. That was the only place to go. Sometimes it was a get-away -- "Lets go take a stroll in Walmart."

One of my mother-in-law's church members offered a house for all of us to stay in (22 in the bus). I think I was at a realistic point at that time because I prayed, "God, I know we don't have any place to stay, but I know all these people are not going to be able to function peacefully in one house." All of these different families together in one house, so I just prayed and asked Him to make a way for us.

My husband Shaun actually had a 4-fold plan and one of the things was to get our kids in school to take their minds off the situation. We didn't want the kids to see mom and dad break down. So it was almost like I had to go hide in a restroom when I needed to cry because I wanted them to feel a sense of security. That was our responsibility; that is what we are here to do -- make sure the kids are comfortable.

Katrina happened over four years ago, so our daughter Bria is 16 now, so she was actually 12 at the time. Our sons, Khari is 13, so at the time he was 9; Kobie is 12 now, so he was 8. They were young at the time, oh my goodness. But they still had in their mind that it was fun because they were with their cousins every day. They weren't worried. But if we had not handled our emotions, if we had acted like "oh my gosh what are we going to do," the older ones would have been a little more concerned.

We were in the process of looking for schools for the kids. In New Orleans, Bria had been attending Metairie Park Country Day School and the boys were at a private school. Bria's sister-school per se was Westminster School in the Atlanta area. So Shaun went there first. That started the beginning of our blessings because the Admissions Director 'took us in.'

When I look at it now, nobody but God provided like that because we went there for one thing to get my daughter in school. Keep in mind, this is the beginning of the school year, so we had just paid tuition. We can laugh about this now, but I said to Shaun, "Make sure they don't want any money, because we don't have any." But they didn't. They got all the kids in school.

But then, the Admissions Director mentioned that there were a whole bunch of families calling in and they were looking to "adopt" and bring in a family to stay with them. She asked us, "Would you be interested?" Well we were in no position to say no.

I was blessed enough to get online to apply for a job and I started teaching in Cobb County. That is one thing about the education field that is a blessing. The lady we were living with, who had "adopted us," was a stay-at-home mom. When I started working, she was like, "Shaun is not going to go get a job?" I told her, "Right now, it does not matter, as long as one of us is working."

But you know, it depends on your culture and how you are raised. It was a concern for her that it should be Shaun going to work and me being at home and raising the kids. At first I didn't understand her concern, you know I was just so focused, "Yes. I got a job, we can get benefits!" My son Kobie is asthmatic and that was the first thing I was thinking about – a job with benefits. And I had some hypertensive medication that I needed and I was like, "I don't have any medicine." So I was very happy to get that job.

That job was something out of my element because I was teaching the second grade. I've never taught second grade ever; I've never taught anything lower than fifth grade but anyway it was a job. One of the friends of the people we were staying with had an extra car – they even provided us with transportation. I was able to go back and forth to work. So, in hind sight, you look at it and you are like, "WOW, it is amazing how it worked out."

Looking back at that year, it is so funny because that entire year I was teaching second grade with little kids that are so needy. I didn't think I would be able to give them what they needed, because I was so needy at that time. But believe it or not, we complemented each other because all they want to do is hug all day. They gave me hugs and they didn't realize that I needed them too at that time. It sustained me that entire year.

I remember when school let out in May and I was home that summer, I finally lost it. Oh my gosh, I broke down and I was thinking, where is this coming from? I finally cried; the sadness was always there but it held up long enough for me to work. But I've always heard, and it is true, that as soon as you slow down and you are able to think about everything, the emotion just comes.

All the stories are different -- how one family can go through so many different things. Even the kids went through a lot changing schools. I heard a lot of stories of students staying in the trailers, and their parents were gone, because they wanted to finish their senior year of high school in New Orleans. That was not safe. Many schools act as safe havens for kids; they go home to sleep but they are right back to school the next morning and get support.

-Shannon Lain

**Meryl**
(great-granddaughter of Odis & Irene, granddaughter of Otis, daughter of Wellington)

When Katrina hit, it was my junior year at Louisiana State University. I didn't have homesickness before Katrina because New Orleans was only an hour away from Baton Rouge. Just about every weekend, I would drive down home; it was no biggie to go home. My grandfather used to tell me, "You keep comin' down here, it's not like you ever left." I would say back to him, "Papa, you're sayin' that, but you're gonna' miss me one day -- watch."

Then after Katrina, I started getting homesick. My mom was in Oklahoma then, my dad and step-mom were in Georgia, and now me and my sister Whitney were in Louisiana. We were trying to figure out how were we going to see family, and how were we going to divide our time up between our mom and dad. As an R.A., you don't get every holiday off, only a few.

That was really rough on me and my sister especially because my parents couldn't quite afford to say, "I'll fly you out to visit." As college students, we had to scrape up what little we had and we really wanted to see them, especially that first year after Katrina.

So Katrina really changed a lot for me. I never thought I would get homesick, but it happened. I reminded my Papa of my words to him that he was going to miss me. Whitney and I always laugh because we said we always wanted to go out of state to college. Now it felt like we really were out of state without even moving.

Watching TV During Hurricane Katrina

It bothered me to watch people on TV that were suffering (right after Katrina hit). I wound up talking on the phone to my ex-boyfriend who was stuck up on a roof at his mother's house in New Orleans East. He cut his foot and he was stuck out there. I found out through his mom that he sat up there for about three days on top that roof and then he was finally rescued. For a long time, nobody was able to get in touch with him.

Watching from a distance, I started thinking about people I wouldn't ordinarily think about. All of a sudden I was thinking, "This person is down there, and that person is down there." It was unreal seeing all this on TV.

It was kind of like, "Is this America? Is this really America? Nah, it can't be." I always feel like as Americans, we are so arrogant. Then I looked at what happened, and I said, "Are you kidding me?" It made me so upset that they were waiting so long to go in to save people. And then being at LSU, I was hearing all kinds of racial stuff and comments like, "That is what they get." I was like, "What? Are you kidding me?" It was just surreal.

I know that if we really wanted to, as Americans, we could have reacted a lot better. Just in our natural sense, not necessarily like, "Oh we have to have a plan, and take a moment." In this case, we didn't have a moment to wait -- just common sense should have made people realize that we needed to get people water and food. I don't just blame Bush, like it was all his fault. Everybody had their responsibility and they failed. To me, it was a pecking order -- you had the city of New Orleans and they should have had their plan together. But the responsibility goes up, up, and up. Still nothing was happening.

We got to the top of the top and they were still like, "What is going on?" The U.S. goes into other countries and can do so much for people and I'm not against that at all, but right here in our own country, we couldn't do anything? Four days.... come on. I think there were a lot of things beings covered up. New Orleans is always known for being all about politics and not about the people.

Katrina happened right before Labor Day and most college students, including myself, go home to New Orleans on Labor Day weekend to get the rest of our stuff from home. So a lot of my stuff was still at home.

I had just moved out of an apartment that was in uptown New Orleans and had moved a lot of my major things, like high school yearbooks, photos, and clothing to my Grandmother Estella's house in New Orleans East. But those things that you hold onto – like your memories – I had just moved into her garage. I did go back to New Orleans soon after the hurricane and I couldn't believe it. It was horrific; it didn't look nothing like where I grew up.

-Meryl Lain

**Raymond**
(9th child of Odis & Irene)

I think a lot of affected people are dying post-Katrina and I don't think anyone is keeping track of that. Someone counts the murder rate, but they don't count the people just dropping dead. It might be from stress, it might be what was in the water, I don't know. The media doesn't publicizze death numbers with natural causes. I think there are a lot more people dying post-Katrina in New Orleans than pre-Katrina. Katrina evacuees don't even have to be here, they might be in another state and drop dead. Someone should be looking at the long term effects of Katrina.

## The Children and Families of New Orleans

I'm a teacher and I think it really, really affected the children. The children are going to be alright, but they just don't act like things are normal. Now they're just not normal, happy-go-lucky kids. I think they have seen a lot of devastation.

Some kids now might not even have a place a stay, bathe or wash their clothes. You don't know what is going on in some of these families. The kids show it; they act out and show it in their behavior. I teach in high school; some of them just act crazy, that's all. I taught before Katrina, and I taught after Katrina and to me, the kids are acting out a lot more now; it's a lot more behaviorial problems. It's just not what it used to be.

In general, I think people want to get out more and do things -- party more, celebrate more. I guess it is to get their minds off the devastation. Even the Saints (football team), before Katrina never had a 'sell out,' let alone a season ticket sell out. Now you can't get the tickets. Now the Hornets (basketball team) are trying to sell out too. Before Katrina, we wouldn't even support a basketball team, but after

Katrina, a lot of people are going to see the Hornets play. Things may not be all that great at home, so you just want to have something to do. Some people go to the Casino to get away. It is just 'escapism' -- like going on vacation for a short time, if only for a few moments or hours to get out and about.

-Raymond Lain

**Alex Nicole**
(grand-daughter of Odis and Irene; daughter of Calvin)

I think people from New Orleans are really strong. To go through all of Katrina and come back to absolutely nothing, you have to be really strong. People from New Orleans are really creative also, opening new stores and businesses. The culture of New Orleans and the togetherness of the people, make New Orleans special. I'm even attending Loyola University here in New Orleans.

New Orleans is a great city to live in because of the spirit here, the food, the beignets, Café du Monde, being able to celebrate Jazz Fest, Mardi Gras, holidays in New Orleans that aren't celebrated anywhere else in the country... Things like that make New Orleans special.

When we found out that Katrina was coming, we were just all at home watching the news. I was only thirteen at the time. My cousins called and they said the hurricane was coming straight towards us and we better leave. So we packed and got in the car and went to Dallas. We have relatives in Houston and some in Dallas, so I think that's why we picked those places to go to. We left on the 27th (Saturday), there was a lot of traffic but it wasn't like traffic on that Sunday.

About two days later, we were watching the news in the hotel and we saw the devastation from Katrina. We were crying. After that it was kind of funny because we went to Walmart and got me a new swimming suit so we could go swimming. We were still very upset though. It didn't really hit me as bad until I had to go to a new school and make new friends. It was hard and I didn't want to go to a new school at all.

The first school I went to was in Houston after we left Dallas. I went to Nimitz High School for 9th grade. I'm kind of shy so it was hard. I wasn't really scared, but I didn't want to be there. The people were really friendly though. They were like, "Oh, you are from New Orleans?" They wanted me to talk and say everything. Like they said, "Can you say baabee?" They were really nice. I was kind of scared just to start a new school.

I was sad during this time because I lost thirteen years of dancing school trophies and all my clothes that I had just bought for the beginning of the school year. But, then I was excited that I got to get all new clothes again. All of our family history and pictures were gone and we couldn't get that back and that was really sad.

My dance teacher ended up about an hour away from where we were at in Houston, so all of us who evacuated to Texas ended up going to her house once a week to practice dance. And we ended up even getting to do a competition during those months in Texas.

We moved back to New Orleans for the first time at the very end of December, for Christmas break. Then I started another new school in January. We had someone go to our house before we did and they actually threw everything out in the trash, so no, we didn't get to save anything. In January, I attended Edna Karr High School in New Orleans on the West Bank. I didn't really like it there. I went to Edna Karr from January to May.

Edna Karr was not hard, but it was on the West Bank of New Orleans, and I'm from the East. We had to live on the West Bank for a while before we could get back in our house. So we didn't really know the people over there. Everyone who went to Edna Karr had gone there before Katrina, so they had already made friends. It was hard to break into their groups of friends.

Then I switched to Xavier Prep High School for my sophomore year. The good thing that came out of Katrina was that I started a really good track career. I had never run a day of track in my life before Katrina. When I went to Xavier Prep, my history teacher was the track coach. He kind of recruited me to come out for track and then I got stuck with it. I run track even now at Loyola University.

Our dance teacher came back to New Orleans about the same time we came back, so I got to keep doing my dance. Before Katrina, I was on the dance team at school, but after the hurricane, I was only involved in private dance lessons.

It was sad coming back to New Orleans at first and living here right after Katrina. Seeing all the buildings that weren't open; it was kind of devastating. There wasn't anywhere to go for food, no Walmart. It was like an hour and a half to get to something that was actually open. Also, trying to buy stuff that we really needed was aggravating. After everything started opening back up and people started moving back in, then it started getting better.

The most difficult part of going through the Katrina experience was watching it on TV-- seeing all the water so high and people on their roofs. I really learned that life is more important than possessions. I was really sad that I lost all my stuff, but then I was just really happy that I wasn't one of those people stranded on a roof. I learned that life is just really the most important thing.

-Alex Nicole Lain

# Chapter 13

## Trying to Make It Elsewhere

**Shaun**
(grandson of Odis & Irene, son of Otis Jr.)

<u>Glued to the TV</u>

My dad was missing. When we were in the hotel room (near Atlanta), we thought he was dead. My mama was crying and we didn't know what to expect because there was a report that 10,000 people were dead and bodies were floating everywhere. My phone went dead that morning at 7:46 when the phone towers went down. Finally, three days later someone called and said they had just seen a CNN report with a guy that said, "I just want to thank Otis Lain for saving my life."

There were so many things reported on the TV; you had politicians making speeches, people crying saying, "This is unreal, this is America" and the news media were calling people 'refugees.' At first we thought that was funny, but when we thought about it, 'refugee' is a person without a country. What is the subliminal thought in that? Are we Americans?

There were so many dynamics going on watching the TV, it was like rapid fire. Seeing houses under water, people on the news, people wading in the water, looting being reported. We knew it was a mis-caricature of New Orleans when we heard that the Coast Guard was trying to rescue people but yet they reported that the people were shooting at them. Now my logic told me, people trying to get rescued ain't shooting at the rescuers. What they most likely did was, 1) they shot holes in the attic to get out, and 2) the National Guard was passing over a lot of people and getting certain people, so the remaining people were like, 'Look I'm here, come get me.'

Because of the systematic, negative mantra of the news media, it creates a certain mindset and people can't even think logically. So during this time period, we were glued to the TV. My wife, Shannon, was numb. I said, "I got to get these kids straight." So my mother started making calls and our old church member said, "We have a house for sale, but if you all would like to stay there, you can. We will take it off the market for now." It was in Fairburn, Georgia, probably about an hour from where we were staying in the hotel.

## Bank Accounts

We couldn't access our bank accounts. We didn't have an ATM. I used Liberty Bank, a local New Orleans bank, one of the oldest black-owned banks in Louisiana. Their back-up system was located in New Orleans. It was flooded and destroyed. Reporters on CNN said the bank had lost all its records. I immediately jumped on the road and went to Baton Rouge, which was the branch that was open to get something out. They would only give me $1000. I said, "We got a lot more than this in the account. What is goin' on?" Bank officials said that is all they could give out because they couldn't verify everybody's accounts.

## Divvying the Group Up

So we started divvying up the group. My Aunt Rose and Uncle Henry was with us; they decided to go up to Maryland and eventually over to West Virginia where he is from. Liz and my grandfather, Odis, were scheduled to fly to North Louisiana where he is originally from. My cousin Tonjolique came and got my Aunt Elynda and Uncle Ed and brought them back to Nashville where they ended up living. So now we had diaspora going on – 'family diaspora'... the disbursement of people all over America.

Because there was a kind of psychological and spiritual warfare going on, I needed people around me who had a solid foundation, especially spiritually speaking. I had to make the break from those who could not maintain civility or their composure. I didn't want to give up on them but I wanted them to go where they could be comfortable. So we started making arrangements for everyone. "You are going here, you are going there."

Some people recognized strength in leadership. They said, "I know Shaun is going to be alright. Let's just stick close to Shaun, no matter what." When the church member came through with the house, that was great. My wife said, "We're not moving in there with the rest. That is a lot of women in that house." It was my mama, my aunts, my sister-in-law, and my grandmother. Shannon said, "That is not going to work." So Shannon had contacted her cousin Iris, who is a record producer for Sony in New York. Iris said, "Shannon what can we do?" She called the famous singer, Montel Jordan who lived in Atlanta. He told Iris, "I'm going to help them out."

Montel came over and gave us money for an apartment. He gave us the deposit money, the first and second months' rent, and the last month rent. He gave us one big check. But the most important thing he gave us was not what he gave us financially. His house had just burned, he lost everything. So his heart was so tender to help other people, "He said the most important thing is for you and Shannon to be close brother, during this devastation." He gave us the Word, I mean, he just preached to us. It was on-time, in-season, everything was right on keel.

Shannon had family, Sissy and Vert, that was in Fayetteville, Georgia. They came and checked in on us and when Montel came, they listened to Montel also. In the natural, people say, "Look, I'm tremendously blessed." I know that the seeds we have deposited over the years, have been manifested back to us now. So we were straight as far as that.

In New Orleans, my boys went to Arden Cahill, a private Christian school. My daughter went to Country Day, a private school. Both of those schools were very expensive. I remembered my mentor from college in Atlanta, Delinda Brown. She told me her son went to Westminster, which was equivalent to Country Day. I explained to the school about our situation and that we were in a hotel room. I left a message that we just needed to get our kids in school and get them settled. Marjorie Mitchell, Director of Admissions for the school, called me back and said, "Listen, we are going to send a car to the hotel. Where are you?" She sent one of the parents over to the hotel to pick us up and brought the kids clothing. Marjorie said, "Shaun, everything is going to be alright. You are going to be alright."

Immediately we got our daughter into school. The school tuition cost $17,000 a year. They said, "Don't worry about the tuition." They didn't have room for the boys but the school down the street, Trinity, that feeds into Westminister, did. Trinity costs $11,500 a year and they waived the tuition for both of the boys. They bought the boys' uniforms. So my children were at exclusive schools right away.

The next thing was a home. Marjorie sent an email out. We're an African American family but forty white families responded to the email to take us in. Of course we didn't know these people. Marjorie picked us up on the eighth day after Katrina and took us to the first house to 'visit' to see if it was a good match, and if we wanted to do it.

We pulled up to this multi-million dollar mansion and the family started taking all our belongings out of the car immediately. They put us in their two-bedroom, one-bath pool house. They had it set up already. They had made arrangements with all their friends to bring us food every night.

We stayed with that family for six weeks, from September 6th until October 18th. Every night we were fed by the finest restaurants in Buckhead. They put an "all-call bulletin" out and their friends were sending us checks, just money. "Hey we are sorry about this but hopefully this will help." We were getting $500, $300, $3000, $5000, $1500. They were just sending us money. We said, "Wow."

This had a double edge. We were in this upper-class household. The wife was a socialite, a housewife. The husband was a very respected lawyer who worked for the largest law firm in Atlanta. He had offices in London, New York and Houston that he was responsible for. We were just talking and he said his property tax for that year alone was $23,000 for his house. I said, "I can't even relate to it man."

So the first night, they cooked dinner for us and said they didn't want us to worry about anything. So I asked him, "Look, we have a lot on the plate. How long do we have to stay here?" He said, "Look, we have talked about it. We're going to give you five years to get yourself together." Shannon and I looked at each other and just laughed.

A friend of theirs just gave us a Ford Explorer, a good car. You have to remember, we evacuated on the bus and we left the Mercedes and the Land Cruiser parked at the Loews Express Building. So we didn't have a car. When they gave us that car, it was beautiful.

Then Trinity, the school where the boys were, gave us a Volvo that we still have to this day. It was titled in our names, so we had two good cars. I have that car and use it all the time; that's my memorial for Katrina.

God is great because I had all these fraternity brothers in Atlanta from Morehouse College. God had already directed it, everything was in order. But at the same token, all these friends gave us checks. Dave Mitchell, my line brother, said, "Here is $1000 man, just call me with whatever else you need." That was it, that was the love that was pouring out. Another line brother, who I hadn't heard from in years said, "What are your kids' sizes?" He is a dentist in Florida. He sent them Nike clothes and all brand new clothes.

All of this benevolence was factoring in. One thing I had to deal with was my pride. I didn't know how to receive. So I had to learn how. I also learned something that was real important - we had people that was close to us that didn't even think about helping, and we had strangers that didn't even know us that were helping. So one thing I realized was, that 'everyone of your color is not of your kind; and everyone of your kind is not of your color.'

We were rapidly going through lessons of life. Just all kinds of things were happening - the dynamics of wealth, the dynamics of middle class, and poverty. I thought I was on one socio-economic level, but now I was in poverty. We had to go stand in line to get a $1600 check from Red Cross. We had to stand in line to get food stamps. I had a master's degree, a physics degree, and now I'm in the food stamp line. I learned that you can't look down on no situation, unless you are going to help.

'There for the Grace of God goes me.' We learned what it was like to go to the clothes bank and the furniture bank. A group from the Universal Church gave us all new furniture. At that time, America was embarrassed in front of the world. They were ashamed because we preach to the world about human rights and yet, America was seeing poverty unveiled by Katrina and it was in everyone's face on the TV. There were people waving t-shirts talking about 'save us' and 'come get us.' It was the 5th day and people were still stuck there in the Convention Center and the Superdome.

Some people talked about what Ray Nagin (Mayor) should have done, or what Kathleen Blanco (Governor) should have done before the storm. No city in the history of the United States had ever been devastated like this. In two hours after the tsunami, we had the Marines in Indonesia – two hours. For Katrina, they waited five days!

People say tragedy brings out who you really are. There was a white Louisiana legislator who said, "There is a God, because reconstruction is over with." He felt that way because the lack of response was purging New Orleans of the poverty blacks and thus, some of the officials would not be able to get elected again. This way the Louisiana legislature could reclaim for whites the true gateway to the South -- New Orleans. A lot of things came out – it brings out who you are, you can't hide behind it.

I implore a lot of people to google things because a lot of things came out that are being shoved under the rug and people don't talk about anymore. If you go to Democracy Now, MSNBC, PBS, and those places, they recount what was done and piece it together. You can get a whole different understanding than how people are trying to recreate history now.

We had the kids in school, so at this point Shannon said, "Look, I'm going to go get a job." We opened up a bank account at Bank of America. The bank manager called her mother who is a 'big-wig' in Cobb County. As result, Shannon got an interview for a teaching job within a week.

We could tell that people were saying that Shannon was working, but what about him (meaning me)? Is he going to go get a job? McDonald's is hiring....

A lot of people don't understand, no matter what their background, that I had been the controller for the Loews Express business and I was responsible for 75 employees. Those employees were trying to get in touch with me because they needed their last check to survive. So I had these dynamics going on; my whole thing was recovery mode and how to get money in for Loews so we could all get paid. We had contracts out and people didn't know how to send us money, so we had to figure out how to get that going. But the idea that you had some housewives, who didn't work, to figure out what we should be doing is funny.

The federal government did supply vouchers for us to get an apartment. My wife and I wanted our own. So in October, I started looking. People can be benevolent for just so long.

Marjorie Mitchell, who just be-friended us so much, not only wanted to help us get stabilized, but she wanted to help my business. Most people can't fathom that. Marjorie made calls to get my business going again. She made calls in Atlanta and she never looked for anything in return. She is just a good-hearted person.

I remember my father used to watch John Cherry on From The Heart (religious TV program). I liked John Cherry and he talked about a lot of current issues and related that to the Bible. So we looked up "From the Heart" and they had a church in Atlanta. I visited a couple times by myself and then brought my family. On Christmas Day 2005, we joined that church. It just happened that the pastor, Charles Jackson, was one of my classmates at Morehouse College. He was a year younger than me but we were students at the same time.

So now, we had a church, we had our apartment, we had Shannon working, and me working on the recovery of the business, and we had schools for the children. We still wanted to get a house. My brother's passion is looking at houses on the market . He was down here in the Fairburn, Georgia area and he started looking in Fayetteville (suburbs of Atlanta). I wanted Fayetteville because I knew that in the following school year, we could not pay for the private schools and we couldn't ask them to let our children go for free another year. So I knew we needed to get them in a solid school system and at that time, Fayette County was the number one public school system in the State of Georgia.

So my brother actually found a house and he told me, "Hey man, come check this house out." We looked at that house, which my parents bought. We looked at another house across the street and my family fell in love with it because it was gigantic. I mean it was six bedrooms, four and a half baths on six acres with a pool. It had a theater in the finished basement and a weight room. So we said, "Look, this is it." Across the street they were asking $420,000 and they were asking $405,000 for this (current home). We offered $380,000, they mulled it over and accepted the offer and they paid closing costs.

We bought our house in New Orleans in 1997 for $85,000. But here's the blessing, we paid for it, we did the renovations on it so the value had increased on it to $200,000. So we had a lot of equity in the house. We were blessed in New Orleans, insurance-wise, because we were one of the few people with flood insurance. Only 17% of the people in New Orleans had flood insurance. People don't realize we weren't required to have flood insurance because the zoning didn't require it, but fortunately we had it.

I reflect back before Katrina on my good friend Bill at the Franklin Avenue Baptist Church. It was like God was preparing us for something that was coming down the line. Bill had been saying, "Look man, you need to look at your insurance policies, and you need to restructure some things. You need to refinance and look at upping your insurance." That is what I learned about listening. The Holy Spirit was using him to speak to me. Had I listened to him, I would have easily collected well over $200,000 in flood insurance by adjusting that. But I didn't listen, I just said, "It will be alright."

-Shaun Lain

## Byron
(grandchild of Odis & Irene, son of Louis)

<u>Arkansas</u>

After getting out of New Orleans, they brought us to a church retrieval site, first in Arkansas where we got off a bus. That is when the workers were separating everybody. They had two sides – males on one side, females, on the other side. The workers fed us breakfast, lunch and dinner. Then they sent us to an Army base.

The base had Internet where we could get in contact with people. I was able to make phone calls. We were able to get some money from the Red Cross. They brought us to Walmart where we could buy clothes.

Maybe three days into it, my girlfriend's brother was saying to me, "We got to get out of here." He was like cracking up, so I told him I would call my girlfriend. Some church members had picked her up from Texas and brought her to Las Vegas. My girlfriend said she would see what she could do for us.

Maybe two to three days passed and that is when they flew us to Las Vegas. The church people brought us to the airport and I believe it was the church pastor who paid for our plane tickets. I was OK with staying in Arkansas, but my girlfriend's brother kept harassing me. All I kept thinking was, "We are safe here."

<u>Las Vegas</u>

So my girlfriend's brother and me went out to Las Vegas and we were fighting every day -- so she kicked us out. That is when he and I got an apartment together and we were still fighting. We were working off that Hurricane Katrina stress. We were like drinking a lot of alcohol – we had been through a lot. We fussed all the time, but we had to try to forget about it somehow. Me and my girlfriend's brother were taking it out on each other. We stayed together for about a month until he moved back to Texas.

I stayed in Las Vegas. I got a job at the airport for awhile until my father passed and I came back home to New Orleans for the funeral in March 2006. I didn't really tell the people in Las Vegas how long I would be gone for the funeral, so I lost the job at the airport. After that, I went back to Vegas and started to work for the apartment complex; the apartment people would pay me for doing work around the apartment complex.

The apartment people told me that they were hiring for a position but I waited too late to fill out the application. A week or two later, I talked to my girlfriend's brother who had moved to Baton Rouge. He bought a bus ticket to Baton Rouge for me just three hours before I left. I didn't give enough notice to the women I was working for and they were mad at me. I figured they would hate me for this so I went on to Baton Rouge. I stayed awhile in Baton Rouge and then eventually made it back to the city (New Orleans).

My girlfriend and her kids all came back to New Orleans because her mom was in Baton Rouge. She said that she missed home and left Las Vegas a couple of months before me. Still, I loved Las Vegas and I wouldn't mind going back there.

-Byron Lain

**Estella**
(daughter-in-law of Odis & Irene, wife of Otis Jr.)

Cobb County, Georgia

I think that it was Tuesday after Katrina and our group went out looking for the Red Cross. We were asking directions and people sent us somewhere in Cobb County, Georgia. We pulled up in the Loews Express bus. We saw police and a dog, and somebody came to the bus and said, "Wait, you all hold up, then we will let you all come in." So we got back on the bus and sat down. Finally someone came and said, "You all can come in."

When we walked in, everybody started clapping, "Yeah, our first refugees." We looked around and said, "Refugees? We are just looking for the Red Cross." The lady said, "Go ahead and look around in there."

They had all these cots laid out, they had food, and they wanted us to fill out some papers. She said, "Just pick out the area you want to sleep." I said, "Sleep? Miss, I can't even get down there on a cot, and if I ever did, I would not be able to get back up."

So we thought that was funny. We did go in and use the facilities and found out some information that we were in the wrong direction about the Red Cross. Then we left from there.

That was something. They were waiting on a bus, apparently a bus that was coming from the airport with people that had been moved from the Superdome and they had flown out to Atlanta. They just assumed we were a part of that group because we were in our Loews Express bus.

So on that first day we tried to get registered with the Red Cross, but the only people that got up there was my sister and my mother. In fact my sister, Elmyr, had to go to the hospital. Red Cross serviced my mother, but my sister took sick. The ambulance took her to the hospital up there in Sandy Springs. So we also had to deal with that.

It took me maybe two to three weeks to finish signing up for what the Red Cross was handing out. I think I may have been the last person in our group to finally give in. It was $300 per person Red Cross was giving out.

I had about a week & half before I knew if my husband Otis was living or dead. I heard from him through Meryl and Whitney (granddaughters) on LSU's campus. They made preparations for him. I heard his story how he barely escaped with his vehicle to get up there to Baton Rouge.

-Estella Lain

**Raymond**
(9th child of Odis & Irene)

Colorado Springs, Colorado

I stayed in Houston a few days. Then I went on to Dallas because Tiny (significant other) had relatives in Dallas. We stayed there for a few days. I left Tiny in Dallas with her people. Some Colorado people had come to Houston and they were sort of recruiting the evacuees to come to Colorado Springs. They promised us a car and stuff, so I decided to go to Colorado Springs.

They did have the Red Cross set up there in Colorado Springs and they did give me shelter. For a little while I stayed in a hotel and then Red Cross gave me an apartment. So I ended up going to Colorado for a car and an apartment -- got the apartment, but never did get the car.

It was the Red Cross who paid for the hotel bill, and then you could get FEMA housing through Red Cross. Within the Red Cross area, different little departments were helping people out: the VA (Veterans Administration) Center, the Health Care for Veterans, the Salvation Army, and a clinic. All of this was to help the evacuees.

So I ended up getting an apartment in Colorado Springs and I signed a six-month lease. I didn't work while I was in Colorado; they were willing to accept my teaching license from Louisiana, but the 'Catch 22' was I had to do long term subbing before I could become a regular teacher in Colorado. That didn't deter me so much, but the salary wasn't that much more than in Louisiana. In fact, I think it was a little bit under what Louisiana paid me. So I passed on that.

Colorado was pretty. I liked the snow. Colorado Springs is about sixty to seventy miles from Denver and there were lots of mountains. It was real beautiful. It even snowed in the summer time, but the snow melted -- it didn't stay on the ground that long. The sun came up and it didn't even look like it had snowed.

I came back to New Orleans maybe in December. I remember spending Thanksgiving in Colorado. I don't think I spent Christmas in Colorado. My school in New Orleans called me and said that I needed to come back to work, and so I came back. When I got back to New Orleans, then the school said I had to get rehired again. I ended up not getting that job. I could of ended up staying in Colorado after all.

After that, I started working with Bobby guttin' houses. I didn't get back to work at the school until that next August. I worked on guttin' houses and worked on my own house trying to get it straight. I was basically unemployed that whole year.

-Raymond Lain

**Sarah**
(4th child of Odis & Irene)

Oakland, California

My daughter Liz and I flew to Oakland and later on I had my car towed out to Oakland. Liz went to school there for a year. That was traumatic; California is not like New Orleans. In California, they are like a bunch of aliens from another planet. People from California think they are privileged. I tease everyone out there about their pedestrians and their right-of-ways. The way Californians do it, they would be drinking their lattes and reading their little books and magazines and a pedestrian would step out in the middle of a five-lane highway in the middle of a block. Traffic would screech to a halt so they could pass.

Now they say California has a population of 46 million, but I think it is probably twice that, like 92 million or something. I tell them to come to New Orleans for one day and tell them that they have the right of way and step out there. Shucks... we could fix that real quick. Squash.... People in California feel they are "entitled" that they should be getting this and that.

In New Orleans, we have black and white and now we have Latino also, but back before Katrina, we had only black and white. Shucks, there is racism all over the U.S. But in the northern states and in California, they are racist, but they grin and laugh and they pretend that they think you are equal. In subtle ways though, you know which way the 'weather is blowing.' But down South, everybody knows where everybody stands. I think blacks and whites have truer friendships down South.

In California, if you go to the Social Services office, they have things in twenty different languages. They have ethnic groups that I had never seen before. The thing that struck me was that if you went in a Walmart down there in

Oakland, you would see blacks shopping in the stores, but you would see only Asians and Latinos working at the cash register, not any black people. Then when you went to Target, Burger King, or a gas station, you would see black people that were panhandling. I didn't see any blacks employed, let alone in professional jobs. It didn't look like they gave blacks any jobs in California. That was kind of strange.

One time my sister, my daughter and I were driving up to Reno and we stopped in a supermarket. My daughter came and said, "Mom, look at all these white people." I mean the cashiers were white, the customers were white, there were no blacks, Asians, or Latinos. It was all white. It seemed like we happened to find a conclave of them.

I asked my brother-in-law Terrance, (who is Caucasian and used to live in that neighborhood), "Can I buy a house around here?" He said "No."

That is the thing I learned about California, they are a bunch of hypocrites. You hear about how liberal the West coast is, but given a choice between sincerity among people, I think I have to take New Orleans over California.

I guess that it wasn't life like I knew it. Then the people in California would say, "I can't believe you are going back there. [New Orleans] Those hurricanes ... you are going to drown. I would tell them, "I would rather live in a bowl than on a fault because you can run out of a bowl, but on a fault you just rock."

I bought a book for $2.50 in Atlanta when I came down to see my brother. It was a great book of maps and it had all the highways and states. I looked at it and decided that I could go anywhere in the world to live. I was looking at all these states seriously. But no matter where I looked every place had its drawbacks. I guess one day, as a creature of habit, I just said, "New Orleans is what I know and what I like and I want to go back there." I didn't want to go up North in the blizzard country.

Looking back on it now, what it costs to live in New Orleans after Katrina, I'm having some second thoughts. I'm not sure I can afford to stay in New Orleans at this rate; the insurance has gone up tremendously, we are about to have our houses reassessed to post-Katrina prices. Where I live in New Orleans East, they haven't rebuilt the shopping centers or anything, so we have to make a trek for any shopping. Before the storm, I had paid off my house in 1990 and so I was able to retire. Now, I have an SBA loan to pay back [used to fix the house].

Last summer when gas went up to $4 per gallon and you had to go to the next suburb to get items, that was kind of trying. New Orleans is still not settled yet. It seems like they have put a few band-aids on, but they haven't really fixed it yet. I think they kind of have the idea that New Orleans is sinking and it's not going to be with us for long, so why spend a lot of money on it. I wish they would just let me know, that's all.

-Sarah Lain

## Otis Jr. (June)
(1st child of Odis & Irene)

Not Going Back

Why didn't we go back to New Orleans from Atlanta? I didn't see New Orleans having a future. The utilities are high, gas lines have water and rust in it. The water system is antiquated -- it's not working right. Sewage is not ideal. The electricity costs you three times the money, insurance on the house costs you an unbelievable amount.

There is also a health factor; I still think there are pollutants in the air and in the soil and in the atmosphere. I think that, when it is all said and done, New Orleans is a good place to visit for family and friends.

For the most part, I just came to the conclusion that we ran from about four or five storms and spent a fortune to get on the highway. For those previous storms, we stopped in Dallas, North Louisiana, and we came up here to Atlanta two or three times. When you start running from Gustav, Ike, and Katrina, you finally say, "Man, this don't make no sense."

-Otis Lain Jr.

# Chapter 14

## Headaches and Tremendous Losses

Recent estimates indicate that New Orleans still has 66,000 unoccupied residential properties – about one-third of all addresses – and many of them are beyond repair.

9/13/09 *The Times Picayune*

## Shavon
(granddaughter of Odis & Irene, daughter of Louis)

I always felt like family was important. But Katrina messed up our bonding in a sense because prior to Katrina most of us was in New Orleans – at least the Lains, my siblings and cousins. Since everyone was in New Orleans you didn't have to worry about traveling that much. After Katrina, everybody disbursed. Now, it is like we have people everywhere. Prior to Katrina, during the family reunions, we said we would go travel around the country. But now, we literally have family that have to come from around the country to see each other.

It was already bad that in February before Katrina, we lost my mom's mom, and then two weeks later, we lost Grandma Irene. I moved to Atlanta in the beginning of June that year. Katrina hit in August and then my dad passed the next March.

I know it had to be hard on everybody. At my dad's funeral in March, was the first time that all the Lains got back together after Katrina. With all these losses happening, some of our worse moments became some of our happier moments because that was actually when we got together and got to see everybody. The city still didn't have anything to offer then because it wasn't that long after Katrina. There weren't hardly any hotels or restaurants in the city.

My dad was sick before Katrina, but he turned worse afterwards. I know a lot of people like that; I have a lot of friends that lost their dads and mothers since Katrina. Grandparents were just starting to die after Katrina. There was a lot of stress. It was more about trying to keep the families together – what are they going to do with the house, with their life? And people just couldn't handle that. The stress was just increasing the illnesses that they already had and were coping with. It was just pushing it to another level. Many people were going to funerals after that and it wasn't just directly related to Katrina.

A lot of people didn't understand why people from New Orleans were stressing, especially because they were getting their rent paid for and they were receiving these FEMA checks. They thought that New Orleans' people were getting all this stuff. They had some bad stories of people going to the mall and hanging out in the hoochy stores and spending their money. If that was how they lived prior to Katrina, then that was how they were living after Katrina.

People get jealous about the material stuff, that they didn't have to pay for rent, they got a new car because their car went down, they got some new clothes because their clothes were ruined. When I tell the story to people, they say, "Oh you are from New Orleans." They automatically think, "Oh you are a little Katrina victim, and you just got all this stuff handed to you." I say, "First of all, I didn't get all that money. I got one check and that was all." I did lose stuff in Katrina but it was material stuff and I wasn't worried about it. I was just thinking more about my family at that time, and that money could have been used for people who truly needed it. I had a place to stay, my clothes and stuff.

But people should understand that when you leave the house with your toothbrush and a few clothes, and think that you will get to go back for the more valuable things - you don't have anything left. You don't have a job because you left that in New Orleans, so now what? FEMA only paid so much and it is not continuous, so now what? Yeah, you were able to go shoppin' but you really don't have too much to do other than to fuss with FEMA on the phone and insurance companies and everybody else. And then, now what? You are in a city, or maybe even a town, or some country road, or you are in a house with twenty other people and it is only meant for five. You're depressed, stressed, and this is not where you want to be. You didn't choose this. This choice was made for you, but everybody else wants to act like you got all this money -- like you just became a millionaire.

- Shavon Lain

**Byron**
(grandson of Odis & Irene, daughter of Louis)

Final Impact & Loss

It still hurts to talk about it. Like if I see an episode on the History Channel, I have tears come to my eyes. I have to change the channel. It hurts to see about Katrina. It hurts to think about all the people that died and all those people that I could not save in the neighborhood and things of that nature. I tried to save people, but I couldn't save everybody.

Some people were not fortunate. There were disabled people -- how did they expect these people to get out? I ran across a lot of old folks. A woman in a nightgown, looked like she was cold standing on top of her roof. Her husband stuck in the ceiling. Oh man, how could they do it?

I think about my grandfather, Feado Estev (my mother's stepfather). His brother, Edward Estev, was sick and my grandfather was trying to stay behind to take care of his brother because he didn't want to leave him behind. The whole time I was in Las Vegas, I kept calling to see what the family had heard about my grandfather. They finally said that he and his brother had drowned. I would have tried my best to save my grandfather too.

And I think about my dad. They said he was supposed to have died from cancer before the storm, but he never did. My dad just kept going. But after Katrina, it was only six months and then he died. I think Hurricane Katrina contributed to his illness; stress can kill anybody. He lost a lot of things. He was always worrying anyway – extra weight on his shoulders.

My mom is still stressing, but she is just dealing with it. She has enough strength to maintain and hold her up for now. I would be in Las Vegas now if it wasn't for my mom being in New Orleans. I try to help her around the house. I do what I can for her.

I'm not really working right now. I could be getting back to work but I don't have any transportation. Right now, I just do odd jobs.

The greatest learning I've has is that if it ever happened again, I would stay and do it the same way. I don't think the city will do what they are supposed to do anyway. I know a lot of people would stay behind with me.

What I learned is that when they say evacuate, go ahead and evacuate. I would say to President Bush – get them out. That is what people elected him to do.

I'm thankful that my father taught me to swim. He always did tell me, "We're already below sea level, so you might as well learn how to swim." I always told everybody before the storm, "We are surrounded by all this water and you need to learn how to swim." I'm glad I was able to help others at that time. I feel like every good thing that I did during those days of Katrina, I will get blessed for it anyway. That is how I look at it. Everything I did to help save people, I got blessed for it. That was the irony of the thing – blessed to help people.

-Byron Lain

**Andrew (Daniel)**
(10th child of Odis & Irene )

The State brought a "shrink" in at work [the fire department]. That is what we call a psychologist or grief counselor. A lot of people that had been involved in the hurricane started committing suicide after three years. When the shrinks come, they bring up things that you have put in the back of your mind.  It is more painful when they come and I say  that's not helpful. I think you have to deal with things in your own kind of way.

I had a lot of headaches like when I had to spend $800 dealing with Allstate. Here I lost over $200,000 worth of stuff and they only gave me $900. Allstate made a profit off of Katrina.  They have shifted the costs off to the taxpayer, and then they get profits off of it. They get premiums for twenty years and then they blamed it on the flood and shifted it to the taxpayers. I was paying premiums for insurance every year with the mortgage and I didn't know that you had to raise the level every year.  So, I had the same amount of insurance when I bought the house back in 1988. I was underinsured.

Allstate was a headache.  Every time I would call, they would give me another claim number. But then the new claim number cancelled the other one out and then nothing would happen.  They were trying to stall. They tried to give me another claim number when Gustav came up and I said, "No way." Then all of a sudden they sent me $2000 for Gustav (from additional damage to the house).

The Road Home program did help out. They gave people money up to $150,000 for reimbursement of their bills.  That really helped.  Another thing I've learned is how to fix a house.  I might become an electrician out of this since I wired our whole house.

-Andrew (Daniel) Lain

## Rose
(6th child of Odis & Irene)

At the time, the mayor talked about commandeering busses to get people out, but basically they were saying up front, "You are on your own." They told us, "If you're not going to leave the city, fill your bathtub up because nobody will be here to help you." They weren't thinking about babies, single moms, elderly people, single people who couldn't fend for themselves. Jennie V.'s stepdad didn't get out of that house. He was in his own house flat on the ground. He couldn't climb up on the roof.

I remembered that during Betsy people got in their attics and survived. But Betsy water stayed a short time and we only had to stay away from the house two weeks before we could go in and clean up. Katrina water sat there. That meant nobody could get out and nobody could get in.

Some people died of heat; Miss Aryis was older and she didn't understand what was going on. She was fighting them when they were trying to bring her out of the attic to save her; she was fighting so bad that she fell in the water and drowned. That is the story I heard. That is how Miss Aryis' life ended. She would have been 90. She lived in the same block where our family grew up.

I think most of the people got out of it, but some didn't like Jennie V.'s dad and the people in the nursing homes. Liz and I had been visiting nursing homes right before the storm because she did her school service work at a nursing home. So we can still picture what it was like to have those people there. Even after the storm, we looked for independent living or an assisted living place for daddy, and they are not there now. They are all shut down and they don't exist anymore.

So a lot of people tried to go back because they love New Orleans, they love being home, this is the place we are familiar with.

-Rose Lain Watts

There were only small differences reported between Whites and Blacks in terms of shock and sadness by what happened in the areas affected by Hurricane Katrina..

People who felt Shocked (Gallup Poll)
80% - Blacks
77% - Whites

People who felt Saddened (Gallup Poll)
99% - Blacks
97% - Whites

Black Americans were much more likely than White Americans to report feeling angered and depressed by what happened in the areas affected by Hurricane Katrina.

People who felt Angered (Pew Poll)
71% - Blacks
46% - Whites

People who felt Depressed (Pew Poll)
74% - Blacks
56% - Whites
(White, 2007)

Terry & his two children, Justin & Kelsey

## Terry
(12th child of Odis and Irene)

I saw the images of Katrina on the TV when we lived in Arkansas. I've always thought that eventually I would end up back in New Orleans. After having lived in Nashville for nineteen years, and then Arkansas for four years, we came back. Just seeing the devastation was traumatic and very difficult because the places weren't foreign to me, they were places I knew.

After Katrina, they were saying that they needed psychiatrists to come back to help. A lot of the medical professionals had left the city and they were in desperate need of psychiatrists. The government gave grants out for psychiatrists to come back. It just seemed like doors were opening, and it seemed like the right time for our family to come back.

When I first came back, I was working in the St. Benard Parish, and it was a very devastated area. A lot of the people that I saw professionally had their Katrina stories. A lot of them were basically going through a lot of depression because they were trying to get their houses back up. They were dealing with things like Road Home, FEMA, and insurance companies. It was really a challenge for them. A lot of their neighbors and family members had moved away. It was like trying to start over.

The people would come into the Center to talk about it. They had a need to share their stories and we prescribed a lot of medication for depression and anxiety. Those services at the time were really needed.

Now I don't necessarily see a lot of the things I saw just a year and a half ago in terms of the symptoms that people were going through then. It seems like a lot of people are now coming back to the city with their children. The children had services before the storm or got services in the place where they have been while they were away from New Orleans. A lot of them are coming back and need to continue the services for their children.

The children are basically readjusting, a lot of the schools have changed. They have the recovery district charter schools and they are really trying to put in a lot of different changes in the school system to help the children. A lot of times the children are having adjustment issues just really dealing with the different changes.

Own Frustrations

It seems like the citizens that really want to come back and be a part of the recovery, have really stepped up for the most part. They are rebuilding their houses or maybe volunteering or doing their part. But it seems like the government, whether the city or state or federal, is still mired and not really progressing. You kind of scratch your head and wonder if it is intentional or what. I think the business community could step up too – like grocery stores or department stores. Those things haven't really come back. That is frustrating sometimes.

Overall I feel more positive. Of course there are days that you drive around and you kind of wonder if anything is happening at all. I believe out of the devastation of Katrina, there are some positive results and changes that have taken place. Those changes wouldn't have taken place otherwise. So I choose to look at it, even during that devastation, that this is an opportunity to change some things that needed to be changed. I don't regret moving back, it has been good.

-Terry Lain

**Tanga**
(granddaughter of Odis & Irene, daughter of Emanuel Sr.)

Emotional Toll

It is very emotional. I have a friend, her husband was one of those in the Superdome, and he still can't talk about it four years later. I want to say that he is just starting to get back to regular life --- it took a toll on him.

One of my girlfriends had two cars. When you evacuate, they tell you not to take two cars because they already have so many cars on the road. That was not her reason for not taking her second car; her neighbor had no transportation. So my girlfriend didn't have much money but she gave the neighbor the car and $50 to put in the gas tank. But the neighbor had nowhere to go. All she had was the $50 for gas; so she opted not to go anywhere and was stuck behind. It kind of upset my girlfriend because now her car was destroyed under water and she didn't have any insurance. But this neighbor was one of the ones that had to be bussed out; but she didn't have the funds. I know countless other stories that the people didn't have the money to get out.

I should say my husband was planning to stay in Atlanta where we evacuated. I wanted to come back home to New Orleans, and I still want to come back home. It is family. Family and people say, "How do you like it out there in Atlanta?" I say, "It is not home." I like it because of the schools, on paper it is very nice. My home there is larger than what I had here in New Orleans. My neighborhood is better there than what I had here; the schools are excellent in Atlanta and my children are in all types of programs; they are thriving. Everything is wonderful, it is like a storybook there. But, I would trade it all to come home to New Orleans.

Because my children's education is important to me, I stay in the Atlanta area. Everyone asks, when are you coming home? I used to say twelve years, now I say eleven because my son is in the first grade. They say, "That is a long time," but it will pass. I do come home to New Orleans every other weekend and I'm here for the whole summer.

## Kids Adjustment to Hurricane

My kids were OK after Katrina because they were young. At the time, I had an eight year old and a three year old. My husband is retired Navy, so my youngest, A.J., was born in Texas in 2002. We moved back to New Orleans in 2003. So really he doesn't know New Orleans; he knows my grandma and my mama. So that was no big deal for him. Devon, my oldest, adapted so well. That is why we stayed in Atlanta. Had he not adapted, we would have come home. He was eight at the time, in the third grade. Only one week of school, one football practice,.... I can't stop hearing about that .... "I went to football practice one time, then the storm."

My boys are now in music and started Ty Kwon Do. A.J. is gearing towards track, and Devon is gearing towards basketball. On the off-season, I'll stick them in any activities so they will keep active.

They didn't have all that in New Orleans after the storm. Kenworth Park, where my sister lives, is back. Now they have a little more activities for the kids in New Orleans. I would say last year, or the year before, they may not have had that. Our parks are coming back. NORD (New Orleans Recreation Department) are doing a great job. More things could be done, but for right now, they are doing what they can.

-Tanga Lain Hale

**Jennie V.**
(daughter-in-law of Odis & Irene, wife of Louis)

The whole thing was messed up. That contributed to all the loss that people experienced. You know, I lost my step-father and his brother. He was stubborn; he never wanted to leave. I figured that we would go out of town, come back, and he would be OK.

I was devastated that both he and his brother drowned. They were as stubborn as could be and they were found both in their houses. They were both in the Upper 9th Ward. They stayed on Pauline Street, not far from Mama Lain and Papa Lain's house, within walking distance.

The stress might have contributed to my husband Louis' death. He was only supposed to live eight to eighteen months when first diagnosed with cancer, but he lived almost three years. He kept pushing; he pushed to the end. After Katrina, the only thing he kept telling me, "We're going home, I want to go home. I got to start working on the house." I said, "Don't worry about the house." He was fighting hard I know. I know that he had to be hurting but he didn't complain. He hung in there to the end.

I found out that I can hang in better than I thought. I think I went into shock that I just couldn't get out of. We had to go places, to buy clothes, you know, things like that. You are not used to doing these things, like going to stand in line for food stamps and going to churches to get clothes, and going through the clothes.

Then you are not knowing where your money is at. At first you couldn't get to your bank account; everything just shut down in the city. You are like, "What are we supposed to do?"

It was me, Angela and her children who found out about the Red Cross and got some money from them in Atlanta. Everything we heard about, we would follow up on. We got plenty enough to last by being four people. The food in Atlanta was not as expensive as it was here. We ate well. The people there was very helpful.

Another thing that upset me was that Mississippi had problems too, but Mississippi was helped. And we couldn't get no help out of Louisiana. I said, "Now this is crazy." We went to Red Cross up by Calvin's (Northern Louisiana) and they said they had nothing to give. Then one lady told us we had to go to Natchez, Mississippi to get help. I said, "Now this is a shame. Mississippi is reaching out to help and our own state is not helping."

Then people treated us like we got all this money. They thought that FEMA and Road Home were showering us with money and that we "had it made." That was so far from the truth; people were still struggling. What little money we got from FEMA, we had to live on. The banks were not accessible and so we had to live on it. We got $2000, but how far can you go on $2000? You can maybe stretch it to two months. People that weren't involved didn't understand. I think we deserved the money we got to rebuild. It wasn't our fault.

It was a nightmare -- people were asking for stuff that went down with Katrina, that we did not have. I thought that was so crazy. We had our driver's license which proved where we were from in New Orleans, who we were and our address. They knew what area was under water. Instead they wanted proof of property. That was aggravating, I think your driver's license should be enough, because that is all we had.

I would say to the workers, "If you can find it in Katrina's damage, then I'll bring it." So when I called the hospital, they sent what they had backed up on the computer only a couple of pages. My chart was not there, it was gone. I couldn't understand people asking me for these things when they knew our houses were under water. I told them, "What I left with was a couple of shorts and a couple of shirts, expecting to go right back to my house. I brought my purse with my driver's license in it. I don't know what you want me to do, but that is all I can do. This is all the proof I have right here. If you go to MapQuest and punch in my address, you are going to find it under water." Things like that really got on my nerves. Sometimes you find you might snap at people that you don't mean to, but you think it is such a stupid question. They knew our situation and that was the only proof we had.

I didn't have a copy of my birth certificate, but I did get that later because I had to get my birth certificate and my marriage license after Louis died. I had to get his death certificate. I was able to get that, I don't know how they do that. Some of the city buildings got water in the basement. That was where my medical records were at and I lost them. But they had just started putting some records on the computer and those we were able to retrieve, but that was it. At first, the city was shut down, you couldn't get through on the phone. But a lot of people did carry their records with them; I didn't. I left my house thinking I was coming right back.

-Jennie V. Lain

## Bobby
(5th child of Odis & Irene)

### Rebuilding Difficulty

When I first looked at the house, I tried to evaluate it. New Orleans had been notorious for termites before the storm ever came. That is what the storm really exposed down in the lower 9th Ward. The termite damage was way more than the storm damage, you couldn't tell the difference. A lot of those buildings fell down because nothing was really holding them up except the termites.

That was the same case in our family house and in Sarah's house. I looked in Sarah's bathroom area and that was all it was, termite mounds holding it up. It was in dire straits and needed repairs.

It took me about three weeks to just pull all the mattresses out of the house. The mattresses themselves

Lain family home being rebuilt (March 2006)

were still saturated with a lot of water and they weighed a ton. I think it took me a whole day to try to drag a king size mattress out of the house by myself. I will never forget that mattress. Then we had a lot of hide-a-bed couches in the living room and those things were huge. I finally got them out to the curb. Once I got those things out, everything else was smooth sailing. The clothes and stuff were just thrown on the curb.

Then I finally got to the sheet rock that was left on the walls and ceiling. I could then see the shell of the house and could see all the woodwork that I needed to replace. But at the time, I saw the opportunity to see that I could redesign the thing. I could redo the kitchen or bathroom. The only thing I really messed with was the kitchen and the hallway. I decided to use more treated lumber for the termites and stuff.

It was nice because Lowe's had opened up. They were one of the first ones to open up and they aren't that far from the house. The lines were long; a lot of fighting was going on over there. A lot of people were stressed out, wild-wild west, long-long lines. Nobody wanted to stand in line; people would jump you and run over you. Everybody had a short fuse. Every time you walked in the store was an adventure. That in itself was a little scary.

The main thing was dealing with the MPs (military police). You would be guttin' the house and every time you went outside to throw something out, they would pull up and want to see your I.D. I think this was the National Guard; it was military. They had all these old jeeps with a blue light on it. It seemed like they were want-to-be police officers. They had assault riffles, side-arms; they were fully armed. It was like being in a war zone. The only thing they were lacking were grenades. Maybe they had those in the jeep or something.

One thing I liked was that they really couldn't do anything to you unless they called the police officer first.

Once the police officer came, he would be like, "Come on, just let him go."

One day I had my truck and I turned the corner and these military guys were two blocks away. They came speeding down the street and they said, "You turned that corner and did not put on your turn signal to make the turn." I said, "How did you see that from two blocks away?" I told them, "I live in this house and I turned the corner to come up here."

First there was one vehicle, then there was two. Next thing you know, I'm surrounded by a whole battalion; they kept telling me to get up against the car and everything. I said, "Get up against the car for what? I live here, this is my house. This is my neighborhood."

There was nobody in the neighborhood as far as you can see. You look down one street and there was no movement. There wasn't even any dogs and cats, no animals. It was during the day time and there wasn't anyone else in the neighborhood.

I told them, "All this devastation and you guys are coming around harassing me? What do you need, someone to harass?" They called in more people, and they ended up with about fifteen of them.

Sarah was back in town. I called Sarah on the cell phone and said, "Uh Sarah, I need some help." Eventually Sarah came and she was asking, "What is going on, that is my brother." The police officer finally came, and the officer told the military to leave me alone.

I told them that I owned a computer business and so they tried to ask me some questions about computers…. It was obvious they didn't know anything about computers. I wanted to laugh, like it was the biggest joke in the world. I think they asked, "What is a microprocessor, or a server?" Something like in computer 101. To me they were bored. One person would set off another person, like they might want to show the other person to be tough. It was a lot of young guys and they came with the mentality that a lot of people from New Orleans were big time criminals or thugs.

Rebuilding

They kept giving these little funds out at a time; originally they gave like $4000 and then it was $15,000, then they turned around and gave you SBA loans (Small Business Administration), and then they turned around and gave you Road Home funds. It was so unorganized and so chaotic with no vision. If they had a procedure in place that people could foresee, half this stuff could have been avoided, and a lot of funds wouldn't have been misappropriated. It could have gone to where the funds needed to go. I think some people got more than what they really needed and some people didn't get anything.

It was really crazy; you had to have a receipt for everything. Everywhere you stayed you had to have a receipt, your utilities, whatever. You were basically homeless and trying to put everything together. You couldn't get food stamps unless you got a utility bill, and it was kind of crazy. It seemed like in everything they did, they put up a lot of hurdles to jump through. Theoretically, they just made it easier for people who didn't need it; those with all the time on their hands could go through all the hoops.

But people who really needed it, they didn't have the resources. Like here I am down here with a trailer, but no electricity, no Internet. So I can't go online. But a person in Arkansas or somewhere, they can go online and fill out applications. They know what is going on, and the people stuck down here in the 9th Ward, we had to depend on word of mouth. By the time I got word of mouth, the event done come and gone. The people in the area fighting the fight were the last ones to get the information about something. Although I was a little fortunate to go out and buy a wireless network. When I got the wireless, I made sure that it was open to the whole neighborhood. I knew how to do that because of my computer background, I was way up on a lot of people.

My friend wound up losing his house; basically he lost it out of ignorance of not being aware of the process. I think other people lost their property simply because they weren't on top of things, they didn't know anything about getting on the Internet and accessing stuff. If it didn't come on TV, or you were not privy to the TV at the right time, you didn't hear about the deadlines. Next thing you know, you find yourself in a precarious situation.

Things would change and pop up all of a sudden. Like with the trailers, one minute they said that we could buy them for $600 and then, the next minute, they said that we got to get out of the trailer and give the trailer back. Now they are saying you can buy a trailer for $6! Most of it was that "NIMBY" thing, "Not in my back yard." The people want you out because they think it will lessen their property value. Just because they were fortunate enough and got theirs fixed first or didn't have as much damage as someone else, now they want to slam the door on everyone else.

People in Jefferson Parish were able to come back in first, so they got the majority of the Road Home money. The people with the most devastation was the last ones to get the Road Home money. I heard that a lot of people let their property go for as little as $5000 or $10,000 because they were so distraught. It was like they were emotionally distressed, and they didn't know which way to turn.

## Computer Business

As far as my computer business, I still service my old long term customers. But I haven't done anything to pursue new business. I just have been keeping the old stuff going. But in the mean time, I still do a lot of construction stuff. I'm doing a lot of home repair. There still are houses out there that haven't even been gutted yet – the same as if Katrina happened yesterday.

## Why come back to New Orleans

As human beings we might go someplace else, but you always have a tendency to want to come back home. You want to be at the place that you know best and feel comfortable. I always intended to come back to New Orleans. It is like a real democracy here. I stayed in California for years, and there were so many rules there. You don't talk to your neighbors. It is like a rat race, everyone is chasing a dollar all day long in California. You are constantly chasing money, it is like high stress. Every time you get more, it is not enough because I got a neighbor who had more than me.

Despite all the craziness in New Orleans, people really are friendlier. You can really sit on your front porch and talk to people that pass by. You can read in your paper about all the crime, but you can walk up and down the street and you really don't feel threatened. You feel safe.

## Collecting Stuff

Now, after Katrina, I don't want to collect stuff, don't even want to put pictures on the wall. Why put pictures on the wall if they are just going to disappear? A picture is just a memory anyway. I don't have the feeling of ownership anymore, like this is my stuff. Even if someone wants to give me something, I'm like hey, you can have it, what am I going to do with it? Maybe another Katrina is just going to come along and take it away. What the heck, why do you want to horde stuff? And I had a lot of stuff, between me and Bro; we had a lot of "stuff"!

I don't know how many computers I lost because I was in the computer repair business. I had just bought a shipment of computers at the time and had bought a lot of parts for repairs. I figure well over $10 – 15,000 in inventory and that is besides a lot of people's systems just sitting right there in the office. Now it is just like, "Ain't there anymore," all just destroyed. It does make life have a whole new perspective when it comes to owning things or just being responsible for things. You just want to have a detachment from things. When I think about traumatization; that is the biggest part of being traumatized because you don't want to own anything.

## Family Get-Togethers

This was the second year that the family has had a picnic on the lakefront. We did have a get-together for my dad's 90th birthday at my sister Elsie's house. Someone has to step up now. Everyone has been basically scattered -- some moved to the Atlanta area. Rose is gone to West Virginia and she has always played an integral part of bringing things together. Things are still a miss.

We used to get together a lot more before the storm. I can see that it is slowly getting back together. It might not be like it was before; the year of the storm, my mom had just passed and she was the one to get everyone together. She would get on the phone and call everyone and tell them this is where we are going to meet and this is what we are going to do.

## Block Rebuilt

Right now on our side of the block, there might be three families back; the rest of the houses are still vacant. On the opposite side of the block, you are looking at about four of the houses are filled and the rest are vacant. So we are looking at about 50% occupancy as far as the neighborhood. Before Katrina, we had 100% occupancy. We had a lot of run-down shacks, but people were living in them. The community was pretty vibrant, there was a lot of activity in the community, but now it is just starting to come back. It is not what it was, but you can see the potential. Slowly and surely it seems to be coming back.

It would have been better if they just allocated all the funds to everybody and just said this is what you get and go fix your property. It would have saved so much money. It was like they kept doing everything backwards. I have to remind myself, that it is not done for the benevolence or the benefit of the people; it is done for businesses to enrich themselves. It is all about keeping the wealth among the wealthy. I guess some people may get some of the crumbs that might fall off the table.

Losing City's Renters

Katrina really exposed how many renters they had in the neighborhood. They had very few homeowners but more people were renting property or squatting on property. Maybe the property was in their family but no one took the time to straighten the ownership out legally. Now in order to get it repaired, it took the cooperation of the whole family. And they don't have that cooperation, so the property is just sitting there abandoned.

On this block, there are several abandoned properties; at least 35% of the properties are in family disputes. Not one person wants to invest money into a property when they know someone else in the family might want to sell it. Before Katrina, they just squatted in the house and didn't do anything to it. One person might live in it and everyone else just accepted it. I think that is a dilemma across the whole city, trying to find out who is the rightful owner of the property; therefore they can go forth and repair the property.

Racial changes

When I grew up, the block we lived on, in the neighborhood, was all black. About a street over and towards the Mississippi River, that was all white. Then during Hurricane Betsy, the area flooded and overnight it became all black, from the River to the Lake (Ponchatrain), the entire 9th Ward. It was an unusual metamorphosis. But on our block, we never had whites living here during my lifetime. Now after Katrina, we have whites on our block, right across the street and around the corner. It is kind of weird -- like a slow invasion. They are coming in mostly in the Habitat for Humanity homes.

Musician Village is also a community not too far from this neighborhood. Most of the prize musicians in the community are now white, so that is a change. I thought New Orleans was known for a lot of black musicians, but apparently there must be a qualification process to live there and the black musicians can't get over the hurdle. That is why I think a lot of these Habitat for Humanity houses are going to whites, it is about 50/50 white and black. But when you consider the neighborhood was previously 100% minority, now it is 50/50%.

Louis passing

Bro (Louis) was shocked when we first came back into the city with Sarah's credentials, before they let others back in the city. He had a lot to lose -- a warehouse, all the stuff in his warehouse, a house and a pool. He just came from having brain surgery. He was a lot more overwhelmed than me. I just thought, "I have a lot of work to do. We have to start somewhere. Somebody has to clean up all this mess."

The water had receded and we just drove slowing through the remaining water and mostly it was just mud. You had to keep driving fast so you wouldn't get stuck in the mud. It came all the way up to the bottom of the car. There was so much mud and sludge on a lot of streets, we had to stop and go back around, working our way around areas.

Bro started to deteriorate after that. He was just trying to work. After he died, I found out that all his medicine was being shipped to the wrong address. I think they brought a whole bunch of it in at the same time. The mail was being held up probably.  But it was all stacked up there. I said, "I guess some things weren't meant to be."

Plus Bro's passing was a big factor when it came to organizing stuff for the family, setting up and doing all the cooking and things that he enjoyed. That is one of the biggest losses from the storm because I believe that he would still be here if he was taking his medication.  But due to the storm, the mail was all out of whack. Especially if you were receiving medication in the mail; then the treatment got interrupted.  You forget how important that stuff is, and next thing you know, he was deteriorating -- it didn't take long.

We've had so many people pass since the storm and most of these people are around fifty years old and younger. It seems like a pandemic. Someone should be studying whether all these deaths are related to the psychological or physical affects from Katrina.  It feels like it is accelerating.

Looking for Leadership

Some times I think the family is still looking for leadership.  My daddy is old, but he never did exercise that quality of cohesion that you need to pull everyone together to get some direction.

There were so many losses - the death of Madear, the death of Bro, Otis being sick, and the devastation from the hurricane. From a family aspect, it has been devastating. It has been four years and the family is still trying to patch things up. And, there is probably really a lot of depression still and no one is really dealing with it.

It has just been a lot of loss, with my sister's husband Arthur passing and stuff like that.  There has been material loss, physical loss, and mental loss. Then it has been a lot of work. Somebody has to rise to the occasion to get some of this work done

- Bobby Lain

## Calvin
(13th child of Odis & Irene)

<u>Daddy stayed</u>

My daddy stayed six months with us up in Northern Louisiana and everyday he wanted to get back to his house in New Orleans. Regardless of what your home looks like, you have a tendency to want to get back to it. I have come to understand that after my accident.

One thing that happened was my daddy contracted shingles. I had never heard of shingles before that. It was at a very advanced stage when he brought it to my attention. So he and I had to deal with that for weeks, changing a bandage on it at least twice a day. We had to put medicine on it to heal itself; that must have taken six weeks to two months to heal.

Shingles are highly likely caused by stress. This was at least the third time in his life of going through the loss of his home: he lost his home due to Hurricane Betsy, he lost his home due to a fire, and now, he lost his home in Katrina. His mindset was probably like he was tired of rebuilding. That was very stressful and probably precipitated him contracting shingles.

I learned that you only get shingles once, and if you have had chicken pox, then you probably won't get shingles. It doesn't cross the whole body, meaning if it starts on the left side of your body, it will just go across the center of the back to the center of the abdomen. His was on the right side of his body. With him having probably about a good 50-inch waist, imagine putting an ace bandage around that to secure the bandages. It had a lot of puss, some blood, scabs and skin peeling. It was just awful. But, he and I adjusted to it and we went through a lot of T-shirts with blood and puss on them. Daddy stayed about six months with us and that is when he ran away.

### Daddy Ran Away from Home

I work for myself and had stayed at home until about 9:30 on one Monday morning. Apparently, daddy left about 10:00 or 11:00 a.m. We had several cars and he took a Ford Taurus. He packed up all his clothes, cleaned out the closet, loaded up the car and headed to New Orleans.

Now, the problem was, I didn't get back home until about 8:00 that night and I was into watching the TV series, Twenty-Four. When I got home, I went straight to the TV and my wife was there. She said, "Where is your daddy?" I said, "Oh, he is probably in his room." Right after the story went off the TV, I went into his room and I noticed there was "nothing." The drawers were empty, the closet was cleared, his chair was gone and the room was vacant.

Keep in mind, at this particular time there was very little contact with anybody in New Orleans. This may have been about six months after Katrina, at Mardi Gras time, late February or early March. Once we realized that he was gone, my wife said, "Come on, we have to go find him." I said, "Josie, do you know how many ravines and canals and ditches between here and New Orleans, 210 miles." And it was dark, about 10:00 at night. We called whoever we could and I said we would wait until the morning.

Finally, I believe it was my brother Raymond found him at 9:00 that next morning. He was sitting in a car in front of our family house in New Orleans. He finally made it back to my house on Wednesday. He hadn't taken a bath that whole time. He thought that he could stay at the Casino, but they put him out about 3:00 a.m. Prior to Katrina, they would stay open all night. So when he came back on Wednesday, this was a pure situation where you have role reversal -- where the son became the parent and the parent became the child.

We were sitting at dinner on that Wednesday night and I'm semi-afraid to bring it up, but the opportunity presented itself and I said, "Daddy, why didn't you tell anybody that you were leavin'?" With his mouth half full of food he said, "I did tell you I was leaving." And then he turned to my wife and said, "Josie, didn't I tell you?"

I have to tell you that my wife was scared of elderly people. Knowing that he didn't tell her that, she still gave him an 'Amen' and backed him up. I just said, "Oh Lord" and left it at that. I had my daddy thinkin' that he told me, and my wife is giving him credibility, so I just left it alone. I think I put him on punishment then by telling him, "You can't use the car except to go to the grocery store." Here it was the child setting the curfew for the parent. It was kind of funny at the time, but everything worked out in the end. He made it back to his home in New Orleans eventually and it is just a story to tell for the ages: 'The Day My Daddy Ran Away.'

They may have had the FEMA trailers delivered on the New Orleans property but they were not hooked up at that time. There was no electricity, no sewer, no anything, I'm not even sure if they had the keys to the trailers. So there was literally no place at that time for anybody to stay.

My uncle lived not too far from our family home in New Orleans. At that time, he would drive down to New Orleans for four hours, take care of some business, and then have to drive back to Northern Louisiana because there was no place, no hotels, or anywhere for people to stay.

-Calvin A. Lain

Homeowners were looking for answers on what [to] do about the toxic drywall in their homes that was imported from China after Hurricane Katrina created shortages of building materials.
.............

After their home in Metairie was damaged in Katrina, Raffy and George Rigney moved to a brand new home on the outskirts of Hammond in May 2006. Since then, their two air-conditioning units have required servicing 10 times. Their washer and dryer died. Their security system failed. The wiring in their home has turned black.

*New Orleans Times Picayune*          September 17, 2009

## Sarah
(4th child of Odis & Irene)

Now people's appliances have been going out and they are having health problems and things like that. They are saying that the Chinese dry wall, used in the construction, might be at fault. It has only been a year since I'm back in my house and the lower oven of my brand new double oven won't work, that was after about four months, and then the top oven quit after about six months; so I don't have any oven now. My refrigerator is making this noise, like "aaaarrgggg," a grinding sound. My washer works pretty good. These were all brand new appliances. The dryer takes almost five hours to dry stuff. So I'm thinking that this all might be due to Chinese dry wall.....

I think I really need to look at my house and see if I have Chinese dry wall. Some people get rashes, breathing problems, some people have had to move out of their houses because they can't take it.

I spent the night in the hospital the other night. I have never had panic attacks before, but it is just like I wake up at night and I can't breathe, my heart is racing. I'm trying to convince myself that I don't have Chinese dry wall. They produce these hydrogen sulfides and it corrodes metals and it gives the person illnesses. It makes you sick.

When people have exposed dry wall in the attic, it will say 'made in China.' I have that foam insulation and it is covered. I think there might be some exposed in my garage, so I need to bite the bullet and have somebody come and peak and see.

When I first bought my house in 1981, my neighborhood was middle income families, with about 90% white. As years progressed, more black residents had moved in. Now since Katrina, there might not be any whites left. My neighborhood has about 75 – 85% of the people back in the homes. The grass continues to be cut on the unoccupied houses. The lawns are still manicured and landscaped.

Since Katrina, I've noticed that the neighborhood is a little less exclusive, it is probably more of the lower middle as opposed to the upper middle class that have moved in. After Katrina, I think the prior owners were so disgusted that I think they literally just about gave the houses away. For example, the lot for the neighbor next to me, and my lot, are worth $75,000, and the owner sold the whole house and lot for $75,000. Now State Farm has my house insured for $325,000; I think that is a bit too much.

We have covenants, like all the homes need to be owner-occupied; you can't rent a home in my neighborhood. We still have a neighborhood association and they still have meetings, but they are not as stringent as they used to be. When the neighborhood used to be white, if you put your garbage out on the curb a minute before 4:30 p.m., you would get a letter in your mailbox. Now I might see someone park a car on the street and it might stay there a while and they don't get up in arms about that. But the neighborhood has not gone to seed; it is still a nice neighborhood.

## The "Road Away From Home" Program

First off, Bush stood in front of the Saint Louis Cathedral and said, "Oh, I'm going to help you all." There was a Republican governor in Mississippi, whereas in Louisiana, we had an image that it was a third world republic, so Louisiana was bending over backwards to show everyone that they were going to do everything right. The Louisiana governor hired a Virginia Company for $100 million to give the money out for the "Road Home" program, whereas Mississippi just said everybody gets $150,000.

Right after Katrina, when stuff kind of poured in, people from Jefferson Parish came back first and they had free gasoline, free clothes washing, and Red Cross supplies. By the time New Orleans people came back, there wasn't a whole lot left. The money was supposed to go to the victims of the Federal levy breeches, who got flooded out. But, since

New Orleans was a majority black kind of town, it didn't happen that way; they lobbied and the next thing you know, Jefferson Parish, who had wind damage, was getting the Road Home money. They were here first, so they started giving them the money.

If you had money from your insurance company for wind damage, then that was going to be subtracted from your Road Home money and then you would get less. What I heard was the people from Jefferson Parish went out and got these private appraisals that said their houses were worth $400,000 and so they could take all their homeowners money and subtract that from the value. Then they still could take the $150,000 from Road Home.

By the time the people from New Orleans was able to apply, the Road Home program would do their own appraisal. Even if you went out and got your own appraisal, it couldn't be 15% more than what the Road Home appraisal said. So they changed the rules. As the Road Home went on, the stuff they allowed in the beginning, started to change as New Orleans property owners were able to get in and start getting work done. As much as two years later, Road Home had a meeting over in New Orleans East, and the New Orleans people, who were mostly all black, had not seen one penny of the money.

I came back to New Orleans about five times during that first year. I was in California and was trying to take care of my property, the gutting and this and that. I would listen to the radio and hear how they would make so many changes to the Road Home program. The Road Home made so many hoops to jump through; if they wrote something down in error, it was hard to work around that. I had a nickname for it: 'The Road Away From Home'.

I got some flood money, but it was three years before I got back in the house. I didn't have a mortgage prior to Katrina and now I had living expenses: I had to pay for those plane tickets to come back from California, to get my car trailered out to California, and to get back to New

Orleans. I think I had to pay $300 for an engineering survey because I wasn't sure if I was going to just demolish the whole house and just start from scratch.

In order to get mitigation money, ($30,000 from the insurance contract to demolish the house) if your house had ever flooded more than once, then you could get it knocked down. If it had only flooded that one time, you had to have something else to go with it --- one thing you could have is to be below sea level. So I paid $300 to hire the engineer firm. They would ask you, "What do you need this for?" Depending on what you needed it for, was how it came out... like they said my house came back as "1/8 inch below flood level."

There were just so many different ways you were fighting FEMA. For example, they said only home owners could get FEMA trailers. I think even to this day, they have never done anything for renters. When I first came back, I rented a townhouse for about $1000 a month in Jefferson Parish. The way I got that townhouse was that I was staying at my brother Raymond's trailer. I went to a trade show down at the Convention Center where they builders had set up booths. FEMA was there, Road Home was there, SBA was there, one-stop.

So I was looking for a place when I first got back in New Orleans... there weren't very many apartments open in New Orleans when I first got back; and those that were open were gouging the renters. Before the storm, something that you would have paid $400 for, now was renting for at least $1500. So at the trade show, FEMA gave me this list of apartments, one was in Jefferson Parish. Jefferson Parish was really against having New Orleans people come out there. You had to really show that you were an "upstanding citizen;" that you went to church on Sunday and you drove very slowly.

I met with these realtors about the Jefferson Parish apartment. I said I was Dr. Lain, I paid the security deposit, the first month, deposits, etc. and they said, "OK, you can move in." Later on, after a couple of months, this older white man moved in down stairs and he had a companion with him. I was talking with him one day and I asked, "Well when is your house going to be finished?" He said, "I don't have a house." He told me that he lived in Jefferson Parish in an apartment that was damaged and FEMA was going to move him to Gonzales or something and he told them he had to stay in Metairie. FEMA was paying his rent even though this guy did not own a house.

FEMA and I had parted company after about the first three months. When I came to New Orleans and I was still trying to get reimbursed for the California rent I had paid, and maybe moving back, they kept saying, send this and send that. I kept trying to go downtown to their different satellite offices and bring all these papers. Each time, I would mail them the entire lease, etc. and still nothing would come. The last time I think I called them on the phone, and somebody with a Spanish accent said, "Why did you go to California? California was too far to go," and they were not going to support me on that. So, I never called them back.

They put people on the plane and sent them to Utah and wherever. I guess that was OK, but it wasn't OK to go to a place where I had support. California was the only place where I could get a school for Liz; she needed special education. At the time, California opened up for her and so I went to California. I wanted to tell the FEMA man that California was a part of the United States you know, but the guy said California was too far and that was the end of that. All this time I paid rent in California, rent in Metairie, bought furniture, made airplane trips and many other extraordinary expenses. For years I also paid for non-existent telephone and utilities in my destroyed home. I just didn't want to lose my telephone number. I convinced myself that this would make everything normal.

Things were still in an uproar at that time – you didn't know if they were just going to raze New Orleans and you didn't know if you had to build at flood elevations: some people said you had to build your home nine feet off the ground, some said fifteen feet off the ground. Then the insurance companies were saying, if you raise your house too much then they wouldn't insure you because people could fall off these high areas. It was just a lot of confusion and a lot of headaches.

I think I moved back in my house finally in August 2008. OK, I made a mistake; I gave the contractor all the money up front and people later said that you never should do that. Consequently, the contractor did not finish everything and I still have a lock box on the back of the door – a year later. And, I don't know what he did with the back door garage opener, so I have to get out of the car and open the garage every-time. There are a few knobs missing and there are a few window frames that still need painting.

I remember that Road Home said my house was appraised at $139,000, so what I got from the flood would cover that, so my first "gold letter" said that I got zero; they weren't going to give me anything. I had lived for three years outside of my house, but I wasn't going to get anything.

Then, finally I made the SBA loan. You had to pay the closing costs, and all these fees to do the loan. We had to jump through a lot of hoops, and then as they gave the money out, you had to send them all these receipts. They wanted letters and documents for everything. It was a lot like those Chinese acrobats with those plates circling on top of those sticks – you had to keep everything spinning and something would fall and break.

I had paid for my home and was living quite comfortably prior to Katrina. During this crisis, at one point I was paying rent and a new SBA mortgage -- prior to Katrina, I had none of these. Needless to say, I am no longer comfortable. Although I've paid huge taxes, I have received next to no government help. I am really much worse off since the storm.

-Sarah Lain

## Elsie
(2nd child of Odis & Irene)

We were staying with my daughter, Drusilla, in Houston. She was really good with taking care of her dad and that helped me and gave me some strength because I was going out of my mind.

In Houston, I didn't have transportation for my husband. He went to dialysis three days a week. There was a dialysis unit not far from my daughter's house, but then we wound up transferred to another unit that was a little further out and I would bring him. Then we had ambulance service that would take him.

I would come back here to New Orleans often. It was just unreal to look at the house, knowing that you were just in a situation where you couldn't even return. There was no food, flies everywhere, gnats eating you.

Thank God time has passed and you don't think of it as much. Just looking around at some of the blight and some of the things that hasn't come back even now, like groceries, shopping centers, and restaurants that were in my area.

When we got back to New Orleans, my husband's condition deteriorated to a point that he needed an ambulance to pick him up and bring him for treatments. At that point, I couldn't do it, there was times that he would actually fall on the floor and I couldn't get him up.

The medical services was out, but dialysis patients just have to be treated; there is no way around that. Other medical services was there, but a lot of people just weren't seeking. But the dialysis was OK. Originally we had to go clear across town to get treatment. The center moved back down here closer to home on St. Claude, which is still not in the East.

Then my husband got to move back up to Touro Hospital for treatment. Once his doctor saw him one day in the hospital, and the doctor said, "Why aren't you here getting your treatments?" My husband always loved Touro and the doctor opened up that door for him to come back up there. He was happy about that.

Now I look at it knowing that you can always replace material things. You know you can't replace life. Even at that, I just went out and bought necessities. I didn't go back high end like I was before the storm. I said, "If it ever happens again, I don't want to be out of a lot of money." I really like a nice kitchen and I said that I could have a $100,000 kitchen alone, but I'm not going to do that. Instead of going Viking and Thermador and all of that, I decided to go Frigidaire.

I don't put too much emphasis on material stuff now, because it can be replaced. I knew, with my husband being so sick at the time I was rebuilding, it was a possibility that he wouldn't be here, and so I thought, what do I need all that for anyway. So I made it just comfortable and nice enough, but not exactly the same quality as it was before. The house is fixed different from the way it was before Katrina. To tell the truth, I probably got a better house if nothing happens.

I miss the kids' wedding pictures, that was the biggest thing that I lost. I lost jewelry and I kind of wished that I had put that up or got that out. My husband had this sear sucker suit that he loved. He always desired that suit; I said that if I had that suit, I would have buried him in it because he loved that suit. He had a cashmere coat, and I wish I could have tried to see if I could have something done with it. But once that mold gets in it, it actually turned to a "rust", and some things you just couldn't get out. So I finally decided at some point, if it wasn't something that could be washable, that had the moldy smell, then it had to go. Even the cleaners couldn't do anything with it

-Elsie Lain

**Shaun**
(grandson of Odis & Irene, son of Otis Jr.)

I had a lot of trouble with the insurance company. However, my situation was a blessing because my father had stayed in New Orleans. So we used his testimony within my insurance document that I came up with.

What happened with my house was that my walls fell down, they were blown away. We indicated to the insurance company that they were down before the waters got there. We got a system engineer to verify that. So we went to court and won. We won our insurance and they had to pay us off. That was a blessing.

It was so much turmoil that we shouldn't have had to go through. If the insurance would have dealt fairly with the people in New Orleans, we wouldn't have needed FEMA assistance. They didn't want to come through with their policies. They didn't want to pay out for the time we couldn't use the property. They didn't want to reimburse for contents. Everything was a struggle. This was a battle that I had to fight and we won in the end. It settled before the trial.

We are still dealing with Road Home right now in 2009. They easily could have just written checks out - $150,000 for each person. But they sliced it, divvied and dimed it, and it felt like they just said, "We can't give these people this money without some torture."

People have gotten cancer and died, and the suicide rate which was not high in New Orleans before, is now high in the middle class. That is a whole other report that needs to be done. Just like a '9-11' Commission, there needs to be a '9-29' Commission. We have to put this in the history books and study this, so it doesn't repeat itself.

-Shaun Lain

## Otis Jr. (June)
(1st child of Odis & Irene)

<u>Lost Businesses</u>

I got insurance money for a vehicle that was in the flood and I bought a brand new truck. I must have put about 50,000 miles in a couple of months on the truck. I rode to Miami, rode to Washington, you name it, I spent a lot of time on the highway. The real convenient thing about the truck -- I was able to recline the seat and I slept in the truck. I went to truck stops, ate and took my shower.

I really was homeless, living on the road, running from place to place; I was running to St. Charles where I had busses parked, out and around Alexandria, back and forth to Pink Panther and then I would come to New Orleans. I found out I was running in circles and not really solving too much, just showing up.

Supplies and equipment were at every location. I spent a lifetime accumulating this stuff. I always worked early in the morning until late at night, and thought one day, my family really would be secure and everything would be OK. But nevertheless, along came Katrina and the whole dream of my life's work caved in.

I couldn't buy my way out of it. I spent a lot of money trying to fix it and appease people and make it right, but in the long run, I did declare bankruptcy just for peace of mind and to stop the phone calls. Was it best for me to do that? No, simply because my financial situation should have dictated that I could get out of this thing. But a lot of this stuff required lawyers and the lawyers were really just taking a fee and not really giving me the service. In the long run, I took the short cut.

Not knowing it then, but in the long run, it may have been a blessing because I had been working fourteen to fifteen hours a day, and I had about a hundred people working for me and I didn't realize that it wasn't really progress. It was just a lot of 'mess' that I was dealing with. I'm calling it 'mess' simply because I did everything to appease people and they really weren't grateful.

I used to tell people, "If you don't mess with me, and you don't cause a disturbance, I will pay you a salary." All I want to do is have harmony, peace. I thought that was a blessing for people, but then I found out that the more you give things without people earning it, the bigger the problem gets. You are not solving anything, you are just adding to it.

Like that old adage about teaching a man to fish, not just giving him fish. That is what I really found out in life. Everybody, everyone, and everything has to be accountable. If you don't earn it, you shouldn't get it. It took me a lot to understand that because I gave away a lot of money, a lot of equipment, and time, to people who didn't appreciate it.

## Pink Panther Park

I had this Pink Panther trailer park in Slidell (just East of New Orleans). It was 78 acres with lots of trees; it was a huge place and all of these people just started coming after Katrina. The park had people everywhere, all these migrant workers I'll call them; they just came in and squatted. The people came from all over the country. These people came with heavy duty equipment, a lot of dragline bulldozers, and all kind of equipment. So I was somewhere in Lake Charles and I got a phone call from my park manager who was trying to control the park and get everything up and running. It really looked like the storm stopped and devastated that place.

I had hired a woman that was a member of the park long before the storm. You could tell that the woman had some type of business skills. So I told her, "Look, I want you to manage the park and try to take care of the basics." We went over all the little details and she started collecting money and for the first couple of weeks, it was unbelievable. We must have collected $14,000 or $15,000, then it was

$17,000 or $18,000. People were paying by the week and the month. All of a sudden, after a month of this, she said nobody paid her and the money disappeared. I asked her, "Where is your husband?" because he used to pick up the trash and go around the park and help to maintain it.

We got very little electricity and they would cut it off. We had people going in the woods defecating. It wasn't the greatest situation in the world, but from day-to-day, I was living in a trailer that was flooded and I felt like I was getting sick from it. I sold the thing for pennies on the dollar. This was a $40,000 unit and I got rid of it because I thought it was making me sick.

Then one of my workers had a unit which smelled a lot better. So I slept on the sofa for a couple of nights in that unit while trying to get the park organized. Everybody kept telling me, "We can get the electricity straight. And we could get the place up and running." In the mean time, I had maybe about $75,000 that I'd collected and I was thinking that I could take that money and put the park back together.

The Corps of Engineers came over and told my manager that they would put the park in order. They told her that they would bring people to stay in the park, and how much I could charge them. So I signed the contract that she forwarded to me. The next day after I signed the contract, they called me and said the contract was void. But every other park in the neighborhood was fixed up by the Federal Government; my park wasn't. Once he found out I was the owner, the next day they called and said they couldn't do it.

I was the only black owner of all the parks in Slidell and I had 78 acres. Everybody knew me and I didn't know that I stuck out like a sore thumb. In the park, after the storm, I would think that 90% of the people staying in the park was white.

I rode around the rest of Slidell and they must have had about ten different parks; they all were fixed up except the Pink Panther. To this day, a lot of people think I made millions off of it. I did not make one dime. In fact, I sunk all my savings and everything I owned into it thinking I could get it back. My problem was that I had people coming into it, taking parts and equipment. This was a place that we had tractors, riding lawnmowers, all kinds of equipment, you name it and we had it. We had to grade the roads, we had to maintain the flowers and the trees, fix up units, and maintain all of the equipment and the trailers we owned.

We must have had about eight people working at that place and we had about three people return. I paid these people and what happened was a dispute about payment; I paid them again. They saw that was an easy thing. We wound up in court and the judge ruled in my favor that I was right because I did everything that I was supposed to do. Later on, the ruling was changed, the judge went back over and she scratched out a lot of stuff because the attorney wasn't satisfied that he lost the case. I've never seen anything like it, but I have a copy of the judgment and I have a copy of the one where she scratched and made the changes. The fee that she awarded them was close to $6000. Just to make it go away, I paid them that fee.

We had a situation where there was a dump right next door to the park and they had been piling this stuff up. So the guy who owned the dump owned half of Slidell. He came over and said, "Look, I will buy this park from you." I didn't know it at the time, but my manager told him that she wanted nine million dollars. He offered three million. By the time I found out he was interested in buying the park, he told me he would offer 1.5 million. I told him I wanted 1.8 million. It was too late because now I had people trying to foreclose on the Lowes Express busses. The park was nearly paid for; I'd been owning the park for nearly fourteen years. The amount we owed was minimal.

It wasn't a situation where you could just go to the police and just go downtown and lodge your complaint. They had this dump right next door and the people started burning stuff which they weren't supposed to do because it was toxic. I told them that we were going to sue them so they stopped burning the toxic stuff and was only supposed to be burning the trees and storm debris that was buriable.

I didn't sell the park, I ended up losing it. A bus company had put a hold on the park like they were going to buy it. I couldn't sell it at the time simply because of technicalities, so they wound up getting this thing for a little bit of nothing. They were still saying that I owed them $600,000, but in essence, everything I bought, I put a lot of money on it.

But now, I had a lot of slip and fall cases, I got my insurance which was sky high - $85,000 a month insurance bill on the busses. I had lawyers that I was giving money to take care of these things. This whole scenario and chaotic situation went down the drain because they took money and went south. I had lawyers in Baton Rouge who I had given $10,000, I had lawyers in New Orleans who I had given $15,000, I had lawyers all over the place. But once people know they can get away with something, it seems like it was 'survival of the fittest.' Only the strongest survive and if you are the lone wolf, you need an army of people to support you.

I was thinking that I should have this stuff paid for in a short period of time. The majority of busses and things that I owned were close to being paid for. But when you go to court, these people put all kind of attachments on the property: lawyers' fees, courts costs, what have you, and it can run up to the $100,000's.

U.S. Bank called and I had a situation where I probably owned them about $200,000 for four busses. They ended up getting $600,000 as a sale from the park. There was a lot of equity involved in the park; I have my wife and my kids and I was thinking it was going to be with the family for a long time. It probably could have been handled a lot differently than I did, I'm not going to go into all the technical details of the lawsuits, but it was a challenging part.

## June-El Refunds

In the mean time, the last business I owned was June-El. We collected a lot of deposit money for upcoming engagements prior to Katrina. I was trying to give these people their deposits back. There was one situation where the guy came in and I said, "Man, now look, we have cleaned the place up and you can still have your engagement." He said, "Look, I just want my money back." He said that he had given $700, but the record said that he had paid $400. We wound up on Judge Judy in New York. He made a case on the Judge Judy TV show that I should return the money. I seemed to lose any situation I had that involved any type of court situation. I was told to return money but I couldn't ever collect any money. This is a still an ongoing process.

## Health

I was dealing with cancer at the time and I have high blood pressure. A lot of days I woke up and I didn't feel like moving. People say, "Why you didn't do this and why you didn't do that?" I was just happy to be able to open my eyes up and just move during each day. We had a lot of jockeying back and forth, and right today, four years later, we still have the effects from Katrina.

## Town Hall meeting

I might have been the laughing stock of the nation because there was a town hall meeting and the New Orleans Mayor had all these people come in that wanted to complain about something. All I said to him was, "Mr. Mayor, all I want is my equipment back. I own Loews Express Bus Company on Chef Menteur. I've been down there for years. Some police officers took my equipment and I would like to have you return it." The Mayor said, "Oh yes, Mr. Lain, we are going to reimburse you. We are going to take care of you."

They assigned a police officer, and to this day, I carry that police officer's card in my wallet. This police officer went around and found like three pieces of equipment, even though it was devastated. One piece was a minivan they brought back on a truck and parked in the bus yard. Another piece was a van that my son got. They didn't even have the keys for that, so they had jeri-rigged it and jumped the switch on that.

I had a Rolls Royce that was in Baton Rouge that cost me $1000 to get out of the police pawn shop. They said someone had it parked on the road. The police picked it up and brought it to the police storage yard and the fees everyday were adding up. They were anticipating keeping this unit. It was a stroke of luck that I found out it was parked in Baton Rouge, so it took me a long time to get this thing out. I tried to tell these people it was stolen; it didn't matter. They were there to collect money. It added up to over $1000. To this day, I'm sorry that I paid and got it out.

We had too many scenarios similar to that, trying to get equipment back and people thinking you don't deserve it or you shouldn't have this type of stuff in your possession. People seemed to put ownership on my stuff without buying it or paying for it.

## Helping Mayor Ray Nagin

Ray Nagin was the Mayor of the City of New Orleans at the time of Katrina. We gave this man free busses when he was running for office. We did everything to support him. A lot of times, they needed a bus and they called us. We didn't get paid for it. I feel like I was beat up by the City of New Orleans big time. When he ran for second term after Katrina, we provided busses from Atlanta. We had people come back to New Orleans all the way from Atlanta to vote.

I feel if there was ever a time I was kicked in the butt by the City of New Orleans, it was this. I personally think

I did everything I could to help the city and the mayor, and when it came time to pay for what they used, they were like, "We don't have the money." To be honest with you, I did send in a formal complaint and I asked for compensation. I found out that if you don't have someone inside working on it, that you are not going to get paid.

We actually did some work for a lot of organizations and people since Katrina that we didn't get paid for. Unless you have computers up, you really can't just write stuff down in a notebook and say, "I will get back to this stuff," because everyday something is happening. Right after Katrina, I was thinking that we would be back in business. I'm spending money trying to change out motors and curls and sensitive stuff that once you get salt water in, to change it out, we spent lots of money. We were trying to paint stuff, and put desaltation type of chemicals on equiptment to keep it from rusting. I hired people to do this, that and the other. Believe it or not, if I had done nothing, I would have been better off.

Emotional Loss

A lot of people don't know it, but emotionally, I've gone through a lot. I didn't grow up complaining. If you cut your foot off, just put a patch on it and keep on going. I have a football mentality that you run through stuff, and the more you run through, the better you get. You will be able to run for a touchdown. That is the way that my life worked. Everything I did was straight forward, try to be honest, pay my bills.

I declared bankruptcy back in January (2009) and my case is still open. Why it is still open? Nobody wants to tell me. I gave my bankruptcy lawyer over $5000, and he said he could handle it. But he won't even talk to me. For some reason, it was 'take the people's money' and 'close the door.' I'm in bankruptcy and as far as I know, I don't have anybody fighting for me. I don't know where this thing is at.

I have a wife and others that were affected completely differently from Katrina than me. I think it was different by me being there and staying in it, and being around all these people. I was in the storm. It wasn't like, I could just say, "Oh I can get over it." Unless you were in it, you don't know. You can't possibly understand it because the story is hard to tell and explain.

The feelings, the mental agony and the stuff you went through. People don't understand the impact when they come at you with a big gun and say, "Hey, what are you doing? Where are you going?" being really aggressive and confrontive. At every exit they had policemen and military men, and it seemed like they all had these big, huge rifles. They were young guys, like twenty-one years old and it looked like everybody had their finger on the trigger. I've seen a lot of that in New Orleans, and it is scary, scary, scary!

-Otis Lain Jr.

**Emanuel Sr.**
(7th child of Odis & Irene)

Melva, my wife, didn't want me to throw any of her clothes away; she wanted me to put them in bags. Then she would go through the devastation. But I waited until she left and I did throw away everything. It took a long time for her to quit talking about it; I don't think she ever forgave me for that. She felt like she could have salvaged some things.

We got maybe about five feet of water in the house and maybe we could have salvaged some things. But when you are gutting a house, that involves throwing away everything in the house. When we came there the house was upside down, the refrigerator and stove turned on the side. We had moved into our house in 1997 and it was an upgrade for us at that time.

I felt like it was a great tremendous loss, I felt like this would take a long time to recover. The whole thing was sad and you know, I thank God for life, but it was very emotional. To lose everything, you just feel almost like it is the end of the world. You don't know how you will make it at the time. The best word I could use to describe it, is "sad" and you feel depressed. You feel like you don't have many clothes except the clothes that people have donated to you. You still go to work every day. You thank God that we are alive and I didn't have to swim through the storm like we did in Hurricane Betsy.

Even four years later, when you think about it, it is still sad. I heard someone say the other day that it is going to take like twelve years before New Orleans really recovers from the storm. I still got a rental property building around the corner from our family home on Clouet Street. It was Melva's grandfather's. I put in a contract to have someone tear it down. That was something that I didn't want to do, but the house was off its foundation and the weeds were growing up high.

I am a minister and I own a church building across the street from our family home. I need to do something with that to bring it back. My church was mainly a family church; my mother, my wife and children and a few neighbors attended there. Hopefully, if it is God's will, my intention is to fix it up someday.

In New Orleans East, we don't have any major stores and we have to travel to the West bank across the River to get things. I really can only take one day at a time. I thank God that we are here and I ask him for strength to face each day because it is still a challenge and hard work.

-Emanuel Lain Sr.

# Chapter 15

## "George Bush Doesn't Care About Black People"**
### - Kanye West,

**On Friday, September 2, 2005, Kanye West went off script on an NBC telethon with actor Mike Myers to raise money for Katrina victims five days after the hurricane hit. In frustration about the lack of response for the victims left in New Orleans, he directs the above statement against President Bush.

New Orleans is the ninth poorest City in the U.S. New Orleans is 70 percent African-American. Louisiana has the fourth highest poverty rate in the country.
(CNN Reports, 2005, p. 90)

Black people comprised more than two-thirds of the pre-Katrina population in the City of New Orleans. Official census data reveal that over the five years that preceded the arrival of Hurricane Katrina, about one-third of the total black population consistently earned incomes below the poverty benchmark. U.S. Census Bureau. 2000. Income and poverty in 1999-2000. Census 2000 Summary File 3 (SF3) – Sample Data. Available at http://www.census.gov (http://www.census.gov) .
(Durant and Sultan, 2008, p. 193)

## Raymond
(9th child of Odis & Irene)

Right after the hurricane, the news was showing how people were drowning and dying from simple stuff like dehydration and lack of food and medical care. If the news reporters were able to be down here, why couldn't the government help the people out? That went on for days. I don't think Bush's response was adequate. Mayor Nagin said, "Bush why don't you get off your ass and come down here and help?" I think Nagin has gotten backlash from that already.

To me it looked like a thing where they were going into experimental mode. It looked like they were experimenting with what would happen if they didn't rescue the people right away. I mean they could have had help into New Orleans within hours. But it took them almost a week to get help down here. That was not necessary.

I basically tried to find out if my relatives were OK and once my own family was OK, I didn't have nobody personally trapped down here. I felt horror, just like the rest of the country, because of what I was seeing on the TV. I knew it wasn't necessary what the President was doing.

Since Katrina, the makeup of a lot of the city neighborhoods is changing. Some neighborhoods don't have nobody living in it. Some neighborhoods now have whites, blacks and Hispanics. There are a lot of whites coming into previous black neighborhoods now after Katrina; you have a lot of Mexicans coming into the city. This section of town, where our family home is located, was all black before Katrina, but now it is mixed: you have Spanish, whites and blacks in this part of town. My neighborhood in Uptown is still mostly black.

Another thing Katrina changed is how high the rent is now; rent use to be cheap in New Orleans. I had a house I rented out for $250 a month before Katrina; now that amount of rent is unheard of. People are not making more money but their rent is going up.  What is going to happen to these people? You are going to have a whole lot of homeless people when all these funds run out.  People will be up a creek without a paddle.

-Raymond Lain

**Elsie**
(2nd child of Odis & Irene)

I think the lack of response to evacuate people was due to their lower class. Poverty played a part in that lack of response. I also think that basically nobody believed that this was really happening. Things weren't done in advance and I know a lot of money was at stake -- once the Governor made a decision to deploy the National Guard that was money out of the State's pocket which they were trying to avoid. As it turned out, the peoples' lives should have been put before the cost.

There was also politicking involved, the Governor was Democratic and Bush was Republican. You know how they do -- they play their little games. The lack of response was just that they were spiting each other and they all ended up taking the blunt end. They could have acted more quickly. I think if we would have had a Republican in [the governor's office], we would have had more recovery money and things would have got done faster.

The Road Home program was a mess – disgusting really. They spent more money trying to keep money out of the peoples' hands. The process to get recovery help to the people took too long. The way they ran the program was not even economical. They could have gone on and given everybody $150,000, been done with it and saved taxpayers money. That is the politicking part that I don't like.

-Elsie Lain Hagan

## Rose
(6th child of Odis & Irene)

Because New Orleans was 65% black, and the people who had the means took care of themselves, there were only the people with no political power, no means, and nobody to care about them that were left in the city. That's why there was a lack of a quick response to rescue the people. There were other people who were in the hospitals and nursing homes, who had told their families, "Don't worry about it, everything will be all right." Then the water came in and you had only the few people that stayed behind to help these people who had no means.

-Rose Lain Watts

## Otis Jr. (June)
(1st child of Odis & Irene)

I personally feel, deep down in my heart, people have a way of placing stuff on shelves: the first, second, third and bottom shelves. The people in New Orleans were placed on the bottom shelf and never were considered above that. When you have something on the bottom shelf, it is not the most important thing to think about. It was an eye opener to most people simply because it wasn't a conscious thing to leave the people in New Orleans behind. The people in power never really had given any consideration to these people.

Is it fair to say that this was right, wrong or otherwise? Just like in the Bible, you want to say that everything in the Bible is equal, but automatically you start prioritizing stuff. Unfortunately, the people of New Orleans just happened to be at the bottom of the list. Whose fault was that? It's just the way it was.

I think it wasn't a black or white issue. I really, really don't believe that any thought went into it because the thought mechanism wasn't even in the process.

At the time of Katrina, we had a Republican in national power, but a Democratic governor and mayor, and people in the city who were predominantly Democratic. This is the way the political process works -- first of all, we help and are concerned about people who are most like us.

When those in power finally realized that if they didn't help this group of people left behind, the whole world would think they were bad, then they finally started to act. If there weren't outside people crying, "Why don't you help the New Orleans people," they would have ignored the people forever, simply because that is human nature. Those in power felt they were better than the type of people left in New Orleans. In the process, the people of New Orleans just happened to come out at the bottom.

-Otis Lain Jr

**Jennie V.**
(daughter-in-law of Odis & Irene, wife of Louis)

I agreed with what Kanye West said that George Bush didn't care about black people because Bush was so nonchalant about the situation. But I'm not as upset with Bush as I am with Blanco (Governor). She tried to stop everything; she didn't think we needed the Road Home money because we didn't know what we would do with it. She acted like we were too stupid to know what to do with it! Now, if we owned a house, why do they think that we are too stupid to get our house fixed? So when HUD had to go and fight for us, Blanco was determined not to give us the money.

-Jennie V. Lain

## Sarah
(4th child of Odis & Irene)

I think the lower economic people got left in the city and the lower economic people happened to be black. But I think it was a political thing too. There are just a bunch of Democrats down here and the powers to be were all Republican, which is too bad that they would just let the people rot you know.

Before Katrina, we didn't have any Hispanic workers in town. Post-Katrina, twenty to twenty-five percent of the population are Hispanic. Now we have Mexican restaurants.

Yesterday (Summer 2009), the City Council had a hearing and they said that the Latino workers would do a job and then once they were finished, the contractors would tell them that they didn't have papers and would refuse to pay them. The workers had no recourse. The city council was going to pass a law to help them.

But, when I first got back, some of the Latino workers said individual home owners would hire them and give them a price. In the middle of the job, then the Latino workers would tell the home owner that it would cost more. The owner would have to pay more or they would walk off the job. So I guess it has been kind of a tug-tug on both sides.

There's been a little tension because of that. It seems like if any other group comes in, like the Vietnamese, they always move up. Now there are a lot of Latinos that own the grocery stores and gas stations and it seems like the black people never get their turn. Other groups seem to get businesses and stores by getting loans from the banks and that is the way it goes.

I heard people on St. Charles Avenue might have had some little flood damage. They had some Israeli type military come in to protect them though. They had such hysteria. Ray Nagin (mayor) wanted 10,000 or 20,000 body bags, I don't remember exactly how many. A lot of people still are not accounted for. They spread people around and no one could really account for everyone.

They are building this big memorial and there is a big rig-a-ma-role, because they don't want to put names on the memorial. I think just because so many more people are dead, and they just don't want to say how many people died in Katrina. There were a lot of people left in New Orleans, and a lot of people didn't evacuate. So I'm wondering what happened to all those people?

I think if it was a bunch of black Democrats in federal office, the response would have been better. The party affiliation had something to do with it,.. but I can't imagine, everything went bad on that Tuesday and Wednesday, but to be Thursday or Friday and still not rescued? And the temperature was very hot that summer. They have found mummified bodies in people's attics.

They wouldn't even drop any water on the people. What was the thinking? Bush, coming back from Crawford, Texas on Tuesday at 37,000 feet, waved at the people on the rooftops down there.

Katrina taught me one thing, you have to take care of yourself. You can't depend on the government; they will forget you. They will wave at you from 37,000 feet while you are down here treading water. I don't know anybody who believes otherwise than that race played a part.

I read somewhere that until they saw on TV what looked like a dead elderly white woman in that wheelchair cast aside, nothing moved (in the rescue effort). If that hadn't happened, how long do you think they would have let that go on? And people were just asking for some water and it had been day after day watching this. That just is un-imaginable, you can't even wrap your head around what happened to people in Katrina.

-Sarah Lain

**Emanuel Sr.**
(7th child of Odis & Irene)

I saw lack of response on the TV. By me being a minister, I was wishing some kind of way that I could be here to help people. Even though I have responsibilities with my family and wife, I wish I could have been here to help. I don't have a boat or anything. You would just cry and feel helpless to see a lot of people trapped in their houses.

My neighbor, who lived directly next to me, was trapped in his house because he stayed, but his wife evacuated. He was on the roof for three days until someone in a boat came and got him and brought him to Chef Highway. There were people at my oldest brother Otis' place. People took refuge in his place.

My neighbor, he is about the closest one that was devastated by the storm. Our sister-in-law, Jennie V McGee Lain's step-father was killed in the storm, and his brother was killed. I know Ervin Mayfield, a jazz trumpeter in the city, and his father was killed. And I might know a few other people who died.

I know we lost about 1500 people; a lot of them were elderly people. I felt real bad that they were stuck in the city. I had a car in my driveway which I wish I could have given to someone so they could escape. A lot of things go through my mind.

I thought the government didn't care; I thought that the government was incompetent. I felt like they could have had a much better response. I think it was embarrassing in the end. I was angry with the government; all three branches really. They were trying to fight over power and so forth while the people were suffering. In 2005, you would think we would have had a better plan to deal with a disaster like that. I don't understand why it was slow and why they were fighting over who was going to get the credit and who was going to do what between the State and the Federal governments.

I think the President was out of touch, the same way he handled 9/11. He was slow. I think once he gets it, then he acts. But he has to think about things; he has to have people tell him what to do, and the response was slow because he was slow. I don't think it was just intentional, but it was just that he didn't get it.

I think it was just indifference, people didn't really care. I don't think they wake up in the morning and be thinkin' about poor people. That's what it was really, a lot of people that was poor.

Personally, I don't think Bush was a racist, I just think he's a slow person to respond. The people around him, that advised him, they probably just didn't care because the people were poor. I think it is more about being poor than being black.

If you are rich and famous you are going to get your attention, but if you are poor, nobody really cares about you. I think the country and the government were embarrassed to see it on world-wide TV. I think it was mostly like a class-type thing rather than a race-type thing.

-Emanuel Lain Sr.

**Calvin**

(13th child of Odis & Irene)

A couple of days after Kanye West had his famous saying that Bush doesn't care about black people, public officials were acting more like they were being attacked as opposed to seeing the need for humanitarian aid. With the prevailing images of a few people looting or hearing shots at night, some people said they were shooting at helicopters, and some people were saying that people stuck on rooftops at night were trying to get attention, like sending up a flare.

Then you add in what people said happened on the Danzinger Bridge -- people getting killed, and the police officers in Gretna where they refused to allow people to literally walk across the bridge to get help. Those things that serve up as proof. Most of the people in the Superdome or Convention Center could have simply gotten up on the elevated interstate and walked across the Mississippi Bridge to get to dry land. They were viewed as all these undesirables; they were not going to let them come across and basically were going to lock them out of the neighborhood.

The same thing happened in Baton Rouge, where you had a black mayor and police chief. The number one concern was law and order. A good example of the sharp contrast was when General Honore came on the scene, then stuff started to be handled. When Honore ordered his men to put down their guns and to grab the babies and pass out water, that was when it really turned into what it should have been from day one -- not an armed military situation.

Prior to Honore's arrival, the local police and the police in Baton Rouge felt more like 'we are under attack by these victims,' as opposed to 'we have a humanitarian crisis.' The rescue response was definitely hindered or significantly delayed by how it was perceived based on racism.

- Calvin Lain

**Darren**
(grandchild of Odis & Irene, son of Elsie)

Bush talked with the Governor on Sunday evening and declared that it was going to be a natural disaster. He heard about it over and over, but chose not to even do anything about it. Not to send help.

There were a number of people left over at Charity Hospital and a few other hospitals. The doctors stayed behind and were still working with no lights, electricity or water. They stayed there trying to assist some real sick people that they couldn't really do nothin' with. As time went on, people just kept checking out, passing. It is pretty upsetting. Almost four years later, you still think about it and see pictures on it, like it just happened today or yesterday.

You never knew that anything would ever happen like this in this country. You see things like that, bombs go off in foreign countries, people outdoors, but you never knew this was going to happen in this country. I felt very angry about it. There is nothing I can do with the anger. Nothing at all I could have done but try to be patient about it.

-Darren Hagan

## Bobby
(5th child of Odis & Irene)

I know it was racism .... a combination of inadvertent racism and politics combined. The politics from the aspect that New Orleans is Democratic and the administration at the time was Republican.

I think Bush was sitting there waiting for Tom DeLay to make the decisions. The decision was, "Hey, we can't let them go back in there." I believe Bush had this kinder and gentler talk... oh, I'm going to practice racism, but it is going to be kinder and gentler. It's like, "I'm not going to cut both yours eyes out; I will leave you one." But still you have an eye gone. So that was the mentality that they had.

First, on TV they showed a lot of black people walking in water, and people see it as a 'black thing.' I believe generally, when white people see something as black they need to consult with other white folks because they don't want to come off as a black sympathizer. So they have to talk to another white man or someone in power, and ask, "Should I help them?" to get permission, then that person has to go and say, "Let me talk to my boss."

They go through a lot of indecision before they do something to help. That seemed to happen a lot with Katrina. They didn't want to come off like helping. Like the history in this country, if you get caught helping slaves, you become a sympathizer and as far as they are concerned, you are like one of the slaves. Then they could get lynched along with the blacks.

I think a lot of Katrina inaction was based on that 'old time thinking,' I can't allow other people to do something. So in the position of power, they couldn't let the boats in because they would say, "Hey no one said I could let you in yet, because they haven't told me I'm supposed to be helping those people."

Then Nagin said to get off their asses and do something and then they showed the image of what they thought was a stranded white lady and that is when all hell broke loose. "Oh, now we are killing white people." Then I believe they said, oh we need to get in there and all of a sudden the planes started flying, the boats started moving. Then they found out, that wasn't a white lady after all.

A lot of people don't understand the black poverty that was in New Orleans at the time. They believed that the people should have gotten out on their own and they didn't realize that a lot of people didn't even have a car. There were a few of us who could escape, but for most of us, we couldn't. But then, a lot of people felt justified that 'they dug their own grave,' but really they are in a cycle that they just can't easily escape. A few got lucky.

-Bobby Lain

**Shaun**
(grandson of Odis & Irene, son of Otis Jr.)

I don't think so much that George Bush doesn't care about black people, I think George Bush doesn't care about poor people. He comes from a different, ultra rich, rim. I think he understands capitalism and how it works and what is needed for it to work. This was an opportunity for a lot of systematic things to take place: for Black Water to get contracts, for Halliburton to get contracts, friends got paid from the Katrina situation. That's what took so long because they had to get certain things in place. So they had to give the impression that they wanted to help, but at the same time, they wanted to get paid.

Barbara Bush gave a million dollars to Katrina, but she said it had to go to her son's fund. Her youngest son had an educational program, so she funneled money to her son in the guise that she was helping out the people of Katrina. She still had the comment that the people from Katrina 'were better off in the shelter than they were before in their own homes' – how arrogantly ignorant can you be?

Race compounded it. We have to understand that race built this country. We don't want to talk about that. We came over with prisoners from Europe that wiped out ethnicity. We killed Native Americans, we slaughtered them, but we don't want to deal with that either.

When Kanye talked about George Bush not caring about black people, I believe George Bush doesn't care about anyone in poverty and it does compound it by race. But what happened was, true America was exposed to the world. So people felt guilty.

It was guilt. Once they felt they had done enough, which lasted about 60 – 90 days, then that guilt turned to anger: "How dare they think we should do more, we have done enough." They dusted themselves off and said, "Let's move on."

Then that same guilt turned to anger and bitterness, and then they got 'Katrina-fatigue.' It is not just whites, it is blacks too. They felt like the federal government would help people from Katrina out, and the mantra of Katrina is "poor and black."

They forgot about the middle class who caught hell because people said, they had insurance to take care of things. They didn't have enough insurance, but they couldn't get FEMA. And people forgot about that. So I didn't get the lump sum that other people got. I had insurance, but then my insurance denied me, so it was a fight.

It is a poverty thing and what we are doing right now in America is that we are cutting the middle class. We are going to have the "haves" and the "have nots" on the extremes. The second law of wisdom is that a person has to always be under control. You can't control nobody else but yourself. So education is your pathway to liberation.

In New Orleans, Ray Nagin said that 50% of the people were unemployed when he took office. 50% of those are unemployable, they have no skills. So they have gone through the whole system and are not productive. They were the ones stuck at the Superdome.

Ronald Reagan always said, "You have to pull yourself up by the bootstraps," but Jesse Jackson said, "Well what if I don't have boots? What do I do?" So that is where we are right now.

We have to educate and empower the people to fend for ourselves. You had some people, on the poverty level, that did better after Katrina when they were dispersed different places. They found the opportunities were better.

-Shaun Lain

# Chapter 16

## Knowledge Learned

**Estella**
(daughter-in-law of Odis & Irene, wife of Otis Jr.)

What I learned through the Katrina experience is that nothing is certain. I felt that I was at a point in my life where I was ready for retirement. We had just paid off our house, and I was ready to just sit back and relax and just enjoy life. But everything is temporary.

I did not go into a depressed state over the loss of material things. If I was to be honest, the Lord was trying to tell me to lighten my load for a long time. So the load was lightened, tremendously.

Nothing is permanent. Also, out of the depths of a disaster, there is life. Even though we may have lost something, I always looked at it as a new beginning.

-Estella Lain

## Bobby
(5th child of Odis & Irene)

Living around earthquakes, living around volcanoes, living in areas with tornadoes; you can't plan for those. I don't think you can go anywhere on the planet and say that it is "safe" ground. There is always something catastrophic that could happen.

I think you can really prepare more for a hurricane; you know they are coming. They can put up barriers in the Gulf and that wouldn't cost that much. Nobody has figured out how to make money at building a barrier reef yet, or it would have been done. When hurricanes hit land, they lose power really quick. It is not rocket science. Wind can't turn like that on dry land. Hurricanes turn the same way each time. It seems like they could figure out simple ways to fix that. Some of these companies make lots of money off of disasters, like Halliburton, and so they don't want the hurricanes to stop.

What I've learned through this experience is that material stuff doesn't matter. Just enjoy life and move forward. Just kick back, relax, and enjoy yourself. You can't take it with you.

-Bobby Lain

**Raymond**
(9th child of Odis & Irene)

The biggest lesson for me is that "You can't take it with you." You spend all your life gathering all these worldly possessions -- see who can get the most marbles. But something like Katrina comes along and wipes everything out. You have to start all over again and you realize you can't take it with you. Nothing is forever. You're going to die even if you get the most toys and stuff, and they ain't going to put it in the grave with you. You can't take it with you, you know.

-Raymond Lain

## Calvin
(13th child of Odis & Irene)

I guess I learned not to have all your eggs in one basket. And, I think I've learned not to take as much stock in "stuff." So many personal items were lost, family heirlooms and pictures. Now there is a tendency not to acquire so much; if it should happen again, then your loss wouldn't be so painful.

You learn to appreciate each day, you don't take it for granted. If you had your house paid for and you are retired and you figure you can just ride off into the sunset, this changed for everybody. It changed their lives entirely. It is a lesson whether you were indirectly affected, as I was, or directly affected. It has and continues to have an impact on your thought process while going forward in life.

-Calvin A. Lain

**Darren**
(grandchild of Odis & Irene, son of Elsie)

I lost all my stuff. It feels very different to me now. The things you once had, you don't have any more. You try to go find those type of things to match them up again, but it is totally different now. I feel very hesitant about new things, because we lost everything.

I thought about moving to another city at times; but I just had a lot of things to do, cleaning houses out and fixing houses. And my job was still here in New Orleans.

There is a lot I have learned through this experience. Some things you can't replace, you just have to move on without it; just let things go. I found strength in myself through all this devastation

-Darren Hagan

## Otis Jr. (June)
(1st child of Odis & Irene)

It cost money, but for the first time in my life, I realized that money is not going to solve all the problems at this particular time. If you are in a society of chaos and nobody is following rules and regulations, the strongest man wins (and I wasn't about to get a gun and shoot anybody.) So I decided that declaring bankruptcy and just driving in my car was the best. I must have spent a lot of time just driving in my car. I spent a lot of time in Houston because that is where I was getting treatment at the cancer center.

I didn't realize how much junk I had accumulated – it probably wasn't right for one man to be in possession of that much stuff. In the long run, even though I feel like I've lost millions, I feel like it has been a blessing in a way -- I can wake up right now and have a little grits on the table, but I can't splurge and do some of the things like I used to do.

Now I have to live within my means, which is minimal -- only retirement. Even though I'm eligible, I still have yet to collect from the Road Home program. But the biggest blessing of everything -- when I learned how to pray and understand that cancer was not going to take my life away and that I can survive it. I didn't do the best job, but I managed to still be here. I'm reminded of a poem I often quoted:

*I do the very best I know how, the very best I can; and mean to keep doing so until the end. If the end brings me out all right, what is said against me won't amount to anything. If the end brings me out wrong, ten angels swearing I was right would make no difference.*

-Otis Lain Jr.

# Chapter 17

## The Importance of Family

## Calvin
(13th child of Odis & Irene)

<u>Large Family Perseveres</u>

Madear passed about six months before Katrina happened and she would normally handle most of the business deals because my dad always worked. She handled insurance and the premium was due in January that year of Katrina. So, when she was sick and died in February, the premium did not get paid. Therefore they did not have flood insurance to pay for the family house.

I think, like many of us think, if she hadn't been sick, or passed away, the premium would have been paid. There would have been insurance money and they would have been back in the house much, much, much quicker. But even if they didn't have it, she would have made it happen to get back in the house.

So I guess some people carried on in the spirit of 'What Madear would do?' Basically, they were in survival and perseverance mode -- where you weren't going to let it tackle you. Katrina put more of a daze on people like, this was the ultimate.

At least with Hurricane Betsy, people had a base to work from. With Katrina, people had to travel four hours or more to get rebuilding work done. There were no close resources, so you had much less to work with to get back to a rebuilding state; hence it took longer.

I guess family members drew on the strength of each other, and they learned from each other in the experience. Everyone pretty much got consumed with a desire to get back home. I think of salmon; even though they know they are going to die and they are swimming upstream, it is in their DNA to get back. I think it is the same thing that we experienced with Katrina that you just had to get your home back.

I'm reminded of my brother-in-law, Arthur. He had been on dialysis for almost 30 years when Katrina hit. He held on after Katrina because he wanted to get his house back. They did eventually get the house renovated and a few months after that, he passed away.

But there is a strong urgency in every person, when you are dealing with a catastrophy like this, to get home. It is something I can't really explain better than that until you actually get confronted with it. Home can be a mansion or a shack in the woods with aluminum foil holding back the elements. In your mind, if that is home, that is where you want to be. Most people, if there is any strength left in their body, they will walk away from the hospital, personally discharge themselves, walk the road, all in an effort just to get back home.

You have to have resources and one thing that happened with our family was, the ones that were able to get back the first became the building blocks for others. So when my brother Emanuel came back first, he had about eight to ten people staying in his house, and that would save them on their trips back and forth and they could work on their house more. So you could develop that "piggy-back" effect.

Now if you were a person by yourself (without family), and you don't have those resources, then you still had to travel from Houston, or North Louisiana, or Atlanta. So you had to spend most of your time traveling because you could sleep in the car only for so long. That definitely played a part in getting the family back into their homes.

-Calvin A. Lain

## Rose
(7th child of Odis & Irene)

My mother passed away six months before the storm; my brother passed away six months after the storm. The funerals were totally different. The second funeral, everybody had to come in from out-of-town, but this is the place we know and we couldn't just have it any old place. We came back to New Orleans for that and we got to see family. The family is spread out everywhere now; they are like scattered to the wind. We have family living in Atlanta, Georgia now, family that used to be just twenty minutes away.

Everything is so different, it's not the same anymore. It's a plane trip to go to a family reunion or a birthday or Christmas or Thanksgiving. It's not just get in the car and drive twenty minutes; it's drive seventeen hours. To drive that far is expensive. So, one blessing we had was our T-Mobile cell phone company gave us all kinds of extra minutes and didn't charge us after Katrina.

Any monies we saved in that way, got spent going back and forth to get back to visit family. One of my first trips back, I was able to just ask the hotel people if they had any discounts for Katrina victims and I was able to stay the night without having to cough up money. After that, every trip costs hundreds and hundreds of dollars. I made quite a few trips because you got to try to take care of business.

What I got from this experience is, 'depend on family and depend on yourself.' I felt privileged that we could get on a bus that was owned by my brother; I felt that we were privileged that we were very comfortable on that bus and that we could get past the traffic faster than the cars; I felt privileged that we were in a hotel watching the disaster on the television and not in the middle of it; we lost a lot and we got a lot of support.

## Help From Others

My brother-in-law took us from the hotel in Atlanta up to Maryland and we stayed with him for a month. I went from October to November and then by December 12th, I was in a job in the Post Office.

We weren't stuck at the Superdome and then we were blessed to have the Frederick Community Association in Maryland furnish us with everything we needed to live in a house: the furniture, the sheets, the towels, the soap, the hairbrush, everything we had lost -- pots and pans, even a blender and a toaster, silverware, furniture. I don't know if it cost them $10,000 or $20,000, or if it was all donations, but it was helpful. They put the donations in an apartment and let us stay in the apartment.

We had tried to look for an apartment before then, but we would have had to start off on the floor. We did get a lot of donations from Henry's brothers and their jobs also. The Red Cross gave us $600 to buy clothes, shoes, and coats and we split it. $600 doesn't go that far.

Barbara Bush said Katrina victims are doing better now than before. That depended. If you were doing OK before, you might have gotten some help. But if you weren't doing well before, you definitely weren't on the list to get help afterwards. Did you see all those people cussing up on that overpass? Four days and nothing; but the worst part was, watching those scenes made me know that there were other parts where people were stranded.

One school teacher stayed in her house out in the East. She got rescued and then she ended up sleeping the night on the ground on Elysian Fields Avenue. The next morning when she got up, she saw a preacher she knew and she went and asked him for help. He got her to a bus that got her out of town. The people at the Superdome were part of the masses and so nothing was happening fast. The individual preachers and people helping other people, could only pick one or two to help. But the masses had to wait. They brought in troops after troops, and the first set of troops were the worst because they had guns on the people.

-Rose Lain Watts

**Shaun**
(grandson of Odis & Irene, son of Otis Jr.)

The gift of time was something we did not take advantage of in New Orleans. We lived in New Orleans East around twenty family members' houses and we didn't visit. Now we are trying to say, "Come back around and let's visit." We do miss family being in Atlanta. I'm fortunate here because my brother lives on my street and my mother lives one mile from the end of my driveway. My kids can walk to their houses.

-Shaun Lain

## Shavon
(granddaughter of Odis & Irene, daughter of Louis)

I was able to help my family when they came to Atlanta and stayed with me. I guess I look at it as a blessing in that we have always been able to lean on each other. I felt like I pulled my weight at that time. But I didn't really feel like I did something life changing, it is just that I had a place where Cynthia and Angela could stay.

They didn't stay in the apartment long. They went out and found their own place and that is when my mom and dad came up to stay. I don't know when Dwayne made it to Atlanta, but he never had to stay with us.

Honestly, when I first moved out to Atlanta, before Katrina, I wanted to go there to get away from family. But then again, on holidays it felt good to come back home. Then I could go back to Atlanta and do my own thing. After Katrina hit, here all my family came. Eventually everyone kind of migrated back to New Orleans. I was hearing all these stories – "I miss home, I miss home." So I said, "OK, I'll move back home to New Orleans."

-Shavon Lain

## Shannon
(granddaughter-in-law of Odis & Irene, wife of Shaun)

Family means being able to stick together when it is important. I think when everything is taking place, you are not thinking so much about relationships. One thing that sticks in my mind is, you learn not to take anything for granted.

In the past, a lot of times I took for granted that my mom was right around the corner, or my mother-in-law was five minutes away, so we wouldn't see each other. But now, when we are miles away, it is difficult.

I have friends who were my friends before the storm, but it has gone to another level. You think you can just live anywhere, but it is hard on Saturday or Sunday, when you can't just decide to stop over at a friend's house or at Grandma Irene's house.

I've never lived anywhere else than the New Orleans' area. I was born and raised there and when it was time for me to go to college, I attended Xavier and then UNO right in New Orleans. I just knew that I wasn't leaving. That is just the close knit nature of New Orleans. I didn't go anywhere.

Now we realize how different our culture is. We go into the grocery store now (in Atlanta area) and you say "Hello" to someone and they are like, "Do I know you?" Whereas in New Orleans, we speak to everybody. And now it is not fun going to the store anymore, cause you're not going to see anybody you know. It is not fun to go into Home Depot because I'm not going to see anybody. So I do miss that.

Not only that, but starting over. I value friendship and love my friends. Now at 41 years old, it is hard to start over with that. I have to find new friends. So this person can be an associate or an acquaintance but it is not that person who you grew up with. It is just so different, you have to start over with that aspect of it.

For guys, I think it is different, if you want to look at gender. It is different with men because they can get some fellows together and go to a ballgame and it's OK. Women are more emotional as far as meeting and going to do things. You just can't do that with anybody. True friends are the people you want to be with, not just associate with. That is different for me. I miss those friends.

-Shannon Lain

**Meryl**
(great-granddaughter of Odis & Irene, granddaughter of Otis Jr., and daughter of Wellington)

I think right after Katrina, our family got closer and realized the value of family. Sometimes I don't think we quite appreciate it as much as we should. People, period, don't appreciate the grace and mercy that we are shown. Because it could have been a lot worse, it really could have.

In my family, both on my mom's and dad's sides, I didn't lose any close family. I thank God for that. I tell people from Atlanta area, Katrina was a blessing in disguise for me. Yeah it was a loss of material stuff, like we had traditions that my sister and I went to the same high school that my parents went to. But I wouldn't trade that for them coming out here to Atlanta. School systems are better; it is a better life for my younger brothers and sisters. They are growing up totally different. I think this is a better life for them. I'm actually happy about that.

When I grew up in New Orleans, granted it wasn't the best city to grow up in, but at the same time, I grew up in the faith. We are closer now, we are all living right together. After moving to the Atlanta area, I am in walking distance from my parents. I am not at all used to that. I see them a lot more than I saw them in New Orleans. It is crazy.

-Meryl Lain

## Elsie
(2nd child of Odis & Irene)

I basically think that we are a strong family and we had that unity and endurance to make the come-back. When I looked at our family house, it is like, how many times have they repaired that house? The house had a fire, almost burned down, '65 Betsy took it, and I can't count in-between, the little rains that flooded the house out. They always managed to come back with it.

Basically, everybody else moved away, they still want to be here and come back. That is how I thought I would be, so I decided I better just come on back. I know people that come here every two weeks. They got a house in Houston and they can't stay away from New Orleans. It'll just be in you, and you really want to come back to your birth place.

I just think it is the way we were built, you know, that we always have the desire and stamina to come back and put your feet to the grindstone and rebuild. I do think the connection of the family had something to do with that. Basically, we have never been a people to give up. Us black people have always been through a lot, so we are used to having to pick up and keep going. Some people look at it as giving up, but no, in the long run, we might have wished we had given up.

But I tell you what, if they announce there will be a bad lightning and thunder storm, I don't want to be in the house. A week out, if they announce a storm, I'm out of here.

If I had to do it all over again, I really don't think I would have rebuilt knowing that my husband wasn't going to live for only such a short time after we got back. I love my house, it is just the idea that it is a lot of work because of the size of the house. It is something to do, but then you can downsize and do less. I think about the day when I won't be able to keep it up.

-Elsie Lain Hagan

**Darren**
(grandson of Odis & Irene, son of Elsie)

We are a strong family to come back and rebuild. My mom and dad's families are big. I have a lot of people from both sides of the family and it is amazing that all of those people, on both sides, made up their minds to come back home and do it again. The strength comes from good spirits, and the pull of family.

-Darren Hagan

**Andrew (Daniel)**
(10th child of Odis & Irene)

I never want to do that again, I know that. You wonder what Madear would have done, because she was like an expert at that, dealing with the government. That was a nightmare dealing with Road Home and Allstate. I mean you had all kind of people, Salvation Army, Red Cross, and the bureaucracy.

Everyone wouldn't still be all over the country if my mom was still here. They would be back. We saw it dealt with before through my mom's example. Other people were burning down their houses because they didn't have flood insurance, some people were committing suicide. Immediately there were fires all over the place but we had helicopters that was droppin' water.

Strength just comes because you wake up and you have something to do that day. You're tired, go home and go to bed, and then the next day, you have something to do that day. If you look at it in the distance, like next week, you would collapse. You have what you have to do today.

I have a cab and would get up and cruise the town with the cab. I would read the newspaper. I went and bought a little TV and watched that while sitting in the cab. There is always something to do. When you don't have things to do, that is when you get in trouble.

-Andrew (Daniel) Lain

## Otis Jr. (June)
(1st child of Odis & Irene)

I think what we really found out was, where this is unity there is strength. One of the things that I can appreciate, and it helped me to understand, that God comes first. A lot of things you do, can be a blessing or a curse, and you need to know the difference of the two. Then everybody gets on the same page, you can't just do things because you want to do it. Everything is interrelated and since we are together as a family, it has made us stronger as a family. If Katrina hadn't came along, Stella had her sorority and all these different activities she was involved in. And I was thinking it was important to get this bus out on time, and get this campground straight.

When you really stop and think, you have to say, how much of that really, really mattered? My life was passing me by and I was doing stuff all the time. On a Sunday, I was too tired to even think about going to church. I didn't go to nobody's church back then, but guess what, God gave us a wakeup call.

Thank you Jesus for peace and understanding and getting things straightened out. My son Shaun is real strong with his relationship with God. My son Wellington and his family started going to church; they never was going to church before. It did make us more of a religious type of family than before. That helped. Two things helped with that: Katrina and medical problems -- my cancer.

-Otis Lain Jr.

**Tanga**
(granddaughter of Odis & Irene, daughter of Emanuel Sr.)

2005 was a difficult year for our family. We lost our Grandmother Irene earlier that year. One thing happened... I'm the organizer of the family as far as picnics and things like that. That year I couldn't do it; so one of my other cousins, Dwayne, said we are going to do something every month. It was at different parks throughout the city; we usually just do it at one park and we have our backup plan. But this time we visited various parks; so we had those memories when the storm happened, we could say that we all came together.

Well in 2005, when my grandmother passed away, I couldn't organize, because it was too much. I did for Easter, like I always do; but I couldn't go on. So, everybody else pitched in. And then we can think back on that year, that Katrina happened, but at least as a family, we did get together from April all the way through August – once a month. We hold on to that.

We had a big block party in April 2006. That was nice. That was our first get-together after the storm. This house (family home) was not even rebuilt yet, I don't even think you could go in the home. Gnats were everywhere; I remember it because I had Guard Drill that weekend. I cooked for the event but I didn't stay here the whole day.

But it was wonderful! Everyone came by, you know, and we just blocked off the street. We had a table in the middle of the street, because you couldn't go on the grass or anything; we couldn't go into the homes; we just had a block party on the street. We had our music and all the cousins gathered, everyone that was in town came by, that was a nice event.

That was our way of rallying around. It was French Quarter Festival Weekend, it had to be the 3rd weekend of April because that is when I have drill with the Reserves. I want to say it was like the 22nd and I remember my cousin Shaun came through with a bus. We made the news because we had a block party. Uncle Calvin said we are going to have a block party and we boiled crawfish and crabs, one of the two, and had the bar-b-q. With all the overgrown grass, and the grass was nasty, it was nothing nice about it, but we got together.

In the past, it usually was the fourteen of them (Odis and Irene's children) and they might lean on each other. But now, they were leaning on nieces and nephews after Katrina. We do have a "pecking order" in this family, you know your place and it would be bad for someone older than you to fall and lean on someone under them. All that went out the window with Katrina; everyone was able to help everyone. If there was a need, someone would help you. It felt great that my family wouldn't ignore me; it was wonderful.

I know my faith -- when I didn't think I had flood insurance and then I saw that paper proving it, I just dropped to my knees and said, "Thank you Jesus." My faith had a lot to do with it. Sometimes I get upset with myself, how come I'm so down when I know the Lord will work it out. But I battle with those issues. I battle with that because I do believe in the Lord and he will work it out, so why am I down? But it is kind of hard when you are away from your family. Not that I need them for support or help, it is just the fellowship that I miss.

But the next time (during a hurricane), I know they are all coming by me in Atlanta, so I wouldn't have that worry. I think it is important to have your paperwork together and have everything in order; I think a lot of people learned that. That "unorganized-organized" book, is now organized. The main thing I would have now, is the Chirp. Whatever they call it these days... Sprint was our link. You could press and talk to them back and forth. I learned to have that so you could keep in touch with family.

I want to say, most people are like that now. With my parents, they left their passports, so they lost those. Time to evacuate, you take all that. And pictures, take your pictures; but everything else is material and it can be replaced.

If anybody knows me, they know how important family is. Even before we learned about the levees, a person asked me, what did you get? I got my family. I have my family, my mom and my dad, I know how important they are to me.

I think we are a strong family. The strength comes from our Grandmother (Irene). She was a strong woman and someone said, "If she would have been here, she would have been able to get this place in shape." She would have had everything together.

I always consider us as a unique family, well known family. A lot of people say, "You aren't going to the 9th Ward are you?" I'm like, "9th Ward, I live in the 9th Ward!" I know anywhere I go, someone is going to recognize me, so I don't fear anything. It is just a unique, strong family. We lean on each other in ways that I don't think we ever did before.

-Tanga Lain Hale

❖ ❖ ❖ ❖

# Timeline of Hurricane Katrina + ^

Thursday, August 25, 2005 - 7 p.m. Hurricane Katrina strikes Florida as Category 1 level.

Friday, August 26, 2005 – 5 p.m. Governor Blanco declares a state of emergency for Louisiana.

+ Timeline results from a combination of sources including CBC News Online; talk@talkingpointsmemo.com (mailto:talk@talkingpointsmemo.com) ; FEMA. Mitigation Assessment Team Report: Hurricane Katrina in the Gulf Coast, Building Performance, Observations, Recommendation, and Technical Guidance, FEMA Publication 549, July 2006.

^There is no independent verification of these exact events, times and dates, however the various timelines corroborate each other. There are many other events that surrounded Hurricane Katrina and the aftermath, but the author has chosen some highlights.

Saturday, August 27, 2005 – Katrina grows to Category 3, eleven die in Florida. Per Governor Blanco's order at 4p.m. contraflow begins. New Orleans Mayor Nagin declares state of emergency, issues voluntary evacuation order at 5p.m.

Sunday, August 28, 2005 - At 8 a.m. Katrina is declared a Category 5 hurricane. Mayor Nagin orders mandatory evacuation at 10 a.m. Residents are encouraged to go to the Superdome if unable to leave the city. Governor Blanco sends letter to President Bush requesting federal aid.

Monday, August 29, 2005 – Katrina makes landfall near Buras, La (approx. 60 miles east of the center of New Orleans) as a Category 4 hurricane with 145 mph winds at 6:10 a.m. Before 8:00 a.m. storm surge sends water over the Industrial Canal in New Orleans and a barge is believed to have broken loose and crashed through the floodwall, flooding 9th Ward and St. Bernard Parish. Approximately 9 a.m., the eye of hurricane Katrina passes over New Orleans. At mid-morning Katrina rips two holes in the Superdome's roof with people inside. The 17th Street Canal is breached in late morning, and is confirmed by city officials at 2 p.m.

Tuesday, August 30, 2005 – 2 levees break in New Orleans and water pours in, covering an estimated 80% of the city. Crowds swell at the Superdome and the New Orleans Convention Center.

Wednesday, August 31, 2005 – Mayor Nagin estimates death toll at minimum of hundreds, most likely thousands. Air Force One flies over New Orleans to view the devastation. The U.S. Army Corps of Engineers estimates it will be 30 days or more before the water can be pumped out. Police are ordered to abandon search and rescue and turn attention to looting. Mayor Nagin calls for increased federal assistance. The Times-Picayune reports just after 11 p.m. that 3000 or more people are stranded at the Convention Center.

Thursday, September 1, 2005 -   At 2:00 a.m. the first evacuees arrive at the Astrodome in Houston. Outside the Convention Center, the sidewalks are packed with people without food, water or medical  care. The National Guard increases deployment to 30,000 because of reports of looting, carjacking and other violence. Congressional Representative Hastert says that rebuilding New Orleans "doesn't make sense." Mayor Nagin calls the situation critical and issues "a desperate SOS." Federal Administration Official Chertoff claims, "I have not heard a report of thousands of people in the convention center who don't have food and water."

Friday, September 2, 2005 – President Bush tours Alabama, Mississippi, and Louisiana to survey Katrina's damage. He states, "Brownie, you're doing a heck of a job." FEMA releases a statement for "patience in the wake of Hurricane Katrina." National Guard arrives in New Orleans. Kanye West states "George Bush Doesn't Care About Black People"  on an NBC telethon to raise money for Katrina victims.

Saturday, September 3, 2005 – Evacuation of people from the Superdome and Convention Center continue. New Orleans police report that 200 of their 1500 officers have walked off the job and two have committed suicide.

Sunday, September 4, 2005 – The last 300 people in the Superdome get out, there are still some remaining in the streets around the Convention Center. Paramedics begin carting away the dead in New Orleans.

Monday, September 5, 2005 – Rescuers in boats, helicopters, and military vehicles continue house-to-house searches. Residents in Jefferson Parish are allowed to return to salvage their belongings and can stay until Wednesday. New Orleans police now say 500 of their officers are unaccounted for. Former First Lady Barbara Bush while touring the

Astrodome in Houston, Texas stated that, "Many of the people in the arena here, you know, were underprivileged anyway, so this, this is working very well for them."

Tuesday, September 6, 2005 – The U.S. Army Corps of Engineers begins pumping out New Orleans. Rescue workers continue looking for survivors.

Wednesday, September 7, 2005 - Mayor Nagin orders police and soldiers to use force if necessary to require holdouts to leave the city. Testing confirms bacteria in the floodwaters at least 10 times higher than acceptable safety levels. Only 23 of the 148 pumps in the New Orleans water system are working.

Thursday, September 8, 2005 – Vice President Dick Cheney visits the region.

Friday, September 9, 2005 – FEMA ends its debit card program and Director Mike Brown is sent back to Washington amid charges he bungled the recovery operation.

Monday, September 12, 2005 – FEMA Director Michael Brown, (aka "Brownie") resigns from FEMA. New Orleans is now 50% flooded.

Tuesday, September 13, 2005 – President Bush takes responsibility for the federal government's failures during the Hurricane Katrina relief effort. Mayor Nagin warns that the city is broke. Owners of St. Rita's Nursing Home in New Orleans are charged with negligent homicide for the deaths of 34 residents who were not evacuated.

Wednesday, September 14, 2005 – Residents from surrounding towns, Gretna, Westwego and Lafitte are allowed to go home for the first time.

Thursday, September 15, 2005 – Mayor Nagin says part of New Orleans will reopen for business in a week.

Monday, September 19, 2005 – Mayor Nagin urges residents to return to the city and they begin streaming in.

Tuesday, September 20, 2005 – Hurricane Rita gathers strength and Mayor Nagin calls off his plan to allow residents to return to New Orleans and urges those who did to evacuate.

# Bibliography

Alexander, D. Symbolic and practical interpretations of the Hurricane Katrina disaster in New Orleans. *Social Science Research Council: Understanding Katrina-Perspectives from the Social Sciences.* June 11, 2006. Retreived on July 20, 2009 from http://understandingkatrina.ssrc. org/Alexander/printable.html)

Barber, K., Hidalgo, D., Haney, T., Weeber, S. Pardee, J. and Day, J. Narrating the storm: Storytelling as a methodological approach to understanding Hurricane Katrina. *Journal of Public Management & Social Policy*, p. 99 – 120, Fall 2007.

Baum, D. *Nine lives: Death and life in New Orleans.* Spiegel & Grau, 2009.

Bengal, J., Shipley Hiles, S., Koughan, F., McQuaid, J., Morris, J., Reckdahl, K., and Wilkie, C. *City adrift: New Orleans before and after Katrina.* Baton Rouge: Louisiana State University Press, 2007.

Brinkley, D. *The Great Deluge. Hurricane Katrina, New Orleans, and the Mississippi Gulf Coast.* New York: Harpers Collins Publishers, 2006.

Brown, D.M. *Hurricane Katrina the first seven days of America's worst natural disaster.* D. M. Brown, 2005.

CBC News Online, *Hurricane Katrina Timeline* (3 Weeks), taken on August 9, 2010 from http://www.cbc.ca/news/background/katrina/katrina_timeline.html

Clark, J. *Heart like water: Surviving Katrina and life in its disaster zone*, Free Press, 2007.

Colby-Bottel, S. Doing anthropology in New Orleans, before and after Katrina. *Anthropology News.* November 2005, retrieved on July 20, 2009 from
http://www.aaanet.org/press/an/1105/Colby_Bottel.htm.

Colten, C. E. *An unnatural metropolis, wresting New Orleans from nature.* Sea Grant Louisiana State University, 2005.

Cooper, C. *Disaster: Hurricane Katrina and the failure of Homeland Security.* New York: Times Books, 2006.

*CNN Reports, Katrina State of emergency.* Kansas City: Andrews McMeel Publishing, 2005.

Cutter, S. The geography of social vulnerability: Race, class, and catastrophe. *Social Science Research Council: Understanding perspectives from the Social Sciences.* June 11, 2006. Retreived on July 20, 2009 from http://understandingkatrina.ssrc. org/Cutter/printable.html.

Draper, R. *Dead certain: The presidency of George W. Bush.* New York: Free Press, 2008.

Durant, T.J. and Sultan, D. The impact of Hurricane Katrina on the race and class divide in America." Marable, M. and Clarke, K. *Seeking Higher Ground.* New York: Palgrave MacMillan, 2008. 193-194.

Enarson, E. Women and girls last? Averting the second post-Katrina disaster. *Social Science Research Council: Understanding Katrina-Perspectives from the Social Sciences.* June 11, 2006. Retreived on July 20, 2009 from http://understandingkatrina.ssrc.org/Enarson/printable.

Erikson, K. and Peek, L. *Hurricane Katrina research bibliography.* Produced by Social Science Research Council, Task Force on Katrina and Rebuilding the Gulf Coast. July 2009. Retreived on December 14, 2009 from http://katrinaresearchhub.ssrc.org/KatrinaBibliography.pdf

FEMA. *Mitigation assessment team report: Hurricane Katrina in the Gulf Coast, building performance, observations, recommendation, and technical guidance,* FEMA Publication 549, July 2006.

*Frontline: The storm* (DVD). Producer Martin Smith, 2006.

Gilman, N. What Katrina teaches about the meaning of racism. *Understanding Katrina, Perspectives from the Social Sciences.* First published on June 11, 2006. Retreived on August 9, 2010 from http://understandingkatrina.ssrc.org

Horne, J. *Breach of faith, Hurricane Katrina and the near death of a great American city.* Random House, New York, 2006.

*Hurricane! Katrina, Gilbert, Camille.* (DVD) WGBH Boston Video, 2006.

*Hurricane Katrina, the storm that drowned a city.* NOVA film. Written, Produced & Directed by Caroline Penry-Davey & Peter Chinn. WGBH Boston Video, 2006

*Hurricane on the bayou.* (DVD) Written, Produced & Directed by MacGillivray Freeman. National Audubon Society. 2007.

*Inside Hurricane Katrina.* National Geographic DVD. Washington D.C., 2005.

Kaufman, S. The criminalization of New Orleanians in Katrina's wake. *Social Science Research Council: Understanding Katrina-Perspectives from the Social Sciences.* June 11, 2006. Retreived on July 20, 2009 from http://understandingkatrina.ssrc.org/Kaufman/printable

Knowles, J. G. and Cole, A. L. *Handbook of the ARTS in qualitative research,* Sage Publications, Inc. California, 2008.

Lain, S. *Hurricane Katrina the Shaun Lain story.* 2005

Lee, S. *When the levees broke,* HBO Documentary Films, 2006.

Lewis-Beck, M.S., Bryman, A., Liao, T. F., Eds. *The SAGE encyclopedia of social science research methods.* Sage Publications, Inc., California, 2004.

Marable, M. & Clarke, K. *Seeking higher ground, the Hurricane Katrina crisis, race, and public policy reader.* New York: Palgrave Macmillan, 2008.

McQuaid, J. and Schleifstein, M. *Path of destruction: The devastation of New Orleans.* New York: Little Brown and Company, 2006.

Montana-Leblanc, P. *Not just the levees broke : My story during and after Hurricane Katrina*, New York, NY : Atria Books, 2008.

Norcross, B. *All about hurricanes, hurricane almanac, the essential guide to storms past, present, and future.* New York: St. Martin's Press, 2007.

NOVA homepage. *Storm that drowned a city/ How the city flooded*, PBS. Retreived on November 28, 2005 from http://www.pbs.org/wgbh/nova/orleans/how-flash.html.

Penner, D. and Ferdinand, K. *Overcoming Katrina: African American voices.* Palgrave MacMillan, 2009.

Rivera, J. and Miller, D. Continually neglected, situating natural disasters in the African American experience. *Journal of Black Studies*, Vol. 37, No. 4, p. 502 – 522, March 2007.

Select bipartisan committee to investigate the preparation for and response to Hurricane Katrina. *A Failure of Initiative, Final Report of the Select Bipartisan Committee to Investigate the Preparation for and Response to Hurricane Katrina.* Washington: U.S. Government Printing Office, 2006.

Sothern, B. *Down in New Orleans reflections from a drowned city.* Los Angeles: University of California Press, 2007.

Tidwell, M. *The ravaging tide: Strange weather, future Katrinas, and the coming death of America's coastal cities*, Free Press, 2007

*TPM Hurricane Katrina timeline version 1.4* | Updated 9/20/05, taken on August 9, 2010 from http://www.talkingpointsmemo.com/katrina-timeline.php .

*Trouble the water* [DVD]. Directed and produced by Tia Lessin and Carl Deal, New York: Zeitgeist Films, 2009.

Van Heerden, I. and Bryan, M. *The storm: What went wrong and why during Hurricane Katrina – The inside story from one Louisiana scientist.* New York: Penguin Group, 2006.

White, I., Philpot, T., Wylie, K., and McGowen, E. Feeling the pain of my people, Hurricane Katrina, racial inequality, and the psyche of Black America. *Journal of Black Studies*, Vol. 37 No.4, March 2007, p. 523-538.

# Family Member Index

Carolyn & Walter

Carolyn & Erin

Carolyn & Dana

About the Author:

Carolyn E. Dallinger is pictured above with her husband Walter and her daughters Erin and Dana. Dallinger graduated with a B.A. degree from Simpson College, Indianola, Iowa in 1980; with an M.S.W. degree from University of Washington, Seattle in 1983; and with a J.D. degree from Southern University in Baton Rouge, Louisiana in 1989.

Dallinger has engaged in a variety of employment positions including an attorney in a partnership with her husband; a supervisor of civil rights investigators in Anchorage, Alaska and Chicago, Illinois; a director of social service agencies; an in-house college attorney; and most recently, a college professor. In November 2010, Dallinger received the Iowa Professor of the Year Award from the Carnegie Foundation and the Council for Advancement and Support of Education.

blurb.com